Understanding Political Islam

COMPRENDRE L'ISLAM POLITIQUE
Une trajectoire de recherche sur l'altérité islamiste, 1973–2016
by FRANÇOIS BURGAT

Manchester University Press

Understanding Political Islam

François Burgat

Translated by Thomas Hill

Manchester University Press

Copyright © Editions LA DÉCOUVERTE, Paris, France, 2016

The right of François Burgat to be identified as the author of this work has been asserted by him in accordance with the Copyright, Designs and Patents Act 1988.

Published by Editions LA DÉCOUVERTE, Paris, France, 2016

First English-language edition published in 2020 by Manchester University Press, Altrincham Street, Manchester M1 7JA

www.manchesteruniversitypress.co.uk

British Library Cataloguing-in-Publication Data is available

ISBN 978 1 5261 4343 3 hardback
ISBN 978 1 5261 4345 7 paperback

First published by Manchester University Press in hardback 2020

This edition published 2021

The publisher has no responsibility for the persistence or accuracy of URLs for any external or third-party internet websites referred to in this book, and does not guarantee that any content on such websites is, or will remain, accurate or appropriate.

Typeset by Servis Filmsetting Ltd, Stockport, Cheshire

Contents

Preface to the English Edition	*page* vi
Acknowledgments	ix
Introduction: Writing the History of a Research Career	1

Part I Discovering the Muslim "Other"

1	Intuitive Accumulation	17
2	Algeria: Approaching the Other	33
3	Prelude in the *Jamahiriyya*	49
4	Egypt, Arabic, and Grasping Difference	62
5	Yemen: Modernization without Colonization	74
6	"Beneath Israel, Palestine"	93
7	Syria and *Bilad al-Sham*	108
8	The Other "at Home," or: Islam in France	132

Part II Political Islam: The Stakes of an Alternative Interpretation

9	Being a Political Scientist of the Muslim World	145
10	Saving the Other's "Others": A French Obsession	160
11	The Political Cost of Dissent	169
12	Between Judges and Spooks	188
13	Wrestling with the Research of Others: Olivier Roy, Gilles Kepel, and Islamism	196
14	The *Charlie Hebdo* Attacks: Failure of Islam, or: Failure of Politics?	212
	Conclusion: Where Do We Go Now?	227
	Index	233

Preface to the English Edition
Pascal Ménoret

What you hold in your hand is the work of a trespasser. It sums up the breakthroughs of a French scholar who escaped a snug—and often smug—Western enclave to research one of the least understood political movements: Islamic activism. In the 1980s, François Burgat was one of the first Western political scientists to actively conduct field research on Islamic movements, and to meet those activists everybody feared, few met, and fewer even understood. This book tells the story of a lengthy trespassing.

French scholars are overwhelmingly white, generally male, and often proud of their liberal heritage, which they dub republican, universalist, and secular. There is a simple reason for that homogeneity: French academia, while merit-based in theory, is extremely discriminatory in practice. It tends to favor insiders, and newcomers to the game—in particular former or current colonial subjects—are few and far between. With his Catholic, bourgeois upbringing, Burgat is definitely a member of the old boys' club. Leaving for Algeria as a young professor, however, he started to trespass against his primary belonging.

"It was only in Algeria that I became political," he writes. "This did not happen, as it did to many others, through putting myself at the service of the political project of the leaders of the country, but by discovering there the scale of the distortion" between mainstream, elite, racist French culture and what his North African experience revealed to him. Reading Malek Bennabi and, later on in Tunisia and Egypt, interviewing Rached Ghannouchi and Tarek al-Bishri, he realized the limits of universalism and secularism. Back in France, he dedicated his career to understanding the one political movement that most visibly questioned Western hegemony.

Burgat's book is unique because it sums up an approach that has been largely missing from mainstream expertise. Most analysts of Islamic movements tend to see them as the latest expression of a medieval Muslim theology represented as naturally violent, sexist, and discriminatory. Those who are not satisfied with this explanation tend to focus on socio-economic marginalization: Islamic activism, for them, is the revolt of the downtrodden. Burgat's research shows the shortcomings of both approaches, and looks for answers in the conflicted relationship between a conquering West, from Bugeaud to Bush and from Cromer to Cheney, and the Arab and Muslim fringe of the Global South, a region whose specificity is less its religion and culture than its position right outside the West's bloody borders.

During the colonial period, Islam was used to mark those colonial subjects who in Western eyes needed to be saved from their own culture and taught civilized ways. During the immediate post-colonial period, religion was often pushed out of the public realm, as many post-independence Arab regimes sought to modernize and develop along European lines. For over half a century, Islamic activists have turned religion from a mark of shame into a badge of honor, a marker of civilization not barbarism, of freedom not servitude. They adopted an Islamic religious lexicon against colonial oppression and post-colonial modernism. Islamic activists are not reactionary or medieval. They strive to create an indigenous lexicon against the perpetuation of European and Western influence after Arab independences.

Most observers think Islamic activism ("Islamism") is mostly an ideology that spreads like a disease through the contagious channels of the madrasas or of the internet. Burgat shows that Islamic movements are not linked by a common ideology. It is impossible to predict what Islamic activists will do by looking at what they think. Some collaborate with authoritarian governments while others oppose them. Some refuse elections while others embrace them. Some throw themselves into the political game while others withdraw from the world. To understand Islamic activism, one need not read the Quran or listen to taped sermons: one needs to meet activists, observe them, talk to them—acknowledge their eminently political quality. One needs to be there and conduct ethnographic fieldwork. Islamic activism is less the result of an ideology than the production of new political identities from one's own ground.

How has religion become so central to political scenes where, from the Atlantic to the Gulf and from Syria to Algeria, leftist movements were once thriving? In the post-colonial context, characterized by the one-party system (as in Nasser's Egypt) or the no-party system (as in Saudi Arabia), religious activities have allowed activists to organize under the radar of the state. Mosque activities, informal religious networks, and person-to-person relationships are hard to crack down upon. Fast urban growth has allowed religious networks to expand and thrive in times of political crackdown, as the state was after workers not clerics, officers not mosquegoers.

Repression inevitably hit Islamic movements, as in Egypt from the 1950s on or in Saudi Arabia twenty years later. Arab states reformed religious education, sometimes claiming to modernize it; these reforms often reeked of repression. States imposed predigested Friday sermons, closed down mosques, threw activists in jail, subjected them to treatment that was ever more sophisticated and cruel. Using force, post-colonial elites in turn justified the usage of force: Arab states often vindicated terrorism at the very time when they were fighting it. "For the colonized man," Frantz Fanon wrote, "life can spring only from the colonizer's putrefying corpse." For the post-colonial man, it can spring only from the destruction of what made post-colonial states violent—Western military cooperation, ministries of interior, police terror, torture chambers. Jean-Paul Sartre, commenting on the Algerian resistance to the brutal French occupation, famously quipped, "One must either remain terrified or become terrifying."

Burgat's book is not only a plea for a better understanding of both spectacular and hidden violence but also a candid exploration of what it means to conduct research on the very political movements that, noisily or in silence, have taken their distances from the West and Western-centric regimes. Burgat shows how political trespassing is an art that involves years of decentering and disorientation. It also entails decades of political struggle against terribly dangerous mainstream perceptions—those which fueled the criminal and useless War on Terror from 2001 on. When leaving his office to go lecture, Burgat often says, "*Allez*, I'm gonna harp on again." This endless improvisation on the necessity of shedding one's civilizational bearings is a salubrious enterprise.

I have been the consenting victim of this harping-on since a stormy day of July 2000, when Burgat, then head of a social science research center in Yemen, took us students hiking to the deserted Jewish village of Bayt Baws, where a torrential hailstorm sent us running down the slope and into the safety of a patio where the political scientist offered us dry clothes and Marseillais Pastis. Following Burgat like a shadow through the meanders of Sana'a's rich prewar social life, from poetry sessions around Abdulaziz al-Maqaleh to late-night verbal jousts in faraway compounds, was the best introduction to political anthropology, this strange discipline where the researcher is to herself her own lab, and where empathy—not necessarily sympathy—is the rule of the game.

Reader, beware: the pleasures of trespassing are contagious.

Pascal Ménoret
Boston, Massachusetts, June 2019

Acknowledgments

If this attempt at understanding political Islam now has an opportunity to be read in the English-speaking world, I owe it first and foremost to Pascal Ménoret. It was Pascal who was able to convey his confidence—as demonstrated by his warm Preface here—to Rob Byron and Manchester University Press, who elected to publish it, and thanks to whom you hold this book in your hands.

Secondly, the successful result owes everything to Thomas Hill, and to his precise and demanding linguist's instincts in navigating the rapids of translating my French style—which my usage may occasionally make more complex yet!

And lastly comes the list of those I wish to thank for helping, first, to develop my thinking and, second, to express it. So: the list of my human debts of all kinds. This is lengthy and diverse—and each and every one played a vital part in their own way.

As with my previous books, this one owes much to those who were by my side when my difficulty in writing both fast and well made me even more nervous than usual. Marie and Camille are among those. Moreover, for Camille's part, her "father's beardies" often kept me far from her (but never far from my thoughts)—and not only during my long years in Yemen.

My most direct debt is towards those colleagues who encouraged me to take on this labor of memory and precision—and who helped me bring it to conclusion. I am therefore most grateful, first, to Rita Bassil, who convinced me to throw myself, in her company, into a book project that was initially structured as a series of interviews. Many others then agreed to critique the various stages of the manuscript, to elicit further inquiry, and—for the more foolhardy among them—to refute some of my hypotheses. They also doled out writing advice and vital encouragement.

I can mention only a few of these here. Valérie Amiraux, Pascal Ménoret, Karima Dirèche, and Sylvie Denoix regularly reinspired in me the self-confidence I lacked. Laurent Bonnefoy was far more than merely my second-in-command in directing the WAFAW European Research Council project, so much of whose work helped develop my own thinking. Robin Beaumont, Nicolas Dot-Pouillard, Vincent Geisser, Sari Hanafi, Stéphane Lacroix, Mohamed Mahmoud Ould Mohamedou, Julien Pélissier, Thomas Pierret, Bjorn Utvik, Mathieu Rey, and Seif Eddine Trabelsi were ever at the ready to respond to my anxious appeals to them.

Not only did Xavier Guignard assist my documentary research and organize my writing but at length—alongside the highly professional Minas Ouchaklian—he then also helped lighten my style, breaking up some of its more fearsome multi-clause sentences. These two discreet heroes of the final stages of my project thereby decisively eased the task of François Gèze; not that this deprived him of the opportunity to put into practice his immense talent, as a demanding editor—and as a friend.

Many thanks are due to Olivier Roy and Gilles Kepel for having inspired in me the irrepressible desire to assert different convictions. In a quite different register, many thanks are due to former French Prime Minister Manuel Valls and to his advisers, the electioneering rogues who staged the pitiful saga of the French government's 2015–16 proposal to reform the constitution to enable revoking the citizenship of French-born dual nationals. They made me even more determined to show why they in fact cost so dearly to the nation they pretend to serve.

To Abdessalam Yassine, Adel Hussein, and Mohamed Qahtan, who have sadly passed away; and to Rached Ghannouchi, Tarek al-Bishri, and Omar Iherchane, I extend my gratitude—and, through them, to all those who allowed me to share in their vision of our world.

Several institutions (including the CNRS, MAE, ANR, and ERC) have granted me the very great privilege of doing the work I love. Especially heartfelt thoughts go out to my colleagues and all employees of the CEDEJ, CEFAS, and IFPO research centers, whose countries endure tragedies seemingly without end. For Syrians, a more heartfelt thought yet. I cannot help thinking that, if we have let their country sink into such suffering, it is at least in part due to Western blindness in the face of the deathly failure that this book lays out: the inability of our "Western" political generation to accept the Other, in all her or his (highly relative) diversity.

Introduction:
Writing the History of a Research Career

> They turn France inside out, they shelter behind the legitimate uproar they have caused, they seal mouths by making hearts quake and perverting minds. I know of no greater crime against society.
> Émile Zola, "Letter to the President of the Republic: I Accuse!"
> *L'Aurore*, January 13, 1898[1]

> One cannot self-proclaim oneself to be universal! [...] The problem is that neither Europe nor France are the world. The problem arises when universalism becomes ethnic. The problem is when identity rhymes with racism, and culture presents itself as having immutable traits.
> Achille Mbembe, 2016[2]

This book, now available in an updated English edition thanks to Manchester University Press,[3] is an attempt to retrace the human and intellectual development that has led me to one very firm conviction. Namely: that the tensions that afflict the Western world's relationship with the Muslim world are at their root political, far more than they are ideological. The obsessions produced by these tensions are primarily "our own"—and not merely, as a self-indulgent laziness leads us to assume, those of the Muslim "Other," whose right to fully "decolonize" her/himself from us we have yet to accept.

In what follows, I have not sought to borrow from the autobiographical genre, noble as it may be—and even less so from the genre of memoir. There will be no incursions into the private sphere here, nor any soul-searching as to time passing too fast, or not fast enough. This book aims to limit itself to a precise scholarly arena: it recounts, as meticulously as possible, the most striking interactions between a personal life history, and professional and research trajectories. This path has consistently centered on how the rise of political Islam has been expressed: first in the Arab world, then in its interactions with French society, and finally in its interactions with other European and Western societies. With a few exceptions designed to contextualize my research work, my focus here is a single subject: "Islamism," to which I have devoted the core of my academic work.

I have laid out my core theses concerning Islamism in three successive books.[4] I return to these here in a way that is doubly new. First, by retracing the historicity of the conditions that produced these arguments, using the conceptual apparatus of the social sciences, but also integrating how I constructed a more private perception of these themes. Second, and more conventionally, I bring up to date the theses that I had formulated in the 2000s, in particular in my book *Islamism in the Shadow of al-Qaeda*, by measuring them up against the lessons of the powerful revolutionary dynamics set off by the "Arab Spring"[5] of 2011, followed by the counter-revolutionary ones.

A Shared "Muslim Speech": Diverse Modes of Muslim Action

In summing up my approach to the rise of Islamism, it appears to me that two key processes are too often confused with each other. To make my approach intelligible, I offer up two distinct levels of explanation. The first seeks to explain the origins of the "turn towards speaking Muslim" in the Arab world. The second examines the extreme diversity of modes of action that this vocabulary has enabled. It thereby underscores that approaches that reduce the motivations of the various players of political Islam to their reference to religion alone are inane.

The first explanatory variable rests on an indisputable fact: beginning in the 1960s, "speaking Muslim" made a comeback in the societies of Europe's Muslim periphery. It seeks to account for the tendency of broad swaths of these societies to rehabilitate a long-occulted vocabulary, in the social sphere as much as in that of political competition. The second level of explanation addresses the issue of where this Muslim speech derives its ability to mobilize from. My hypothesis is that the "lexicon" (or vocabulary) referred to here is a symbolic and normative universe that is perceived as endogenous, "homemade," not imposed: neither from the outside, nor by the former colonial power, nor by elites from above. In the aftermath of colonial domination, the culture of the defeated was marginalized, "indigenized" and "folklorized." Its mismatched symbolic attributes were *de facto* forbidden from taking part in the production of meaning, or in expressing values eligible to being perceived as universal. The symbolic universe of Islamic culture was confined to the role of makeweight. Gradually, it could serve only to underline the humiliating centrality of Western culture.

As soon as the Muslim Brotherhood appeared on the scene in Egypt in 1928, a long process of retrieval was undertaken by political activists and intellectuals throughout the colonial period. This process continued after independence, now directed against nationalist elites who were perceived as having been won over to the colonizer's symbolic universe. Direct colonial presence was unarguably the most brutal carrier of this acculturation. It also, however, then found effective representatives among some of the post-colonial elites. Their Islamist challengers accused them of confusing "modernization" with "Westernization." Imperialist domination and too explicitly Western-oriented "modernizing" leanings thus contributed to widen an identical breach. While the peoples of Turkey, Iran, Afghanistan, and Saudi Arabia escaped the violence of being directly colonized, they suffered no less from this process, in which, to their eyes, their private political vocabulary was denied access to the status of the universal. After a long eclipse, the rehabilitation of a symbolic universe perceived as pre-dating the colonial era logically inscribed itself within the framework of a comforting historical continuity.

First of all, I have argued the case for considering the mobilizing virtues of this rediscovered Muslim lexicon as being rooted less in its *sacred* dimension than in its *endogenous* character. I have documented a hypothesis: that, among those who have adopted it, the key appeal of the Muslim lexicon inheres in a key fact. Namely: that they perceive it as more closely tied to their *inherited culture* than were the other political vocabularies—in particular, Marxism or nationalism. For a time at least, the latter had confiscated part of the centrality of the Muslim lexicon—only to be perceived, in the wake of the crushing colonial defeat, as being imported, or even imposed. I have proposed thinking through the dynamic by which the Islamist lexicon has been reintroduced, not as a *break with*, but actually as the *extension of* the dynamic that successfully fought for independence. The process of distanciation from the colonizer that first operated in the political sphere through the vocabulary of independence, then in the economic realm through the nationalizations of oil, agricultural lands, the Suez Canal, and so on, was extented in the cultural and symbolic arenas.

Finally, I have suggested that the dynamics of Islamist movements have sustained a complex relationship with values that are (often restrictively) considered "Western." This is a far more complex relationship than the indiscriminate, reactive rejection with which it has been identified, both by the Western gaze and by part of the rhetoric of assertion of Islamist identity. Rather, the overwhelming majority of these relationships led to a process of "reappropriation" of these so-called Western values. Moreover, this process of "reappropriation" was not slowed by these relationships. Rather, it was eased by the "Islamization" of the lexicon in which these values were expressed.

This process, initiated by the colonial onslaught, and that began with the first sparks of reformist reactions, played out across several generations, and in several successive historical configurations. From Jamal al-Din al-Afghani, the reformer of Iranian origin (1838–97), to the Iraqi Abu Bakr al-Baghdadi, leader of the Islamic State ("IS," "ISIS"), and amidst local and international political contexts enduring deep transformation, the identity-based alchemy pushing these players to use the Islamic lexicon has become perennial.[6] In what follows, I set out three stages to historicizing this latest version of the phenomenon of Islamism, which is now intrinsically part of its structure.[7]

At the outset, faced with what part of these societies perceived as the danger of *Westernization*, Islamist movements consisted of reasserting the political role of the resources of the endogenous culture, including its religious dimension, in the resistance to colonization. From 1928 on, in the political field, the Muslim Brotherhood laid out the challenge of an existential question: how can we mobilize our own ideological resources to organize the resistance to the Western push for hegemony? The question had already been put by Jamal al-Din al-Afghani, Mohammed Abdu (1849–1905), and Rashid Rida (1861–1935). Unlike the intellectuals who had preceded him to Europe, al-Afghani had perceived the danger of Western hegemony quite naturally, since the colonial adventure that had begun in Algeria had just spread to Tunisia (1881) and Egypt (1882). As the British historian of Lebanese origin Albert Hourani (1915–93) so rightly pointed out in a foundational remark, it was at this point—and not when the Muslim Brotherhood was founded—that the essential historical fracture opened up, after which in the Middle East, political thought would never be the same again.[8]

From the independence era to the early 1990s, Islamism then deployed itself, no longer directly against colonial power, but against the native elites that succeeded colonialism. Deep upheavals notwithstanding, a generation after the Muslim Brotherhood had been founded, the national and international environment had retained certain structural constants. While several states had achieved independence, that independence was fast considered incomplete. Borders, nations, and spirits were soon shaken as much by the creation of Israel as by the bellicose responses provoked in the West by the rise of Arab nationalism, from the tripartite expedition of 1956 (by the United Kingdom, France, and Israel) in response to the nationalization of the Suez Canal, through the brutal repression against the Algerian National Liberation Front (Front de Libération Nationale, FLN) until 1962.

During this second stage, choices as to how to subscribe to the Islamist vocabulary promoted by the Muslim Brotherhood would be highly diverse, both individual and national. In order to "return" to the world of religious thought, Nasserists, Baathists, and Communists (whether in Egypt, Syria,

Iraq, or North Africa) followed distinct paths to those who, in Sudan, departed from the matrix of the great Sufi brotherhoods (who at the time monopolized the organization of the political field) to "take orders in Islamism." Despite their diversity, these "neo-Islamists" all demanded that their national elites continue the process of self-distancing from the colonizer that had begun through independence and the processes of nationalization, on both ideological and symbolic fronts. In North Africa, the persistence of official and public usage of French made this schism explicit. In those places where states kept speaking French, secular elites gradually became denounced as the "party of France."

The third era of Islamist movements began, to my mind, with the interventionist and unilateralist turn in US foreign policy that was enabled by the collapse of the USSR at the turn of the 1990s. It appeared on the sidelines of (undercovered, but real) progress in the "normalization" of Islamist groups in parliaments and governments (in Jordan, Yemen, and Kuwait). It came on the sidelines, too, of the transnationalization of repressive policies initiated by the Sharm al-Sheikh anti-terrorist summit of March 1996. This stage was marked by a revolutionary transnationalization of radical groups. Emerging from Afghanistan, they spun the web out of which was to emerge, out of the heart of the Iraqi then of the Syrian crisis, al-Baghdadi's caliphate.

The Omnipresent Diversity of Contemporary Islamism

A second explanatory method provides me with my other major hypothesis. By now, this has been largely vindicated. It highlights the fact that, throughout these successive stages, the suppleness of the Islamic lexicon has enabled its adherents to enlist it in the service of extremely diverse social practices and modes of political action. In other words, "speaking Muslim" is a vocabulary, not a grammar: it is a means of naming things that ties them to a symbolic universe that goes beyond the strictly normative. It thus allows many ways of conceptualizing those things—and of acting upon them. Here, we glimpse the reasons why, from the Taliban to Erdogan, the search for a single causality that would rely only on their use of an identical "Muslim speech" is radically inadequate to explain the positionings and modes of action of "Islamists."

Close observation of the Islamist landscape since the "Arab Springs" has only bolstered this hypothesis of an *omnipresent diversity* of the Islamic lexicon. Tunisia's Rached Ghannouchi was once ostracized around the Mediterranean, from North to South, for his "Islamism." Today he leads a party, Ennahda, which forms part of a government close to the regime that was overthrown by the revolutionary wave of 2011.[9] Decades of propaganda had convinced the world that, were Ennahda one day to win a majority at the ballot box, it would apply the sinister principle of "One Man, One Vote ... One Time." Instead, once it had made a decisive contribution to the adoption of what was considered the first truly democratic constitution in the Arab world, it yielded without argument to being outvoted.[10] In May 2016, Ennahda's 10th Congress enshrined a strict separation between its political agenda and its religious agenda, the latter being demoted to the status of a reference value. These particular "Islamists" made especially inclusive use of their "Muslim speech." Conversely, from the throne of his "caliphate," Abu Bakr al-Baghdadi enlisted the same vocabulary from the other extreme of the Islamist spectrum, using it to especially radical and openly exclusivist ends, and preaching an open schism with the categories of the Western political inheritance.

Taking this extreme suppleness of the Islamist lexicon into account quickly led me to practice a strict analytical separation. On the one hand lie the fundamentally identity-based causes that explain its exponential spread. On the other lie distinct causalities that clarify the diversity of the uses made of the former. The explanation I propose—the widespread resort to "speaking Muslim"—accounts for the relatively commonplace desire of the peoples of the West's imperial periphery to restore a (religious) culture that had long been perceived as having withstood its Western competitor's attempts to replace it. To resort to "speaking Muslim" thereby enabled putting an end to the era of European symbolic hegemony. The explanation for the ways in which this lexicon was appropriated, and for their diversity, must, however, be sought in fundamentally lay causalities. As against the claims of the culturalist approach, these causalities in no shape or form derive from any specificity inherent to Muslim religion or culture.

Measuring these hypotheses against the development of radicalizing fractions among the political players of the Muslim world has more than ever led me to defend one argument. This is the idea that understanding this phenomenon requires focusing, not on the "Islamic" character of the vocabulary of those rising up, but rather on the social causalities of their actions—and, even more so, on their political causalities. By radicalization, I understand here the fact of adopting a rejectionist language and strategy that implies a split and, ultimately, a confrontation, with the (Shia) Muslim or non-Muslim environment—and with the Western environment in particular. These paths thus differ from the approach of simple self-differentiation. Most often, through the rhetoric of "Islamization," the "differentiation" approach opens up onto the process of "cultural reappropriation." This can be said to characterize the bulk of the Islamist movement.

Over the sweep of the past half century, studying the founding intellectual histories of this type of radicalization, from Sayyid Qutb to Osama Bin Laden, has convinced me that these were most often of a reactive nature—that is to say, that their founding motivation was an initial act of violence.[11] My approach thus insists on the need to expand the scope of observation beyond the actions of Islamist actors alone, and to include in it their non-Islamist interlocutors too, be they local, regional, or international—as well as, more broadly still, their non-Muslim ones.

This brings me to put forward an analysis that undercuts the dominant reading of the mechanisms of sectarian radicalization. The *doxa* of common sense, which is especially endorsed in the thesis defended by Gilles Kepel, holds that sectarian radicalization is the prerequisite of political radicalization, or its cause.[12] I offer a strictly opposite interpretation. In no sense is sectarian radicalization—that is, adopting demeaning or even criminalizing categories to define the Other's sense of belonging—the trigger of political violence. Rather, it is merely an auxiliary or incidental factor, far more a product than it is a cause. This is old news that few, however, wish to face up to. It can be summed up as follows: the assumption that what is required to calm tensions is to reform radical religious thought leads down the wrong path. The region will not be pacified by reforming religious thought. It is by pacifying the region that religious discourse can be reformed.

My student backpacking days sowed the seeds of what I later felt to be a phase of intuitive accumulation. It gave me the opportunity to encounter cultural and religious Otherness in every shape, form, and historical configuration, from the Arab Mediterranean to Nepal and Japan. It made me more or less consciously internalize the conviction that cultural and religious differences were in no sense incompatible with my inherited, universalist humanism. In other words, I internalized the proverb that says "Never judge a book by its cover": a self-evident fact that is seldom easily acknowledged as such.

An extended period of teaching and PhD research in Algeria (1973–80) then enabled me to embark on a more theoretical and historicized analysis of Otherness. The French National Center for Scientific Research (CNRS), to which I was admitted in 1983, gave me the opportunity to spend several lengthy and successive periods of immersion in the field: both the field of my research and the field of Otherness. It was in Egypt (1989–93) that I began this process of frequently lifting anchor that nurtured the comparative dimension upon which my approach came to be built. Later, in Yemen (1997–2003), Syria, and finally in Lebanon (2008–13), I continued on this path, making frequent shorter research trips (from Sudan to Iraq) from each of these postings to most of the surrounding countries. In between these extended postings, Islam in France—the "Other at home," as I perceived it at the time, along with most of my compatriots—began to constitute a new chapter of my research.

In parallel, presenting this research enabled me to interact with the academic worlds of each of the twenty-two Arab countries, as well as with dozens of others, from Australia to Chile through South Africa. Without spending an extended period of expatriation there, finally, two other theaters took up a more structural place within my research interests. These were, in chronological order, the experience of "revolutionary" Libya, where I led my first research project when I first joined the CNRS, and the second, longer-term arena was, inevitably, the Israeli–Palestinian conflict. That conflict gradually came to appear to me as being a persistent echo of the old colonial disposition at the heart of the Arab world.

Between the Hammer of the Algerian Eradicators and the Anvil of French Islamophobia

In the second part of this book, I come to the circumstances in which my research choices led me to interact—often tensely—with my media and political environments, and with my key academic interlocutors. From my very earliest work, I grasped first the intellectual then the political price there would be to pay for my approach to Islamism. Those who did not share this approach considered it to be too complacently analytical. This cost soared from the early 1990s onwards, in successive contexts that warrant a brief recapitulation.

In Algeria, the repression that struck the Islamic Salvation Front (Front Islamique du Salut, FIS) in the wake of its parliamentary election victory of 1991 marked the onset of a lengthy civil war. This founding page of contemporary Algerian and regional history thoroughly confirmed that most French media embraced a simplistic and one-sided understanding of the Islamist trend that remained dominant since the Iranian revolution of 1979. In hindsight, the protest wave that the Algerian FIS then harnessed at the ballot box, followed by merciless counter-revolutionary repression, can be seen as the harbinger of the "Arab Springs" that flourished then faded twenty years later. Apart from the referendum of July 1, 1962, that was held in a very different context, these were the only non-rigged elections in Algerian history. Quite legally, they brought the opposition to the gates of power.

The prospect of a legalistic transfer of power was, however, entertained only very briefly. With the unfailing support of the West, with France and the European Union leading the field, the Algerian military establishment shifted a fight that it knew it had lost in the political arena into the security arena. To this end, it managed to impose an utterly falsified representation of the crisis. In the establishment's narrative, the Islamists threatened "democracy" and the "freedoms" that it suddenly pretended to embody, even while these values had been quite alien to its past practice. This vision was fervently relayed by a small section of the French-speaking Algerian intelligentsia. In Europe, it was internalized wholesale.

The party that had won the elections was purely and simply banned. There followed extrajudicial executions, forced disappearances, and the generalization of torture, in tandem with the systematic manipulation of the violence of "armed Islamist groups." Much of this violence was later shown to have consisted of "false flags" organized by the army. The Paris attacks of 1995 and the assassination of the monks of Tibhirine in 1996 were archetypes of the kinds of violence that the regime practiced with complete impunity, even while blaming it on its opponents. They exemplify the practices of a long civil war that would cost over 100,000 lives, including thousands of disappeared.[13]

Come 2019, despite a plethora of investigations and thoroughly documented confessions, the vast majority of French public opinion still refuses to accept the overwhelming responsibility of the junta in power. Imagine, then, at the onset of the 1990s, the level of resistance encountered by a researcher who contradicted the official narrative, and who dared to convey the narrative of the "victims," whom he had met in their various homes in exile. He could only become the target of violent protests, both within the academy and in the media and political arenas. Such, indeed, was my case. Far from ebbing, this tension only increased over the next two decades.

On the initially "Algerian" battlefield of the 1990s, the camp of those who proposed an over-ideologized reading of Islamism received very powerful backup from the Levant. In response to the Palestinian Islamist party Hamas asserting itself, the powerful mobilization of the pro-Israeli camp dramatically enhanced the imbalance of power. Condemnation of the entire Islamist generation, a condemnation that was exclusively ideologically based and stripped of any nuance, became the very core of an Israel-centered discourse. That generation was represented as made up of "fundamentalist enemies of peace." An authentic partnership was then forged between the Arab, Israeli, and Western players of the anti-Islamist struggle. The Sharm al-Sheikh anti-terrorist summit of 1996 made this partnership explicit and, to a degree, institutionalized it.

In this play to criminalize the Islamist camp, Israel then joined forces with those authoritarian regimes that I have termed the "Arab Pinochets." At the time, they sought out Western blessing, or even support, to contain their respective opposition movements. The anti-Islamist paradigm would henceforth become an essential cog in the self-justifying narrative of the most authoritarian Arab regimes. The effectiveness of raising the gauntlet of "It's me or the devil!" became unstoppable. The later landmarks of this trend were accelerated by the attacks of September 11. They are well known. The very next day, Israeli Prime Minister Ariel Sharon proclaimed: "Everyone has his own Bin Laden. Our Bin Laden is Yasser Arafat." It was within this analytical framework that the European Union denounced the Palestinian parliamentary elections of 2006—on the grounds that the Islamists had won them. This even while its own observers had certified that these elections had been free and fair.[14]

In the meantime, since 1989, France had fallen prey to its recurrent "[Muslim] Veil Crises," then to the controversy surrounding the cartoons of the Prophet Muhammad in 2006. These foretold the reactions to the first Islamist election victories in the wake of the Arab Spring of 2011. It then, of course, endured the terrible series of murderous attacks perpetrated by French terrorists "in the name of Islam," from Mehdi Nemmouche (May 2014 in Brussels) to Abdelhamid Abbaoud (presumed to be the mastermind of the terrible Paris attacks of November 13, 2015), and Mohamed Lahouaiej Bouhlel (July 2016 in Nice), through the Kouachi brothers who, in January 2015, assassinated the journalists of *Charlie Hebdo*. This succession of attacks led whole swaths of public opinion and the political classes of France and Europe, first, to tense up—and then to lurch into a process of Islamophobic radicalization.

Very early on, the French left, with a few exceptions (among them the Green Party and the New Anticapitalist Party) gave the impression that, in the race to retreat into the shell of identity politics, it meant to play the hare catching-up with the tortoise of the right that had set off earlier. It launched itself into the competition to reconquer the voters it had lost to the National Front. As Pascal Ménoret and Baptiste Lanaspèze wrote in 2006, "From Matignon [the office of France's prime minister] to the French Academy, via Sciences-Po," a single idea became hegemonic: "Muslims contain jihadists like chrysalids contain butterflies." More than ever before, "to seek to defend Islam from the accusations leveled at a billion and a half Muslims" comes with a steep price-tag attached: "To be exposed [...] to the accusation of 'Islamo-leftism,' of having Islamist, i.e. jihadist, sympathies—in short: of treason."[15] For my part, I remain ready to pay that price. Even if, to my mind, what is at stake is not "defending Islam." Rather, it is explaining how and why the Islamic vocabulary came to be the mode of expression of present-day rebellions that are far more political than they are religious, crowning historical processes that are perfectly amenable to being deconstructed.

From Al-Qaeda to ISIS: Islamist "Revolution"—or the Exacerbation of Western Failures?

This book has one last ambition. The breakthrough of ISIS in 2013, its regional expansion in August 2014, and its later recourse to international terrorism provide the opportunity to reassess the analytical leads that I had sketched out in *Islamism in the Shadow of al-Qaeda* and other writing since 2011, against what may seem to be a "shift" in the historical trajectory of Islamism.

The spectacular breakthrough of ISIS from May 2014 has likely not revolutionized the Islamist landscape as much as has been suggested.[16] Rather, it remains inscribed within the orbit of transnational radicalization, launched in the late 1980s by the founders of Al-Qaeda. The emergence of ISIS can be correlated with the same failures of political representation that first produced Al-Qaeda. Even the strategy of anchoring their fight within a given territory, represented as an absolute ISIS innovation, is not all that new. It bears recalling that Ben Laden himself, despite his reluctance to acknowledge the nation-state, sought to build himself a fortified redoubt in Taliban-ruled Afghanistan.[17] The major novelty of ISIS is twofold. First, given the Iraqi context, is the weight that it gives to its anti-Shia sectarian variable. Second is that the choice of the radicalist option—followed by initial and growing success—is no longer at the periphery of the societies in question. It is deep within them, too.

This process of political radicalization is first and foremost defined by rejecting the inclusive stance towards the reappropriation of democratic thought that had been initiated by the Muslim Brotherhood. It replaces this with an exclusionary condemnation of political thought as the merest impiety. Its logical corollary is the turn away from the ballot box—that is to say, away from the option embraced by the Muslim Brotherhood, at the other end of the Islamist spectrum, and which the Arab counter-revolutions in some sense confirmed was unrealistic—in favor of an armed struggle represented as unavoidable. This is the dynamic expressed by those who remind us that their respective strategic choices enabled the jihadists of ISIS to occupy half of Iraq. Meantime, it enabled the Muslim Brothers to occupy ... almost every prison cell in their country.

The novelty of ISIS lies less in its ideological or political hardening than in the abrupt increase in the mobilizing capacity of the radical Islamist fraction. For a long time, "Islamist radicals" in some sense respected the territorial limits determined by their local conditions. Their hold was limited to the periphery of the societies that had seen them arise. The entrance of ISIS into Mosul in August 2014 was cheered by at least some of its residents. It underscored a deep-rooted illness that consumes many regions of our globe. In Iraq, in Syria, but also in Yemen, in Mali, and likely in Nigeria too, extremists have entered into active synergy with whole swaths of local populations that are the victims of the institutions of their respective states, which are very deeply dysfunctional. The dead-end of institutional mechanisms has let exclusionary forms of management, whether "Shia," "Arab," or "Christian," erode their credibility. The archetypes are well known. Had they not been durably and intensely ostracized by the authorities in Bamako, never would the Touareg of northern Mali have entrusted their hopes to the *jihadi* groups returning from Libya. Nor would the first successes of ISIS have occurred absent the context of a reaction to the sudden downfall of the Sunni minority, under the blows of American purges in the wake of the invasion of 2003. That Sunni minority had, under Saddam Hussein's regime—notwithstanding its secular pretensions—*de facto* grown accustomed to the comforts of hegemony.

"Islamic" violence does not, therefore, emerge from "Islam." It is produced by the recent history of Muslims, and by the multiple authors of that history—very much including the Western neighbor.

Nearly thirty years on, the paragraphs with which I closed *The Islamic Movement in North Africa* seem to me as relevant as they were then:[18]

> In the great game of ideologies, the great producer and exporter of these ideologies—the Mediterranean North—has for years now had to contend with a rival. From the South, this rival has set about undermining the West's certainties, and competing for its constituency. Address the newcomer in French; it replies in Arabic. For "secularism," it hears "materialism"—and replies: "spirituality." It hears "state"—and answers "*umma*."[19] To "democracy," it prefers "*shura*."[20] For a decade now, the arguments exchanged by partisans and opponents of these new references have resembled a perfect dialogue of the deaf. To the modernizing elites of the South, these sounds—that is, the activist language of political Islam—are a threat. To the ears of the North, the Islamists' "Long live God!" rings as a message of defiance and rejection. Against the backdrop of economic uncertainties, political frustration and cultural crisis, Islamism, the new voice of the South, forges on regardless. [...] First, one independence at a time, it set about disconnecting its political future from the West's. Then, one nationalization at a time, it expressed its desire to recover more autonomy in managing its material resources. Now, it is starting to reconquer the ideological territory once lost to the North.
>
> Islamism is not the endpoint of the process through which the dominated South has repositioned itself vis-a-vis the North. But as the "third stage of the rocket of decolonization," it accelerates that process. Within a political environment that is unreceptive to challenge, it has sometimes made the choice of a violence that only states authorize themselves. As nationalist breakaways became routine, the "bogeyman" box in the Western

imagination had been left vacant. It was swiftly filled again by the figure of the indispensable "fundamentalist" so dear to it. No doubt, a temporary weakness in the North's ability to understand the South then increased the North's difficulty in grasping the reach of this self-emancipation. The 1970s underlined the West's struggle to, if not anticipate, then even so little as to follow the mutations of the Arab and Muslim environments. The efficiency of its domination had for a time given it the illusion of control over those environments, in each of the media and political spheres—and, to an extent, the academic sphere too.

On the right of the political spectrum, the Islamist bogeyman came to shore up already well-anchored dogmas. To its left, those who had once showed understanding towards nationalist self-emancipation often remained, precisely by virtue of this, convinced that they were "on the right side of history"—and that they were, as such, history's only legitimate actors. From the Islamist crucible, however, the conditions might emerge of the socio-cultural equilibrium that these societies have been in need of for so long: societies that skipped without a beat from the Big Sleep of decadence to the storms of colonization. Behind the mask of "fundamentalism," a synthesis is developing that, over the past century, neither colonial violence nor nationalist counter-violence proved capable of achieving.

Notes

1 Émile Zola, *The Dreyfus Affair: "J'Accuse" and Other Writings*, ed. Alain Pagès, trans. Eleanor Levieux, Yale University Press, New Haven, CT, 1998, p. 46.
2 *Libération*, June 1, 2016.
3 Together with a new Preface by Pascal Ménoret, the French version published in October 2016 (*Comprendre l'islam politique: une trajectoire de recherche 1973–2016*, La Découverte, Paris, 2016) features several updates for this English edition. Key chapters have been brought up to date with the most important recent developments and factual data. New analytical material and bibliographical references have been added, in particular in Chapter 14. A few sections deemed to be of less direct relevance to the English reader have been cut.
4 François Burgat, *L'Islamisme au Maghreb. La voix du Sud*, Payot, Paris, 3rd ed., 2008 (1st ed., Karthala, Paris, 1988), translated as *The Islamic Movement in North Africa*, 2nd ed., University of Texas Press, Austin, TX, 1997; *L'Islamisme en face*, La Découverte, Paris, 2nd ed., 2007 (1995), translated as *Face to Face with Political Islam*, I.B. Tauris, London, 2003; *L'Islamisme à l'heure d'Al-Qaida. Réislamisation, modernisation, radicalisations*, 2nd ed., La Découverte, Paris, 2010 (2005), translated as *Islamism in the Shadow of al-Qaeda*, University of Texas Press, Austin, TX, 2010.
5 The term "Arab Spring/s" has been subject to some debate. Nonetheless, I use it here to reflect the fact that it remains the shorthand for these events that is arguably still most widely used by the protagonists themselves.

6 A more systematic attempt at historicizing this process is forthcoming in a collection co-edited with Mathieu Rey, titled *From Al-Afghani to Baghdadi: A History of Islamist Movements*.
7 François Burgat, *Islamism in the Shadow of al-Qaeda*; and "Les mobilisations politiques à référent islamique," in Élizabeth Picard (ed.), *La Politique dans le monde arabe*, Armand Colin, Paris, 2006.
8 Albert Hourani, *Arabic Thought in the Liberal Age, 1798–1939*, Cambridge University Press, New York, 1962.
9 See Anne Wolf, *Political Islam in Tunisia: The History of Ennahda*, Hurst, New York, 2017.
10 Rory McCarthy, *Inside Tunisia's Al-Nahda: Between Politics and Preaching*, Cambridge University Press, Cambridge, 2018.
11 See François Burgat, *Islamism in the Shadow of al-Qaeda*,
12 "For Gilles Kepel, radicalization does not precede islamization. [...] [It is] the weight of Salafism [that] constitutes a radical cultural breach with the Republic. The new recruits, imbued with this ideology, [then] turn on the society that gave rise to them" ("Interview with Gilles Kepel," *Revue des Deux Mondes*, May 2016).
13 See in particular: Salah-Eddine Sidhoum and Algeria-Watch, "Algérie: la machine de mort," October 2003, https://algeria-watch.org/?p=52437 (last accessed June 15, 2019).
14 Nathan J. Brown, *When Victory Is Not an Option: Islamist Movements in Arab Politics*, Cornell University Press, Ithaca, NY, 2012.
15 Pascal Ménoret and Baptiste Lanaspeze, "Attentats: Daech, le résultat d'un vice de l'islam? Une idée reçue nourrie d'ignorance," *L'Obs/Le Plus*, March 27, 2016.
16 Pierre-Jean Luizard, *Le Piège Daech. L'État islamique ou le retour de l'histoire*, La Découverte, Paris, 2015; Abdel Bari Atwan, *Islamic State: The Digital Caliphate*, Saqi, London, 2015; Myriam Benraad, *Irak, la revanche de l'histoire. De l'occupation étrangère à l'État islamique*, Vendémiaire, Paris, 2015.
17 Mustapha Hamid and Leah Farall, *The Arabs at War in Afghanistan*, Hurst, London, 2015.
18 The original published translation has been slightly adapted.
19 World Muslim community.
20 Islamic principle of consultation.

Part I
Discovering the Muslim "Other"

1

Intuitive Accumulation

You think that it's you making a journey—but very soon, it's the journey that makes you—or unmakes you.
                                            Nicolas Bouvier, *L'Usage du monde*[1]

When I call on my memory, it tells me that I became absorbed in the Arab world one layer at a time. In various ways, these strata wound up occupying whole swaths of my life—and not only my professional life. Towards the end of the 19th century, around 1875, a branch of my father's family, which swiftly became a distant one, had emigrated from their native Savoie to Algeria. Over a century, the links between us had stretched to airy thinness—such that they have today vanished entirely. But as a child I regularly heard speak of these "Algerian cousins." They had left poor—likely after the economic catastrophe of losing part of their cattle that accidentally fell into a ravine on the road back from an alpine pasture. Family tradition recounts that two of them then took the road for Marseilles, and emigrated to "North Africa." Two or three generations later, at least some of their descendants had made it in Algeria. By the turn of the 1950s, one of them had become a senator and mayor of Souk-Ahras, the ancient "Lions' Market." Another was an Algiers municipal architect.

My family's mentions of these distant cousins were half-envious, half-reproving. Some of them had repatriated their earnings as early as the end of the 1950s and lived in the heart of France, in a small manor lodged amidst a vast cereal-growing estate. After all: Had they not "made the burnous-wearers[2] sweat"? The phrase was reported by my mother, who had heard it used by the "Algerian cousins" during a rare visit. She did not, in passing, necessarily betray true shock at it. It spoke of "the Arabs, for whom we built so many roads and schools, and who now reveal themselves to be so ingrate." The extended family went on to produce several of the countless shades that make up the palette of the French–Algerian relationship. There were cousins who had been "called to serve under the flag" during the Algerian War of Independence, and who took part in its worst episodes of violence, actively and without qualms. Other, women cousins filled the ranks of the first columns of "development" workers to replace France's retreating soldiers: part-adventurers, part-idealists, part-"pieds rouges,"[3] part-leftist Christians. As if, on this dispossessed land, the latter were tasked with redeeming the behavior of their own brothers—or of their ancestors. It was this pied-rouge network that was to become my own, one autumn morning of 1973.

That autumn morning, I walked away from the "Sarrasin" tower erected in my native Savoie, not far from the "Maurienne" ("Moorish") Valley. These were the products of a mixed history of which, at the time, I had almost no grasp at all, plunged as my adolescence had been in the discovery of the wider world.

At Home with the Other

My first encounter with the Arab world was not in Algeria, the country that later came to be central to my scholarly work. It occurred much further to the East, in the Orient of the "Holy Land" that was held out as being my own. In March 1964, for my sixteenth birthday, an aunt of mine—my baptism godmother—had proposed that I accompany her, via Beirut, to Jerusalem, in a mysterious—and so a magical—"Pilgrimage to the Holy Land." This land that we were to discover was not the Orient where the Other lived. Instead, it was to be the land of my Christian roots. The Orient that I first set off to encounter was therefore a curiously "dis-Oriented" one.

For a very long while, I remained unknowing of the fact that history had long since weaved a fine thread between my childhood hometown, Albertville (which was until 1835 known as L'Hôpital, "The Hospital") and the distant Orient. The small plateau sheltered from the flooding of the River Arly and that had, in the 12th century, at the foot of the village of Conflans, acquired its first church, had long been named "Jerusalem." As early as the 12th century, pilgrims on their way to the Holy Land via Rome had been cared for by the knights of Saint John of Jerusalem. The order had built a "maladrerie" or "maladière" (hospice) for them: one of the institutions designed to ease the passage of travelers through one of those routes ("maupas" or "malvies") crossing the especially difficult barrier of the Alps. "Thus did L'Hôpital-sous-Conflans come into being, which is first mentioned in the charters in 1216."[4]

The "Holy Land" that I discovered was thus one where, for the needs of the holy cause, the Muslim Others had been demoted to the status of passive spectator. In the best of cases, they became part of the décor. In the worst, they were a spoilsport to Christianization. On March 21, 1964, I flew in from Beirut to "Jerusalem Airport" at Qalandia that was to be shut down in 2001. (I have, since then, proudly told my Palestinian hosts that I used the airport at the time when their fathers were free to use it too—and to visit the Dome of the Rock as they pleased.) In the course of this first encounter, I understood little of that Orient. Little in it was Arab—and even less was Muslim. That Orient was primarily Christian, peopled by a few folkloric Jews in their "Orthodox" getup, countless nuns of all nationalities and orders, Jesuits and monks wandering in a décor strewn with churches, monasteries, convents, and basilicas far more than it was filled with mosques. On returning to France, rashly encouraged by my scoutmaster, I nonetheless inflicted my "explanations" of Palestine here and there on a few dozen resigned victims. These came built upon a peremptory argument: "I was there." Long before the age of social networks, I drove it home through the formidable means of literal "slideshows." Unlike printed photographs, these enabled the presenter to show off their ignorance (or to reveal their narcissism) to a captive audience …

Nonetheless, I did bring back in my luggage some early intellectual spoils from "Palestine"—mainly, an anxious feeling of dissonance. The understanding of the world that I had gathered from my family environment was based on *Paris Match*. My history and geography lessons had not added much to it. Concerning Israelis, I had mainly learned that they had "made the desert bloom"—and that this "desert" was a land in which, for centuries, the Arabs had contented themselves with meandering the dunes atop their dromedaries. This when they were not making the Americans extract from said dunes the oil that made some of them as scandalously rich as Emir Mohammed Ben Kalish Ezab, one of the heroes of Tintin in the *Land of Black Gold* (1950).[5] In Jericho, while on a search for cold drinks, our bus had by chance dropped off its pilgrim passengers near a "Palestinian refugee camp." An adolescent approached me, not scared off by my blue blazer, elasticated Scottish short-tie, and my Ray Charles or Paul Anka sunglasses (I forget which). In just a few words, he threw me into a world of perplexity: "The Jews took my country!" I was no more ignorant than the next high schooler. I had never yet heard that aspect of local history spoken of. The West Bank was still part of Jordan. The streets of the Holy City were still so narrow, and so steep, that the enormous American limousines that had been converted into collective taxis could barely drive past one another. The neighboring hilltops were not yet crowned by the invasive settler housing projects that were planted there much later, amid the oppressive atmosphere of the settlement era.

My second encounter with the Arab world was more intimate, but no less superficial. It took place between 1966 and 1973, in the name of a religion that I adopted for at least six or seven years: hitchhiking and "the road," Kerouac style or very nearly.⁶ This was the kind of long-distance journey in which the number of miles clocked up, ideally on the back of a truck, was worth more than any learned field trip. I came to realize only much later that I owed far more to this procession of hurried snapshots than a mere patchwork of miscellaneous memories. This phase of (very) intuitive accumulation was far from objective. It was, though, very intensive and, unbeknownst to me, beyond instructive.

During the Easter holidays before my baccalaureate, my parents paid for a language-study trip in Germany, the aim being to aid my final revision. The trip was nearly cancelled when my host family pulled out. The fallback solution suggested at the last minute was called *Jugendherberge*: a youth hostel. There, spellbound, I discovered a world of travelers whose strikingly varied itineraries were to become my own. "Where are you coming from? From Rome ... I'm going up to Stockholm ... I'm coming from Amsterdam, headed for Istanbul. You?" It became impossible not to throw myself into the same adventure.

Little could I have predicted how much this minor decision was to leave enduring marks on my future interpretations of the world. One morning of April 1966, a first, ludicrously easy hitchhike propelled me from Mannheim to the border with Denmark. It was then that I pledged to taste such pleasures again. Three months later, I made a trial run to Scandinavia's North Cape. Amid the fog of the Norwegian town of Honningsvag, the mythical goal of Europe's backpackers, I came to the firm conviction that the world was terribly small once one really decided to roam it.

My second great voyage came very soon after, at the end of July 1966— and this time, it involved leaving Europe. My baccalaureate under my belt, my backpack crowned by a duvet bedecked with the six, tricolor letters of the word "France," I reached the shores of the Arab Mediterranean, via Sicily, then Tunis. My goal was more ambitious yet. I was bound for Baghdad, a magical name that everything I was ignorant of as a fresh graduate converged upon—and so, therefore, did my every desire. Thus it was, during this ("petit") tour of the Mediterranean, that I came to be acquainted with the world that was to become my own.

"How Will You Be Able to Speak of the Orient, Once You Have Been There?"⁷

My first "discoveries" were modest. When an 18-year-old stepped out of the France of the "Trente Glorieuses" to live a little of Tunisia, Libya, Egypt, Lebanon, and Jordan, the "Arab" in the "Arab world" was less of a discovery than was (to me) the unusual market economy of what was then called the "third world." Some political rudiments did work their way through to me, for instance in Libya under the old king Idris Senussi (1889–1983). Libyans were to wait another three years for Gaddafi's "Great Revolution of September 1." Stunned, I observed the calm perversity of the king's customs officers as, one by one, they pierced wretched cans of tinned food. Palestinian and Egyptian migrant workers, white with rage under the sun and in the face of this insult, had brought these from their homeland. "Chak!" the tip of the blade sounded, as it pierced the lid of each tin of peaches in syrup. "Cruik!" the blade itself concluded, as, in the blink of an eye, it punched a triangular hole into the metal, destroying the can. The customs officer then sarcastically dipped an inquisitive finger through the hole before returning the can to its owner.

Inevitably, at the heart of any discovery of the Orient lies discovering the legendary geography of the desert. The traveler who follows Libya's Mediterranean coasts merely grazes that world. My real encounter with this mythical symbol of the Orient's geographical Otherness came only in Yemen's Hadhramaut, the legendary desert valley in the country's east. Far more so than in Algeria between Touggourt and Biskra, it was there that, between 1997 and 2003, at the wheel or in the back seat of indefatigable Land Cruisers, I came to fulfil my childhood dreams of dunes, sand, and starry nights.

In 1996, however, the real surprise to me came from the peculiarities of local shops. I could buy just a single "Vache qui rit" cheese, or just two cigarettes. A juice carton past its sell-by-date exploded as I tried to open it, on the banks of the Nile, at the foot of the old Egyptian ferry that then served as a youth hostel. Here was the truly new! Here was the breach with the Old World! How was I to imagine that, a quarter of a century later, in 1991, flying an antique motor glider, I would often overfly this same majestic corniche of the Nile in order to get my *taleb tayyar* (student pilot) diploma, by landing my handsome white-and-red bird, engines off and airbrakes purring, in the heart of the densely populated Embaba neighborhood—a stone's throw from Cairo's famed camel market? (All this without prompting too much protest—or too many corrections—from my instructor.) Or that, one dark day, this instructor would take a student even clumsier than me up into the clouds, and that adventure would end in tragedy ...

For the time being, the exoticism of that foundational summer of 1966 lay elsewhere. It inhered, for instance, in the young woman who, at a time of day when no sane creature would brave the heat, surreptitiously came to place a plate of cold fruit in front of the hitchhikers baking under the sun, without leaving them time or means to thank her. Or the ghostly customer who vanished after having paid for the foreign travelers' sandwiches. These were tales that handily filled the ancestors of text messages and other cyberchats: those nearly forgotten things called "postcards."

For the hitchhiker coming from Cairo, discovering Lebanon and Syria above all meant encountering the constraints and aberrations of the region's geopolitics—in the most brutal way, and so in rather traumatizing fashion. Lebanon was within touching distance. But getting there was out of the question by road: the "Israeli obstacle" made this impossible. From then on, a feeling hung over my every visit to the region: the Middle East, already so tiny, was extremely constrained by Israel—or by the conflict sparked by Israel's presence. The "near abroad" is radically near—as I was reminded when, many years later, as I drove "home" to Amman from Damascus, my car radio tuned to the Syrian state-owned station suddenly picked up an Israeli song, from across the waters of Lake Tiberias ... Near the Dead Sea, "Welcome to Israel!" adverts from Israeli cell phone companies flashed up on our phones. In the Quneitra area, facing the Golan Heights that Israel has occupied since 1973 and unilaterally annexed in 1981, the inhabitants exchange surreal greetings by waving their arms from either side of an iron curtain that splits their land in two and separates their families. At such moments, the absurdity of the political situation in the region emerged in full.

Very rarely, a border with Israel opens. For instance: the border with Egypt in 1981, after the Camp David Accords of September 1978. Just one morning on a bus, as short and fascinating as the road that crosses the Sinai desert, became all it took to get from Cairo to Jerusalem. I experienced this startling geopolitical shortcut several times. This was also the case each time I would cross one of the bridges that link the two banks of the Jordan River, and the two worlds that, from each side, eye each other with especially palpable tension: at the legendary ex-Allenby Bridge, or at its northern counterpart, Sheikh Hussein Bridge. Crossing the bridge sometimes allows one to take the pulse of the political moment. I once waited there for over seven hours. Granted, this is very far off the "records" that, in this depressing respect, the locals beat on a regular basis—as does any European citizen with a Middle Eastern-sounding name.

In July 1966, I arrived in Beirut. I did not yet know that, in his time, the poet Alphonse de Lamartine ("Allamartine" to readers most intimate with him), as he disembarked there, had described the city as "Syria's largest port."[8] Nor did I know then that it was French leaders who had drawn upon the map of the old Ottoman *Bilad al-Sham* (the Levant, i.e. the "Greater Syria" that encompassed, beyond today's Syria, the historical territory of Palestine, Jordan, and Lebanon), the dividing lines that matched their vision of the world so well. It was only forty-five years later, in 2011, that an advisor to President Michel Sleiman gave me the following abrupt—but enlightening—summary of Lebanon's political and confessional history: "The history of Lebanon is, first, the history of the political hegemony of the Christian community for whom the French created the country. Then, the history of the political emergence of the Sunni community. We are now in the third stage, that was delayed for so long: the self-assertion of the Shia community."

In 1966, close to Beirut's port, the great "Martyrs' Square" (formerly "Cannon Square") was still standing. Its name paid homage to the heroes of anti-Ottoman Arab nationalism. For once, it was not the French who had set up the gallows, or lined up the firing squad. How could I imagine that, twenty-six years later, I would wander in the exact same spot amidst the terrible field of ruins on the edge of the "demarcation line" between the two sides that had fought each other during the tragic Lebanese Civil War that left at least 130,000 dead between 1975 and 1990. In 1992, before he resolved to drive me there, from Muslim Hamra towards Christian Ashrafieh, my taxi driver broke down sobbing: "Fourteen years ... My God ... Fourteen years that I haven't been there ..." And a few days later, in Nabatiyeh, passersby exclaimed as I walked by: "A foreigner! See? The war really is over."

A member of Hezbollah then drove me at length around the "Dahiyeh" (the majority Shia southern suburb) before leading me to an unremarkable apartment on the third floor of a high-rise. There, I had the privilege of meeting the "Seyyed" (descendant of the Prophet) Hassan Nasrallah. Aged thirty-two, he had just been appointed Secretary-General of the Shia movement. Before we got there, the driver explained: "He never stays in a place at street level, to avoid being shot at directly from the street—nor on the top floor, to avoid air strikes." As I emerged from a long and fascinating meeting, I was more convinced than ever: my analytical framework for interpreting Islamism, as the new language of the old anti-colonial dynamic, then the anti-imperial one, was far from being the least insightful one available. My admiration for the beguiling figure of Nasrallah only increased over time. It culminated in 2006, when the Lebanese singer Julia Boutros, of leftist Christian political origin, composed a song (*Ahiba'i*) out of a few impassioned verses from one of the Seyyed's martial speeches. This was shortly before the determination of his troops earned them spectacular victories over the Israeli brigades that had unwisely come to measure themselves against Hezbollah on Lebanese soil. At the time, this "ecumenism" fleetingly swept aside the barriers between sects and confessions. It did not, unfortunately, survive the "Syrian Spring" of 2011—a subject I will return to. Hezbollah had been the fleeting hero of the Sunni world. It became the paradoxical ally of the repression led by the regime of Bashar al-Assad. And, everywhere except in Lebanon (where its alliance with the Christian Aounists endured), it *de facto* came to lock itself into the sectarian ghetto of its Shia identity.

Hariqa and the Forgotten Fires

In July 1966, the road that wound down into the Bekaa Valley, towards Baalbek or Damascus, was a wholly new experience to me. (Over forty years later, I was to drive it countless times to travel between branches of the French Institute in the Middle East (Institut Français du Proche-Orient, IFPO).) The pink Impala Chevrolet that had hoisted me up to the crests of the Dahr al-Baydar pass gave way to a Peugeot 403, whose driver, in his efforts to impress me, went on to drive standing upright on the front seat, very far away from his brakes, and with the tip of his right foot only. My later memories of this spectacular descent into the Bekaa—that also leads to Baalbek, the "stronghold of Hezbollah," as French television was soon to term it—also draw on the insistent presence of the memory of war in Lebanon.

In 1992, while I attended an Arabic language course in a country that had barely emerged from its terrible civil war, the driver of one of the countless Mercedes whose various models punctuate the history of Lebanon reminded me, after his fashion, of the violence of the conflict that was drawing to a close.[9] To use the steering wheel and gearshift, he had only two fingers of one single hand. My fellow passengers in the back seat pointed this out in anxious tones. Sat in the front, I could unfortunately do nothing to reassure them. As for maneuvering the brake, the clutch, and the accelerator, the driver, who had survived a grenade exploding, had only one leg left.

Damascus and its mosques—but also, as in Beirut, its churches—played host to me in the most fleeting way. The most destitute travelers slept on the hotel roofs. Under the stars, they were not necessarily the worst housed. From this first visit in 1966, I took away only a few fleeting images of the Great Souq. At the time, I did not even know that the name of the neighborhood in which the souq was located, *Hariqa* ("The Fire"), had something not-so-pretty to do with the history of the French presence in the region. Thirty years later, Syrian society reminded me in style of this not-very-republican duplicity on the part of know-it-all France. No more so than it had in colonized Algeria did France, entrusted with the League of Nations Mandate over Syria from 1920 to 1946, abstain from (ab)using the shortcuts of sectarianization—nor those of the most abrupt hard power. How many of those who discovered the great Hamidiyyeh Souq, the commercial and touristic temple of Syria's capital, knew that the neighborhood into which they are led by Midhat Pasha Street—the ancient Roman *Via Recta*—is called *Hariqa*, "The Fire"? How many of them knew that, in October 1925, the cannons whose salves set off the fire that ravaged the neighborhood were French? Or that, as they razed to the ground the handsomest examples of the town's bourgeois architecture, the Mandate power's weapons, which were theoretically entrusted with guiding the country towards independence, left behind nearly 1,500 casualties, in under 48 hours?[10] As he visited Damascus in September 2008, President Sarkozy nonetheless felt the need to proffer France's support to Syria to "help it remain on the path of secularism (laïcité)." These words sounded strange to the ears of those who had not forgotten how, a few years earlier, it was the selfsame France that had worked to divide Christians and Muslims, Kurds, Druze, and Alawis. It had thus sacrificed the humanist principles with which it purported, both at the time and to this day, to "civilize" the world, at the altar of its basest mercantile interests. No more so in 1966 than in 2008 did France's Mandatory past dim the warmth with which I was welcomed as a French visitor. Invariably, the three colors of the flag on my backpack were welcomed quite spontaneously. In 2019, what remains of such trust—in every corner of the political field?

In Amman, I attempted to sleep on a terrace of the lower part of the city. Jordan was infernally hot, and far too hermetic for me to be able to grasp any of the social or cultural nuances of the city. I did not yet know that it was extremely young—nor that most of its population consisted of Palestinian refugees. Nor could I imagine that its being Israel's immediate neighbor would so cruelly affect its history a year later, in June 1967. At the time, Iraq was quarantined, prey to a cholera epidemic. I soon gave up the eight-day wait for a second jab of the required vaccine, in a border post where the customs officers and other soldiers' interest in my youthful blondness became a little too intense. I was to wait forty-four years before reaching Baghdad, in 2010, on the back seat of an armored car, escorted by two members of the GIGN (France's SWAT teams) who enabled my visit as Director of the French Institute in the Middle East. In the meantime, the Arab world—from Algeria to Yemen through Libya and Syria—had swallowed me up almost entirely. But my first Mediterranean tour had not yet delivered up all its lessons.

On the road back from this first adventure in "Arabia," the chief impression made upon me by Aleppo was that it was guilty of being excessively ... normal. As I sat on the stone bench of a square at the edge of the Old City, I could scarcely overcome my surprise that so many passersby from this part of my world could, a few differences in dress aside, have been walking the streets of my native Savoie without prompting the least curiosity. "One in three Syrians has the face of a minister" was among the other souvenirs I brought back with me. To Aleppo, I was to return often. On one of the last occasions, in 2010, it was to listen to Mufti Hassoun explain to me that, during his studies, he had lived "in 'F' Building of Paris's University Village in Antony." And thus that he had moved, as he pointed out insisting on the "F" in each, "from 'F' Building to Dar al-Ifta," the House of *Fatwa*s. The quip was funny ... and the hell of the civil war in which his son was to be assassinated did not yet rear its head above Aleppo's Citadel, which overlooked his office. My instinctive feeling of closeness with many of the people of Aleppo (and with so many other Syrians) played its part in the depth of the dismay I have felt since, as, with such absolute impotence, I witnessed the slow agony of their country.

In Istanbul, at the close of my first journey of the summer of 1966, my finances came perilously close to going in the red. I discovered with fascination that the word *chai* crossed the boundaries of Arabic, and still allowed me to order a glass of tea. But I had yet to truly understand what Constantinople had represented, and how the history of the Ottoman Empire and the deep footprint that it had left across nearly the entire Arab world interlocked in the history of the region. For the time being, I ended my journey in Turkey's imposing capital, with an experience whose exoticism had little that was Orientalist about it. For a whole week, twice a day from 5 p.m. to 11 p.m., from atop an overheating circus tent, headphones on my ears, eyes blurry from sweat, I wielded a giant—and recalcitrant—projector. Its beam, that could change both size and color, lit up the beaming sketches and artificial mishaps that dramatized the show put on by the skaters of the "great American *Holiday On Ice* troupe." To refill my pockets, I had let the American West steal from me five days of the Orient ...

The Orient Without Arabs

But I was swiftly to get on the road again. For I was then only at the very beginning of this very lengthy "way of the world" of mine. Other "highways" followed at great speed, in every sense of the word. A year later, after a reunion with Turkey, it was first onto Iran, then Afghanistan, India from north to south, and, inevitably, Nepal. This itinerary had been the road taken in 1955 by my illustrious predecessor Nicolas Bouvier, whom I came to see as the grand master of travel writing, at the wheel of his tiny Fiat Topolino. It had not yet become entirely commonplace. Bouvier's radiant formula, "it is when the sacred is threatened that one comes to discover that it exists,"[11] was not yet ringing in the head of the worshipper of the road and future "Islamism-ologist" that I was then.

The year was 1967. Two more years were to pass before the release of the cult film that made the French dream of the "Roads to Kathmandu."[12] To fund the next journey, it was enough—for those who dared—to resell a few blocks of brown paste or (my only option) merely an Afghan coat made of embroidered Astrakhan fur. Gaunt hitchhikers roamed the ancient stage of Afghanistan, whose sugary tea, rice, and bananas were not always enough to calm the ravages of dysentery. Clearly there were many lessons to be learned there. The state, bereft of any authority, had not yet succeeded in imposing the rule of its representatives. Below the windows to my Kabul lodgings, a policeman of distinctly unimposing bearing attempted in vain to apply the highway code to a (not-even-shiny) Mercedes—and to a driver who clearly denied it the right to exist. Applying his bumper to the knees of the representative of the law, the driver suddenly sped up, flinging the unfortunate policeman onto the hood. He just as suddenly applied the brakes, thrusting the symbol of state authority into the dust of the main street, at the feet of a crowd of gawking onlookers. In neighboring Pakistan, at the edges of the tribal areas, which had not yet been made famous by the "War on Terror," I sat in front of one of Pakistan's fascinating artisanal arms-reproduction workshops. A society torn between the extremes of its accelerated mutation passed before the eyes of the old schoolboy and apprentice political scientist that I was still. What a harvest! What a quantity of things to think through, to historicize, to understand ...

"Why does he not speak our language, since you tell me that he went to school?" an imposing bearded elder demanded to know of an air force pilot. Said pilot had sparred with a businessman for the privilege of inviting me—with a consideration and delicacy that left me speechless. *"Made in France, Mister?"* or *"Change money?"* the curious little children systematically asked foreigners passing through. I had reached a highly distinctive country for whoever has an interest in how Muslims confer political interpretation upon their religious doctrine. The "Land of the Pure" had come into being barely a year before I had. Like the "Jewish state," it was one of the rare states to have been founded on the basis of religious identity—in this instance, that of the Muslims who chose to grant themselves a destiny different to that of their countrymen in the rest of India. Today, it is fascinating to note that, in the space of half a century, the founding common denominator of Muslim identity has become diversified into the widest possible range of modes of political appropriation of Islam, from "seculars" to *"jihadis"* through, of course, the inevitable Sufis—and even the fascinating "Sufislamists."[13]

To this day, I likely have not yet quite clarified to myself all the diverse and contradictory lessons that I learned from my first contact with the "Indo-Pakistani" sub-continent. What does one "learn," exactly, by the Varanasi train station, coming upon a newborn abandoned at the feet of the passersby, a few dozen yards from yogis as radiant with serenity and wisdom as they are skeletal? What does one feel as one's eyes follow a bloated corpse, stomach-up, slowly floating down the Ganges in which thousands of pilgrims are bathing? Or in crossing the large black eyes of a charming young lady unselfconsciously defecating in the middle of the street ...? Here was material to argue for cultures being different indeed ... Might we, after all, not be quite the "same"?

And yet, beyond such striking sights, which widened the feeling of a cultural gap, I slowly came to acquire a more structural interpretive framework. Discovering the social and cultural codes of India and Nepal prompted an instructive comparatist instinct. For Delhi's urban elites in need of social self-assertion, whisky from the West was a modernist transgression. For the rest of the society, hashish was as ordinary and popular a national escape mechanism as the most commonplace bottle of red wine was back home. Even this realization came with lessons attached. One day in his dark and narrow lodgings in Kathmandu, my Nepalese Sanskrit teacher told me: "One thing I'll never understand is how you Westerners can drink alcohol without worrying that you'll then produce deformed children ..." In the same breath he explained, ceremoniously stuffing a black ball of opium behind his molars: "It's excellent for digestion! Didn't you know?"

The following year, in 1968, the ORTF, the French public TV and radio service at the time, awarded me a "Green Light for Adventure" bursary. The time has come to confess it: this was thanks to the pulling of strings by the Secretary of State for Tourism, mayor of Chambéry and a loose family acquaintance. I had also earned a comfortable sum from five pleasant weeks spent on the slopes of the ski resort of Chamrousse working for the US network ABC on their coverage of the Grenoble Winter Olympics. This let me plan to take off for Manaus. My project to film the depths of Amazonia came not only with this bursary, but also with the advice of the filmmaker François Reichenbach (1921–93). He was to advise me as I produced a little 16 mm documentary.

But into this spring of 1968—I had just turned twenty—the protest movement of May '68 came to the boil. At the University of Grenoble like elsewhere, the exams for the third year of my BA in Law were put back to September. It was now out of the question to leave for too distant climes. I had to be in a position to be revising from the beginning of August. That year, I nonetheless invested my Olympic winnings into discovering Iceland, a universe that was both distant and a little less so than my hoped-for destination of Amazonia. The great adventure was only delayed. Between June 1969 and September 1970, I extended these first milestones of my "intuitive accumulation" into a mythical "round-the-world trip." These two words were the stuff that my dreams were made of.

This grand tour opened with a hard-working but lucrative period in several American restaurants and hotels. It was followed up by two months on the road in Mexico and Central America, at the wheel of an unlikely Willys Jeep that the US market had, in its wisdom, chosen to adapt for civilian use, and that broke down constantly until it gave up the ghost along with three out of its six cylinders. These fourteen months in America followed by East Asia (from Denver to Tokyo via Honolulu; then from Japan to the Bosphorus) drove an exceptional—if largely subconscious—learning curve. This later proved decisive when the time came to add a more developed interpretation of the Other to the loose impressions of the backpacker.

From Discovering the American "Overlords" ... to the Orient, With and Without Muslims

Credit where credit is due. In the first of a long series of encounters with the United States, these offered up both the best and the worst. With impassioned surprise, I discovered there everything that unstoppably came to define everyday European "consumption," both material and cultural—and the secret of the positionality of the "dominated" European with respect to the New World's "master" or older brother. Already at the time, and notwithstanding certain obvious contradictions, American self-assurance inhered in the "rainbow nation" that Europe in the 2000s and 2010s was still struggling to understand and to develop—especially the fearful France of ex-prime ministers Manuel Valls, Éric Zemmour,[14] Caroline Fourest,[15] Marine Le Pen, and so many others.

In 1969, working in the US hospitality sector had the happy distinction of bringing the newcomer into contact with a very broad social and ethnic range of humanity. In Denver, right at the bottom of the pyramid of the division of labor, the potwasher, who scours by hand the pots that are too big or too burned to go through the dishwasher circuit, could be an East Asian who did not yet speak a word of English. Next up the chain came the dishwasher. Then the bus boy: S/he who sets up and takes down the tables, and whose only contact with customers was to bring them their sacrosanct glass of ice-cold water and to fill up, again and again, their indeed bottomless cup of coffee. Then the waiter, the captain, and the headwaiter, the "maître d'." This pyramid made room for nationalities considered more "noble" in the US, from American proletarians and students to Italian and French backpackers or immigrants. At the top of the pyramid, the managers, if they were not American, were often Germans. Finally, hotel work provided access to the whole range of guests who were most often Americans, and only very rarely foreigners.

Thus did the Albanian owner of "Café Prômeunade" on Larimer Square in Denver, CO, meet with great success whenever he solemnly introduced me to his customers as "Frannnsoua from Greunobeul, home of the 1968 Winter Olympics" ... And so did I—since my tips went up as a result, bringing ever closer the next stop on my itinerary.

But the deeper lessons provided by this youthful discovery of our American "overlords" lay elsewhere. The key discovery was likely the "well meaningly" racist disregard for the rest of the world, Old Europe included. This was often startlingly uneducated—"Do you have running water in your home?"—if not wholly ignorant: "What language do you speak in England?" or "To drive to Mexico, where will you take the boat?" Far more so than long speeches, the ill-informed disregard which deepest America locks itself up in enables measuring the limits of this intuitive deprecation of the Other, produced by ignorance of the Other's reality. In the relationship between the dominated and the dominant, it is not always as obvious as it might seem which of the two is most abused. Between the insulting party and the insulted one, the roles are sometimes reversed at the expense of the stronger party. Stronger not always meaning the most "intelligent."

On the next leg of my trip of 1969, my discovery of Southeast Asia turned on its head my understanding of the symbols and other markers of religiosity. In a previous glimpse of Oceania in Hawaii, I had come across a subdued echo of the great drama that had sent the survivors of the American and Canadian conquests of the West and the Far North down to the lowest rung of the social ladder, forever branding them with the trauma of their encounter with the "made in Europe" ogre of "civilization." I was to encounter this striking marker often as I came upon each new continent and new range of players of a "civilization" that had come at the expense of others: the despised *Indio*s in Chili, Aboriginals in Australia who had been driven alcoholic; blacks and mixed-race South Africans, whose apartheid regime determined how much and how well its prisoners could eat based on their skin color. What was the common denominator of this global drama? The "civilizing" parties had all come out of Old Europe.

Conversely, Japan provided a counter-shock as welcome as it was unexpected. This was the first occasion on which cultural and religious difference went hand in hand with a level of technological modernity that left a French student hopelessly behind the times in the great race towards progress. This was especially striking as soon as night fell in the Tokyo suburbs in which I had lost myself, pitifully confusing a hotel for public baths. The train that carried me to the World Fair in Osaka sped over 125 miles an hour. As they reversed, taxis blared out an electronic warning that I found especially fascinating. Not to mention the ingenious rods that allowed their back door to open automatically.

In Laos, on the road to Vientiane, a different lesson was no less instructive. In the fog of dawn, the driver stopped his truck in order to throw a string of firecrackers upon the statue of a topless goddess. Bare breasts and firecrackers made strange bedfellows in my "religiously correct" imagination. Yet it was indeed a prayer that the Other had just performed, a little like the fleeting "Hail Mary" that my own father might have recited, hands joined together, before one of the little shrines that dot France's roads, to conjure away the dangers of the adventure of taking his family on holiday.

Fruitful and unforgettable lessons, these. The culture that I had inherited did not have the monopoly of progress. To my mind, the conclusion had become obvious. To many of my contemporaries, however, it was none too obvious. This was a fact I was to have to get used to accepting—for a very long time indeed.

Notes

1 Nicolas Bouvier, *L'Usage du monde*, illustrated by Thierry Vernet, La Découverte, Paris, 2e ed., 2014 (1st ed, Droz, Geneva, 1963).
2 Traditional North African robe.
3 "Red feet," in reference to the "pied-noirs" ("black feet"), the French settlers in Algeria.
4 Joseph Garin, *En Savoie, la région d'Albertville. Son aspect, son histoire ses enfants*, Syndicat d'initiative, Albertville, 1928. In 1835 the king of Sardinia, Charles-Albert, who reigned over Savoie from Turin, decided to unite the twin towns of Conflans and L'Hôpital under the shared name of Albertville.
5 Louis Blin, *Le Monde arabe dans les albums de Tintin*, L'Harmattan, Paris, 2015.
6 Jack Kerouac, *On the Road*, Penguin, New York, 1999 [1957] (French edition *Sur la route*, Gallimard, "Folio" collection, Paris, 1976).
7 Heinrich Heine to Théophile Gauthier (quoted by Mathias Énard, *Boussole*, Actes Sud, Arles, 2015, p. 69).
8 During his journey through Syria in 1832 and 1833, Alphonse de Lamartine was told that some of his physical characteristics (especially the shape of the arch of his foot) indicated that he was of "Saracen" ancestry. "You may believe that you are of French ancestry, but you are not," two of his female interlocutors suggested to him. "If you go deeper into your genealogy, you will certainly discover that you are a Saracen. [...] I began to be struck in turn by the miraculous intelligence behind these two young women's recognition of physical signs," the celebrated traveller noted, continuing: "For it was not so many years ago that the true name of my ancestors was Allamartine, and, according to tradition, they had come from a large village in the Mâconnais [in the Burgundy region of the south of France], a colony that had remained exclusively Arab to this day, and in which no unsuitable marriage had mixed Arab blood with Gallic blood." (Alphonse de Lamartine, *Voyage en Orient*

(1832–1833), edited, introduced, and annotated by Hussein El-Mudarris and Olivier Sahnon, prefaced by Mahat Farah al-Khoury, Dar al-Mudarris, Aleppo, 2009).
9 See Hadi Zaccak's film *Mar Sedes*, Beirut, 2012.
10 See the reissue of the book first published in 1927 by Alice Poulleau, *À Damas sous les bombes. Journal d'une Française pendant la révolte syrienne (1924–1926)*, preface by François Burgat, L'Harmattan, Paris, 2013.
11 Nicolas Bouvier, *L'Usage du monde*.
12 *Les Chemins de Kathmandou* (1969), released in English as *The Pleasure Pit*.
13 See Alix Philippon, *La Politique du PIR. Du soufisme au soufislamisme: recomposition, modernisation et mobilisation des « confréries » au Pakistan*, PhD thesis in Political Science directed by François Burgat, Institut d'études politiques, Aix-En-Provence, 2009. Published as *Soufisme et politique au Pakistan. Le mouvement barelwi à l'heure de la « guerre contre le terrorisme »*, Karthala, Paris, 2011.
14 Eric Zemmour is a far-right polemicist who promotes a theory alleging the "Grand Replacement" (of so-called "de souche" ("trueblood") French by immigrant populations of Muslim culture).
15 See Chapter 11.

2

Algeria: Approaching the Other

In September 1973, after this "round-the-world trip," I moved to Algeria. Since my PhD also involved teaching at the Law faculty of the University of Constantine, this also meant leaving strictly student life behind. It is at this stage that I took up a less impressionistic, more professional, and more systematic approach to knowledge.

Algeria—which had, via cousins from there, filled my adolescent imagination—was no longer quite unknown to me. It had not been a part of my "small" tour of the Mediterranean. But, in the spring of 1968, I had got to take a first look at it. During the Easter vacation, I hurtled down to the end of the Nationale 7 motorway, hitchhiking. A ferry from Marseilles then led me to Algeria, along with the Germanophile friend who had accompanied me to Nepal a year earlier. One of my cousins hosted us there. My host and guide had become wedded, in some order, first, to the country in which he had fought the war; next, to business; and, finally, to the wife he found there. On the public square of a village in Kabylia, one of his friends or clients insisted on hosting us. We first walked for a quarter of an hour on a steep path, at sunset. Then, at nightfall, we were invited to enter a low-ceilinged room in which a good dozen guests of all ages were already seated. At the sight of us, an incredibly wrinkled little woman pronounced a few incomprehensible words that, as they emerged from her toothless mouth, triggered general hilarity. The friend felt obliged to translate what all those who lived through the seven rough years of the War of Independence will already have guessed: "So, these three: we don't slit their throats?"

This was the country that I settled in five years later, in 1973. I was to stay until 1980, during which I would teach a little—and learn much more.

The Other's History: An Other History?

I was not in Algeria searching for anything specific. Becoming a *coopérant*,[1] as we called it then, was above all a means of escaping active military service, as an overwhelming majority of my fellow students of the time sought to do. On enlistment day, an officer asked those interested in "advanced military preparation" to make themselves known. Not one of the thirty deferred conscripts present raised their hand. He had taken this very badly. Such was the spirit of the times. In fact, I was nearly declared unfit for service. One of the mysterious notes scrawled by the psychiatrist on my medical fitness report mentioned a "tendency to uncontrollable laughter." Worse still, in my attempt to understand this diagnosis, I had been unable to contain myself from … roaring with laughter. After a few years spent discovering the world in the breaks between my law studies, faced with the deadline for obligatory military service, I had very conventionally opted for deferment.

Once the deadlines for enlisting ran out, I signed up for "Volunteering as Active National Service." This made me, for a year and a half, a "VSNA." I am often asked: "At what point did you begin to feel especially drawn to the Arab world?" Periodically, some even dare to ask: "When did you begin to feel drawn to Islam?" In truth, going to Algeria was not a choice. Not a moral one—nor a political one. On the Ministry's forms, my wishes had been very clear. It was Argentina that I wished to go to—or, failing that, to Chile. And, like a few thousand others of the post-1968 generation, it was to Algeria that I was assigned for two years. So it was in Algeria that my intellectual trajectory began to take shape. By chance at first, and more consciously thereafter. After a year and a half of VSNA, I chose to extend my stay for five years, primarily to write my thesis. The Algeria of the 1970s was to offer me my first and most marking opportunity to build up an analytical distance from the pillars and certainties of my inherited culture: intellectually, in organized and conscious fashion, and no longer simply intuitively, as I had through my first adventures.

In fact, my political consciousness was very slow to take shape. Unlike that of most of my classmates, it had not crystallized in response to the disparity in wealth distribution that was the classical jumping-off point for the paths of leftist militants. It was only in Algeria that I became political. This did not happen, as it did to many others, through putting myself at the service of the political project of the leaders of the country. Rather, it was there that I discovered the scale of the distortion between my inherited culture and the one that was born of my first readings in history.

Franco-Algerian history had been present in my family and educational environment only through references to the Algerian war, to *"fellagas,"*[2] to "ingrate Arabs," and to the "pieds noirs." But the roles (and the responsibilities) of each party had been curiously miscast. The script of the nineteen years of the conquest, with its procession of massacres and systematic destruction, was absent. Absolutely key episodes of repression had barely entered into my knowledge of Algeria, such as the massacres of North Constantine in May–June 1945, at the very moment when Paris was celebrating the Nazi enemy's surrender. Neither had the especially shameful episodes of our treatment of the *harkis*. In fact, the central importance of this major (if not foundational) episode of our modern history—the violent domination of one society by another—had not yet been faced up to. (In 2019, this is likely still not the case for many French citizens.) In Marseilles a few years later, I interacted with high schoolers who were children of *harkis*, and who were torn between Algerian nationalist violence and the upfront racism of their supposed French compatriots. I was then able to grasp the scale of a terrible waste. Unsurprisingly, the internal convulsions of the French national fabric would soon become its echo chamber. In 2005, it was only natural for me to sign the call of the "Indigenous of the Republic" movement, as it was to publish in the first five issues of their journal. From very early on, their struggle was mine, too.

In Constantine, starting in September 1973, I read the memoirs of the French officers of the army of conquest. This initiated a deep reconstruction of my slender historical knowledge. More even than mere violence, this reading enabled me to glimpse how efficient had been the work of all those who had made it their task to conceal this history from me. Then came the writing of the historians, both French (Charles-Robert Ageron,[3] Charles-André Julien[4]) and Algerian. In turn, these allowed me to decipher the mechanisms of the land and economic dispossession that had followed the crushing of resistance by military force, and to grasp their impact.[5] The "History of the Other" was not all that complex after all. France's "civilizing presence" had been asserted through the pillage of land, pure and simple. "Everywhere there is good water and fertile land," General Bugeaud wrote, "there we must settle. Without seeking to know to whom the land belongs, it must be distributed as if it were indisputably ours."

Last but not least, other writings, from Pierre Bourdieu to Malek Bennabi,[6] while waiting for Edward Said, brought the final touch to my historical reconstruction—and my political self-construction. These were by far the most important touch. They granted me access to a third stratum of understanding. Namely: to the complex (and less immediately obvious) deculturation that had crowned the military rout and the economic and social disaggregation of the defeated. Only then did the impact of 132 years of colonization, following on from 19 years of conquest, appear before me in its full sweep. Upon the ruins of the great Abdelkader's resistance, Algerian society had been inexorably crushed.

It was a shock to discover the double violence of the conquest—military, then economic—that was so often euphemized by official "French history."

I then began to process the decisive importance of the third, cultural level of colonial domination—and the complex interlinking between the contradictions that are to this day spread by this third dimension, contradictions that are as enduring as they are deep. It was with respect to this field of symbolic violence that I would gradually develop my first hypotheses.

The paradigm of cultural dispossession is less tangible than was political domination, or the dispossession of land and economy. This remained unspoken for decades. In Europe, it was even praised in the name of "civilization." Yet it is through this scale of dispossession that the dominated society slowly acquired the sense that its symbolic universe was being discredited, made peripheral and marginalized, and that it was starting to become "indigenized." Its entire symbolic universe was reduced to the role of foil of the "modernity" of the dominant society's universe, which henceforth monopolized the expression of universality. It was my awakening to this hidden, cultural level of colonization that would structure my nascent political consciousness.

Reading the great Malek Bennabi, one of the greatest—but also the least-acknowledged—Algerian intellectuals of his generation, later enabled me to refine my understanding of the implacable mechanisms of cultural domination and symbolic violence. One after another, the economic and cultural frameworks of the conquered society succumbed to the imported models. As Bennabi deciphered the process in a striking phrase, the dominated society "keeps its appearance" but "loses the substance." As the "social and moral orders" were transformed, "outward appearance itself began to change." "Society [...] was being vulgarized from the top, and impoverished from the bottom." Even men's clothing underwent "this degrading evolution," unstoppably overcome by "the European clothing of the Marseilles second-hand shops." "The town, too," was becoming split "into two worlds: indigenous life was becoming confined to the alleyways and dead-ends of Sidi-Rached."

Nor did the arts escape the symbolic violence of imported innovations. On the evening of July 14, Bennabi's grandmother, "hearing the brass, the percussion and the bass drum of a music whose echo spread throughout the town into the marvelous summer night of Tebessa," invariably said something like: "How barbarous!" Enrolling in the victor's army then became the final refuge of those whom the system had pushed to its margins, whether they were dispossessed peasants or ruined artisans. "Impoverishment ['clochardisation'] entered into everything."[7]

I thereby discovered the problematic of identity politics. This was the least immediately apparent component of systems of domination. It would soon help me to lay out the foundations of my interpretation of Islamism.

The cultural dispossession inherent in colonial domination ultimately nurtured an inverse dynamic. Namely: a passionate, emotional, and thus often a proactive reunion between the dominated society and the symbolic universe of the "father's culture": that which the foreign intrusion had for a time managed to "folklorize." On the part of the "dispossessed" former colonizer, this dynamic provoked a rejection as violent as had been his fugitive dream of conferring the monopoly of universality upon the culture of his powerful "tribe."

The Enlightenment for Some ... but Not for Others?

The political duplicity of the colonial policy of "my" France was boundless. Its echoes would ring long after independence in the dominant political and historical discourse. They thus became the foundation stone of my intimate, private political self-construction. The history of "the Other" mainly revealed itself to be an "Other history." It had been purged of the devastation caused by the blinding one-sidedness of the history written by the colonizer. This had all but systematically excluded from it the lived experience and suffering of the colonized. The latter were viciously euphemized, manipulated, denied.

This duplicity would gradually appear to me as a kind of trademark, a shameful flaw of the French Republic. Thereafter, and to this day, I would look upon that Republic as a kind of champion of double standards. Could it be that France was the country of the rights of ... some men only? Did its Enlightenment values, brandished by the French rights-of-man *doxa*, shine only upon one of the two sides of the road of history: its own? Were its purported universal values not subject to a pitiful double standard, the victims of a kind of ethnic or tribal confiscation that stripped them of meaning, and destroyed their significance?

From 1973 to 1980, then, my car bore the license plate "CT—DZ." DZ stood for "Al-Djaza'ir": "Algeria" in Arabic. (As I was soon intrigued to discover, this was the plural of *djazira* (island): a first invitation to interpret the world beyond the limits of my mother tongue.) "CT" stood for *coopérant technique* ("technical volunteer")—or, as some of our much worse-paid Algerian colleagues quipped at the time, *course au trésor* (gold-rush). Here was a first prompt to grasp the Other's gaze in its full complexity and ambivalence. All the more so when one is naïve enough to believe that one is getting closer to it. The barriers, and the cultural barrier especially, remained far higher than I could imagine at first. In 1976, in Algeria, Fridays replaced Sundays as the weekly day of rest. The monopoly of universality that the Lord's Day had held in my eyes until then was suddenly removed.

My relationship with Algeria was complex, the country's diversity disconcerting. Primarily, it could be written in the tone of a reassuring proximity and complicity; intimacy, even. Such was the case with young friends and teacher colleagues at the university. But this could also extend even to the "oldies" who had known every aspect of colonization, including its darkest ones. They knew full well how dehumanizing it had been. But they had also lived it in its quotidian complexity. This could not be reduced to the requirements of official nationalist discourse, which was compelled to foreshorten perspectives and not encumber itself with the complexity of individual perceptions. "Look at my leg, it's Captain Michel who did that to me. It was the war; that's over, today." What, then, could one say when "Michel," "François," "Maurice," and "René," to greet us, happily started ... barking and pulling at their leash? It wasn't their fault if their owners, our hosts in Constantine, all of whom had been National Liberation Front (FLN) guerrillas and boar hunters, had given them the names of French officers stationed in the region. But even those memories contained shades of gray: "Captain Michel, he was a good guy, he was."

What could be said of the unflappable politeness of a young bookseller of Constantine's rue des Arcades? One question too many from me revealed that he had fallen victim to the endless parade of humiliation and violence. This had not been during the War of Independence—but just the week before, in 1975. It was the treatment reserved for immigrants by the French Republic of Valéry Giscard d'Estaing, which at the time was increasingly deporting such undesirables.

There were, of course, a few exceptions to the general rule of courtesy expressed towards the citizens of the former colonial metropole. Because they were so rare, and therefore unexpected, these exceptions were devastating. I was spat at, at the entrance to the old city of Constantine, to the sound of a ringing "Race of murderers!" Out of the blue, a slap traumatized the girlfriend from Grenoble to whom I had hoped to show the medina.

The contrasting lessons that I learned during my long years in Algeria were foundational. This Algeria, its men and its women, their beliefs and their expectations, like their hopes that were so often disappointed by "my" Republic's catalogue of failures, settled very lastingly in my imagination. They would forever shape my later relationship with the Arab world.

For a foreign academic, to teach law in Algeria was also an invitation to reflect upon the content and the political significance of such teaching, in the light of the country's social realities and the reformist ambitions of its rulers—in ways that were rarely possible in French universities, and no matter how clumsily. Within the interactive setup of teaching sections, it also meant learning from the broad spectrum of students I engaged with over seven successive years. Finally, to teach in Algeria at this juncture meant to open oneself up, beyond the host country itself, to the many nationalities of one's teaching colleagues: Syrians, Egyptians, Palestinians, Iraqis, Lebanese, Romanians ... These forged a lasting network of relationships and friendships. A decade later, I would head to Amman to meet up with Abed al-Alami, a Palestinian economist. Two decades on, I traveled to Nabatieh, in neighboring South Lebanon, to reencounter Ibrahim Kubeissy, another of my Algeria-period colleagues. In the meantime, he had become the influential rector of the great Lebanese university there.

The Algerian Regime's Third-Worldist Self-Assertion

Before the Islamic Salvation Front (Front Islamique du Salut, FIS) suddenly entered the political scene in 1989, then defined it during the 1990s, the Algeria of the 1970s was defined by the Agrarian Revolution and heavy industry. These were the two pillars of development upon which the country sought to emerge from its dependence on hydrocarbons, and to perfect its independence. For the countries that the Cold War had thrust into the "third world," this was the time of popular anti-imperialist mobilization, in order to join the countries of the "Free World" and the "Communist Bloc" among the frontrunners of economic development.

Among some of the defenders of Western hegemony, the premonition that these wretched of the earth would inevitably challenge it prompted irritated and alarmist reactions. In 1959, the foreign correspondent Jacques Benoist-Méchin (1901–83), once a senior civil servant of the Vichy regime, and just back from several months primarily in the Middle East, published his *Arab Spring*. In the region, he had come to understand the obvious that perturbed so many of his compatriots: "The scale of the human masses that people the extra-European world. It struck me [...] directly, almost physically, as did their increasing refusal to be governed by us. This is a factor that escaped my notice 20 years ago, because it was not so clearly apparent."[8] In a mixture of naïvety and cynicism, if not simple distress, he betrayed the master's anxiety at the irrepressible self-assertion of the dominated. The anxiety was proportionate to the realization that Western leaders no longer had the means to oppose it:

> To strive to prevent this world from growing and organizing itself would be as vain as to fit a butterfly back into its chrysalid, or to fit a tree back into the seed from whence it sprang. One would have to have never invented the radio, that spreads ideas; nor the press, that governs them; nor the aeroplane, that eases interpersonal contact and allows the human groups most distant from each other to discover their common existence and to measure up their points of view. One would have to tear up the telephone and telegraph networks, abolish schools, close mosques, forbid access to

university, and systematically raze the factories and building sites. That is to say: to sterilize every place in which opinion is formed. Not only would this be odious; it would also be ineffective.[9]

Nationalist self-assertion developed in a Franco-Algerian atmosphere poisoned by resentment. In April 1975, the first visit to independent Algeria by a French head of state had failed to quell the fallen colonizer's discontent. Quite the contrary. Instead of feeling honored by the exceptional presence of his host, Houari Boumediene, at a reception held at the French embassy, Valéry Giscard d'Estaing preferred to convey his irritation at Boumediene's "Gaullian" tone. In the plane that flew him back to France, the French president was reported to have let loose the hostile sarcasm of a former proponent of *Algérie Française*, in front of journalists including *Le Monde*'s correspondent Daniel Junqua: "Every country must have an enemy ... Well: ours will be Algeria!"

I intuited very early on that the colonized of the "third world" would nurse the legitimate ambition of taking a slow but inexorable revenge over the nations of the "first world." The cultural aspects of this rehabilitation, however, appeared to me only much more gradually. So did the unexpected role played in it by the vocabulary of "endogenous" culture, and of the elites long considered as the guardians of "tradition."

During the 1970s, Algeria was the archetypal model of an economy and political society tightly conditioned by oil rent. A sort of "force tranquille"[10] of third-worldism defined the times. The Algeria of Houari Boumediene (1932–78) was an "Algeria of certainties." These certainties leaned on the limitless means provided by oil rent, especially in the wake of the price shock following the 1973 Arab–Israeli War. Granted, the country's institutions were not exactly those of a representative democracy. But they were at least coherent with the reality of the exercise of political decision-making. The reigning institutional leader, the head of state, held most of this power. The country had not yet entered into the institutional schizophrenia that began with the death of Houari Boumediene in December 1978. (Boumediene was never really replaced by the pale Chadli Bendjedid (1929–2012).) This ongoing period witnessed the dissociation between the formal titleholder of power and the real decision-makers: the army and the intelligence services. The "Algerian Way"[11] of the 1970s still seemed clear. It aimed at development, and internal debate was dominated by economic questions. Countries built "heavy industry" and waited, as promised by the Grenoble economist Gérard Destanne de Bernis (1928–2010), for their "industrializing" potential to be revealed. Far removed from questions of identity and religion, the only ideological debates concerned the nuances of the socialism that was being built. The debates that stirred the intellectuals I knew mainly concerned the choice between giving priority to the "development of the means of production" or, more "politically," to the "transformation of social relations."

Every year, generously endowed construction and facilities-building projects were launched. These included the Agrarian Revolution in 1971, of course—but also the Trans-Saharan (highway) to connect Algiers to Tamanrasset, the "Green Dam" that was to slow desertification in the north, and so forth. In theory, the property regimes that had been inherited from capitalist colonialism, rightly condemned as predatory, had been abolished. The world of education, in various ways, rubbed shoulders with the world of "development policies," and put its players at the heart of its projects. The University of Constantine hosted a research center, the CURER, also called a "production" center, that was the potential general contractor of development in the agricultural sector.

It takes as long to measure a policy's impact as it does to put it into practice, and hydrocarbon revenues allowed for deferring the time when a stringent accounting would be demanded. The Algerians of the time, both governing and governed, could therefore live in the almost complete illusion that it was all going to work out. The warning bells of the downturn in oil prices, and the parallel outburst of disillusion, had not yet tolled. A "Berber (but Berber-only) Spring" was to set the tone for the awakening of a society that, in 1980, suffered from a deficit in political participation. The great adventure of the first "Arab Spring," inaugurated by the electric shock of the riots of October 1988, had not yet been brutally crushed in an ocean of disinformation and blood.

A Thesis—but What For?

For the time being, both my teaching responsibilities and my thesis research were sending me in quite a different direction. I taught primarily as a teaching assistant in administrative law, to second-year BA students at the Law Faculty of Constantine University, on "Public Policy Organization and Action," two themes beloved of French jurists.

Nothing very stimulating to see here—except that Algerian law, close to French law, had nonetheless tried to distance itself from the French model, primarily in jurisdictional matters. I then taught a research seminar on planning and decentralization, the subject of my thesis on "The Socialist Villages of the Agrarian Revolution." To teach in Algeria was, above all, to engage demanding young people several times a week, on shifting themes. Like everywhere else, this required healthy efforts to frame and express oneself effectively. The constraints of didacticism conventionally require clear thinking—and therefore to clarify and to frame one's knowledge at least a little. I favor an aeronautical metaphor that highlights these valuable requirements of pedagogical vulgarization: "To fly low, you need powerful engines!"

The subject of my thesis did not remain my core concern for long. Electing to study the "Agrarian Revolution" launched in 1971 by Houari Boumediene's team was not exactly revolutionary, given its centrality to the regime's discourse. It did, however, respond to the authorities' appeal to participate in the research effort at the local level. Incidentally, for anyone contemplating a career in French law faculties, to choose an "Algerian" subject was not so common or recommended as all that. Beyond this, it was an attractive challenge: to try to answer the request to think through the "socialist" transition in which this moment of Algerian history was inscribed, "ideological" and didactic as it may have been. Fresh out of a Masters of Advanced Studies in Urban Studies, I subscribed rather spontaneously to this didactic vision (perhaps a little naïve as it was), which made a "revolutionary" urbanism one of the priorities of the country's post-colonial reorientation. In the discourse of its creators, the decentralized administration of these "socialist villages" was designed to crown decentralization and (a buzzword yet to be invented) the empowerment of the rural populations. These had benefited from the redistribution, no longer just of the colonial domains—that had been done as early as 1963—but also of part of the lands confiscated from Algerian landowners.

At the turn of the 1970s, my supervisor François d'Arcy was among the first jurists to have opened up nascent "juridical science" to the multidisciplinary demands of urbanistic reflection. The goal was to make the concept of juridical norm attain the rank of being considered an "expression of social balance of power." Legal research was stepping out of the splendid positivist isolation to which it had long been confined, to take up its rightful place in the field of sociological inquiry.

As the limits of my approach in dissecting a draft administrative and urbanistic law became swiftly apparent, I learned more by comparing the state's proactive discourse with the sociological reality that it purported to transform. I did not possess the language skills with which to conduct direct fieldwork with members of the cooperatives. Nor did I even have the methodological tools. Two Algerian colleagues from the sociology department, Abdelmajid Merdaci and Farid Benachour, generously helped me to formulate my research questions and, via their students, to put them to the respondents. We expected the results—but they far outstripped our expectations. The peasants were light-years away from the "socialist" consciousness that state discourse and its local surrogates ascribed to them. They were entirely disconnected from the revolutionary dynamic which they were supposed to be the heroes of.

I had fleetingly subscribed to a kind of Marxism, which came out of my first efforts to think through how my legal teaching related to a society "building socialism." This was shaken for good—and to very good avail. One milestone of this break with Communist *doxa* had nothing theoretical about it. In 1974, *La Nouvelle Critique,* the would-be academic journal of the French Communist Party, published a report on the visit of a delegation of the party's leadership to the cooperatives and villages born of the "Agrarian Revolution." This "report from the field" simply paraphrased the regime's triumphalist discourse. In the "analysis" of these brilliant organic intellectuals, the already-gaping cracks between the project's didactic aspirations and its confused and contradictory implementation were nowhere to be found. My discovery of this posture, with its overtones of imposture, if not forfeiture, was magnificently productive. The data collected thanks to the surveys that my colleagues had enabled confronted me with a substantially different reality: first, with the limits of state didacticism, no matter how seductive its reformist discourse may have been; second, with those of a perversion of Marxism from which I would thereafter distance myself for good.

Some years later, when I began to construct Islamism as the subject of my research, I would similarly distance myself, this time from the American political science canon that held sway at the time over French academic work on Algeria. In the nascent field of the study of political Islam, the theoretical bent of my political-scientist elders struck me as more cumbersome than it was enlightening. At the time, I used a quite radical metaphor to denounce the blatant limits of an unconvincing school of thought: "When theoretical crutches are too many and too tall, they become stilts. The researcher's feet no longer touch the ground. He is then cut off from the field." The current excesses of American quantitavists have since pushed me further towards a certain wariness and—without falling into the excesses of the "finger in the wind" approach—towards a certain methodological pragmatism.

The Waiting-Room for the Study of Political Islam

Berber linguistic and cultural claims were already discernible in the 1970s—but so were political ones, like those of the Kurds in the Middle East. These, however, remained concentrated around Algerian Kabylia, and so struggled to appear as a national alternative. As for religion, it was at the time completely bypassed by the *moussayrin* (managers) of the ruling elite. For over two decades, its presence in public debate remained remarkably discreet. Following in the steps of Habib Bourguiba (1903–2000), Houari Boumediene had clearly proclaimed that the more material demands of development took priority. He had unhesitatingly declared that "The suras of the Quran are not enough to feed the people." In the alphabetical index of his collected speeches of 1970–2, an entry for "Islam" is resplendently absent. At the letter "I," one finds only entries for "industrialization" and "institutions." And at the letter "R" for religion, one finds only "revolution (agrarian)" and "realizations" ("implementation"). On the international stage, in tune with the Nasserist revolution, Algeria was concerned above all else by reconquering its economic resources.

The breach that the emergence of Islamism over the next decade would reveal to the light of day was itself barely perceptible. In those days, it partly matched the demarcation line between partisans and opponents of the policy of "Arabizing" education in general, and higher education in particular. But only partly: the first crystallizations of Islamism took place in the French-speaking sections of the University of Algiers. Tensions and rivalries between Arabic speakers and French speakers were the tip of an iceberg whose shape was ill-defined. At the University of Constantine, as elsewhere in the country, the nascent Arabic-speaking sections primarily comprised the underprivileged: those who had been unable to access the French-speaking degrees. These were considered more "noble" and *de facto* granted far more access to the professions—since French very clearly remained the language of the political and economic elite.

I would later discover the extent to which these linguistic and cultural rifts cut across the entire globe. In Quebec, on the sidelines of a meeting of the Middle East Studies Association (MESA), a seminar at McGill University was disrupted by the aggressive protests of French speakers, frustrated at seeing the hegemony of English encroach there. More unexpectedly to me, another such episode occurred in Mauritania, which I discovered only late, in 2013. Several of those present at a conference that I gave in Nouakchott ostentatiously left the room when I accepted a request to answer the audience's questions in Arabic, the language of the Moors, rather than in French, as used by the southern ethnic groups. My very first awareness of the substratum of the emergence of Islamism probably came from the (at first confused) impression that the Arabic language contained a reservoir of meaning that remained out of reach of all foreign observers. In their overwhelming majority, they had deemed it superfluous, or beyond their abilities, to make Arabic an instrument of their political interpretation of the "Arab" world.

Even if the image is reductive, on each bank of the Rhumel, the symbolic architecture of Constantine confronted the tower of Ayn al-Bey University, completed in 1973 by the Brazilian architect Oscar Niemeyer, with the minaret of the great Emir Abdelkader University-Mosque, the bastion of "Islamist" teaching. The naysayers said that the construction flaws of both these architectural symbols—which some wished to interpret as opposites—would send both of them to the bottom of the deep gorges of the Rhumel River. As early as 1974, a seminar on the burning question of family law gave the embryonic Islamist camp the opportunity to make a spectacular coming-out. The university's rector, and professor of medicine, Abdelhak Berehri, drew on his karate-champion skills to push back the troublemakers. In French, these were called the "FM" (for "Frères Musulmans," Muslim Brothers); in Arabic, the *khwanjia*. This reference to the Egyptian Brothers was not entirely reductive. Many of the professors recruited in the service of the Arabization policy in higher education were Brotherhood activists, recently freed from prison by President Anwar al-Sadat, Nasser's successor, when he came to power in 1970.

In the field of political economy, a divide split partisans and opponents of the "Agrarian Revolution." The ideologues of Algerian Islamism condemned such socialism as a collectivist heresy.[12] For my part, however, I had not managed to construct the exact wording of this nascent split in academic terms, or of the formidable political potential that it contained, except in its obvious linguistic dimension—which was, as I have said, dangerously reductive. I remember only impassioned conversations according to which, even if it was obvious that Arabic-only speakers cut themselves off from whole swaths of the knowledge and labor markets, the French speakers should not lock themselves into the ghetto of monolingualism. The logic was that this risked depriving them someday soon of essential resources—political ones especially. In 1976, a philosopher colleague, Jacques Bouveresse, is said to have made a mysterious-sounding remark, with a premonition I envy. This as he watched a thickly-bearded young man walk past on the mythical Place de la Brèche (next to the Old City), where he was savoring the traditional "crêped" lemon sorbet: "One day, this country will have to contend with a terrible crisis."

The Language of the Other

My quest to learn Arabic took root in Algeria, as I discovered the cultural backstage of colonial domination. It expressed my will to go and see—and to read—this country more closely: a country I had ambitions to see more of than the main road trips allowed for. This quest stayed stubborn. To this day, it remains partly unsatisfied. Becoming able to express myself publicly on subjects tied to my research was eventually some reward. But my access to written sources remains tightly conditioned by the linguistic register, whose level of difficulty shifts entirely, from the median register of media vocabulary to the infinite traps of religious or other literatures—and, more so still, of poetry. Primarily, then, this never-ending learning process gave me reason to develop a sense of humility, and to be painfully skeptical as to the length of the road that always remains to be traveled, as soon as one steps off the beaten path of the relatively familiar registers of media language.

One of those who instilled in me the will to make progress, Henri d'Alverny, a Jesuit, had warned me. At the end of his magnificent *Arabic Language Course*, d'Alverny writes:

> And now, to progress with surety, take up the schoolbooks of children preparing for the Arabic primary school graduation certificate (9th, 8th, 7th years ...), read the texts with their explanations in Arabic, look up the meaning of new words, do written exercises. You'll make quite swift progress. If you continue like this for ten years, making progress each year, striving to express yourself and to have your expressions corrected, you'll begin to think in this language, and its treasures will be opened to you, along with the hearts of many men. It is worth the effort.

True, the satisfaction provided by the first achievements, no matter how modest, is immense. Ah! To have it confirmed that it is in fact "Coca Cola" that is written on the familiar bottle, and "Tunis" on the road sign that guided me back from Bizerte! Then, a few years later, when one's interlocutor adds a vibrant "Mashallah!" (literally: "what God has willed," an exclamation used to express admiration) when our conversation can actually go beyond the few Arabic words that the tourist generally likes to brandish, or the fragments of English or French that one has had the courtesy to let him use. Or when, on the shores of the Arabic-Persian Gulf, one has the satisfaction of being told: "No but really, we've had lots of French guest speakers. But this is the first time that the students respond!"

None too surprisingly, the linguistic common denominator collapses at least part of the barriers erected by politically correct communication with the "foreigner." I was to confirm this comforting fact a hundred times over. So it proved in 2010 with the taxi driver who, in the dead of night, drove me from my Damascus home to Amman Airport. Along with English, he slowly dropped the formulaic register of conversation about the road, or the country's touristic marvels. As we swallowed up mile upon mile, he morphed into a voluble activist, exasperated by the endless litany of injustices and insults that he had suffered in silence since he had been expelled from Palestine with his family. It was enlightening, too, to hear another of his colleagues exclaim, as we approached the grandiose remains of the Roman city of Jerash: "To you I can say this: why should *I* be proud of the ruins of Jerash? Jerash isn't me: it's you! Why should we be proud of the traces of your occupation?" In London in August 1999, I participated in Ahmad Mansour's flagship Al-Jazeera program ("Bila

Hudud," "Without Borders," a live 90 min show). A few days later, it was also gratifying to see that some of its millions of viewers seemed to have arranged to meet in the streets of Sanaa to greet me, with a touching complicity and, quite clearly, exuberant affection.

Of course, knowing the language does not always and everywhere provide comfort. Sometimes, it's better not to understand everything. "Shuf al-gawri-edhek!" ("Deal with the *gawri*"—one of Arabic's pale equivalents to nicknames for Arabs in French) rang out in the office of the Algerian Ministry of Culture into which I had ventured, in the early 1980s, to seek out statistics on the publishing sector. But granted: *gawri* is hardly all that harsh.

For many of us, researchers included, Egyptians do not have a president, as we do—but, rather, a "*ra'is.*" And Muslims do not worship God, but "Allah." And so on. When it is wielded from the outside, one of the most insidious traps of linguistic difference is that it is sometimes used to assert and to exploit a difference that translation can, in fact, perfectly well fill in. There is a paradox to this persistent presence of untranslated Arabic terminology in journalistic discourse, and sometimes in the social sciences. It is often those who are least fluent in the language in question who most feel the need to punctuate their analyses with it. They who have not taken the time to learn the Other's language maybe hope to paper over their deficiencies by lining up deceptive references. But there is also another interpretation. Why, in French, should one refer to a divisive "Allah"—when translating the word, which contains no hidden traps, would allow us to speak of the "God" that unites us? In practice, asserting the Other's irreducibility to a shared conceptual universe often conceals a more or less conscious desire to reinforce Otherness, rather than to reduce it. Unless, in fact, it reveals that very desire.

Notes

1 French equivalent of the British Voluntary Service Overseas, or the US Peace Corps.
2 *De facto* "Freedom fighters," pejorative in French.
3 Charles-Robert Ageron, *Histoire de l'Algérie contemporaine (1830–1988)*, PUF, Paris, 1990; *Les Algériens musulmans et la France (1871–1919)*, PUF, Paris, 1968.
4 Charles-André Julien, *Histoire de l'Algérie contemporaine, tome 1, La conquête et les débuts de la colonisation (1827–1871)*, PUF, Paris, 1964.
5 Djilali Sari, *La Dépossession des fellahs (1830–1962)*, SNED, Algiers, 1975.
6 Malek Bennabi, *Mémoires d'un témoin du siècle. L'enfant, l'étudiant, l'écrivain, les carnets*, Samar, Algiers, 2006; *Vocation de l'islam*, Seuil, Paris, 1958.
7 Malek Bennabi, *Mémoires d'un témoin du siècle*.

8 Jacques Benoist-Méchin, *Un printemps arabe*, Albin Michel, Paris, 1959.
9 Jacques Benoist-Méchin, *Un printemps arabe*.
10 François Mitterrand's winning campaign slogan for the French presidential election of 1981.
11 Kader Ammour, Christian Leucate, and Jean-Jacques Moulin, *La Voie algérienne. Les contradictions d'un développement national*, Maspero, Paris, 1974.
12 See, e.g., Abdellatif Sultani, *Al-mazdakiya hiyye asl al-ishtirakiyya*, Algiers, 1974 (François Burgat, *The Islamic Movement in North Africa*).

3

Prelude in the *Jamahiriyya*

> Ben Ali exiled his opponents, he wound up in exile, Mubarak imprisoned them, he wound up in prison, Gaddafi assassinated them, he wound up assassinated.
>
> Abdelhakim Belhadj, Libyan ex-*jihadi*, 2013[1]

Why did I first become interested in Islamists? I have been asked the question so often that I sometimes dream of being able to provide an unexpected answer. No, Archangel Gabriel had nothing to do with it! No—I did not hear voices. Nor did any celestial sign irresistibly call out to me to "turn towards Islam." My attraction towards the object that was to remain the core of my professional life for the long term was more prosaic. It emerged from a conjunction. On the one hand was the rise to visibility in world media of a new generation of political players. On the other, in the context of the 1980s, was my encounter with the Tunisian version of that dynamic. Beneath the thick veneer of its bureaucracy and its authoritarianism, the "socialism" of the Algerian state that I had studied throughout my PhD had quickly shown the limits of its revolutionary potential. Once that had been demystified, it lost a large part of its appeal to me. In the immediate aftermath of the Iranian revolution of 1979, the admirers of Imam Khomeini (and these were not only Shia) seemed intriguing newcomers to the Arab political scene. The Islamism of the Imam from Qom was ousting the Arab nationalism of Nasser's disciples. Muammar Gaddafi (1942–2011) himself—the "fiery colonel," as some journalists then described Libya's leader—had sustained himself in power since his 1969 coup. But even he was on his way to being demoted to the category of outdated versions of Arab political exoticism.

Field Trips in Tripoli

When I arrived at the CNRS in 1983, my research project did not center upon Islamism. This was a subject I was still coming to terms with. I was assigned to the Center for the Research and Study of Mediterranean Societies in Aix-en-Provence.² Aix-en-Provence was where the colonial archives—the so-called "Overseas Archives"—had been deposited in 1962. The project I proposed to the CNRS was to work on comparing Algeria, which I had just left, with "Gaddafi's Libya." In 1966 I had been able to cross what was then the kingdom of King Idriss Senussi, and later, in 1978, the great *Jamahiriyya* ("State of the Masses"). This had been the name chosen a year earlier by Gaddafi—who appointed himself "Guide of the Great September Revolution"—to convey the purported transfer of the exercise of power to the people. So I set about throwing myself into this, the second stage of my Arab peregrinations, in comparatist mode. Despite much media coverage, Libya remained much understudied in France. It had no colonial past there, excepting a fleeting presence in the Fezzan during the Second World War. At the time, bilateral relations oscillated between contentment in the business realm—this had culminated in 1973 with the sale of a hundred or so Mirage fighter jets by President Georges Pompidou—and armed skirmishes (especially through the proxy of Chad) through which France fought Libya's expansionist ambitions (unless it was the other way around).

I also recall, one day in February 1986, coming upon the political advisor to our ambassador in Tripoli. He had set himself up in the courtyard of the nearly deserted embassy, in front of an imposing brazier upon which piles of documents were going up in smoke. "There are, my dear Burgat, certain circumstances in which certain things must be done ... and not spoken," he enigmatically replied to my curious inquiry. The answer very quickly emerged of its own accord. Other Mirage fighter jets—these had very much remained in French hands—were readying for "Operation Sparrowhawk." They were to target Libyan facilities in Chad's Aouzou Strip, which the Colonel had his eyes on. The embassy had had its fingers burned before: the French consulate in Benghazi had been ransacked in 1980. It was now preparing for the worst, by burning all its documents.

My access to the field in Libya came without the institutional base that my teaching post in Algeria had provided me with. It was therefore subject to many constraints, mainly of the security variety. The *Jamahiriyya* was also among the small (but, alas, ever-growing) number of countries that were largely inaccessible to foreign researchers in the social sciences. In our profession, the question of access to the field is essential. It was to evolve fast, and not only for the better ... At the time, to work on Libya was quite career enhancing. The competition was almost nonexistent, and—as I was discover to my advantage—the one-eyed man could become king. The country's university infrastructure had been tormented by extreme politicization, in the most destructive sense of the word. The

Center for the Study of the Libyan Jihad against the Italian Aggression (today's Center for Libyan Archives and Historical Studies) was an island of relative institutional calm. It frightened the embassies, including the French embassy, since they all thought that it was one of the regime's many terrorist front institutions. But the Libyan Studies Center, as it was less officially known, was willing to host foreign researchers. This enabled them to obtain the indispensable visa. The Center's director, the very welcoming Dr. Mohamed Jarari, had managed to develop a remarkable library there, enriched by an impressive collection of oral testimony gathered from players in the resistance to the Italian occupation. Taking up political questions head-on remained difficult—especially when these concerned the opposition, which one could only document through activists in exile. But the country nonetheless let itself be approached.

"You do realize that you meet more Libyans in eight days than I do in a year?" So a cultural attaché, disillusioned by the sterile climate of bilateral relations, complained to me one day. What I should have replied to him is that my depth of understanding of the *Jamahiriyya*'s society still remained very limited. On this subject, I remain clear headed. Even intense, regular visits will never attain the quality of prolonged periods in the field, such as those I would later spend in Cairo, Sanaa, and Damascus. But brief as they were, these visits nonetheless enabled me to collect an overwhelming range of publications. These ran the gamut from reprints of local and regional history classics, through the Guide of the Revolution's novels, to Libya's "Big Green Book," the *Sijl al-Qawami*, an exhaustive collection of the Guide's exuberant political thought.

The air embargo on Libya (1992 9) came to strengthen the trade embargo imposed by Reagan as early as 1982. More than once, this compelled me to transit via the island of Djerba, making my collection of this (often stodgy but nonetheless essential) documentation still more difficult. I did, however, gather up a significant number of publications, not only for the CRESM-IREMAM library, but also for a librarian at Harvard, who was barred from access to the *Jamahiriyya*. For a time, my interest in Libya led me to publish regular chronicles in the *Annuaire d'Afrique du Nord*, a journal then edited yearly by the CRESM, and later to a small primer that the French University Presses (PUF) suggested I write.

Behind the "Power of the Masses," Gaddafi's One-Man Show

When I began to take an interest in it in 1983, the Islamist trend in Libya was latent. It did not yet have the centrality that it was to acquire much later. For a time, repression in the *Jamahiriyya* had focused on the Baathists and Communists. Very quickly, it moved to concentrate especially, if not exclusively, on the local disciples of Hassan al-Banna (founder of the Egyptian Muslim Brotherhood in 1928) or those of his less well-known rival, Taqiuddin al-Nabhani, the Palestinian who founded Hizb al-Tahrir al-Islami (the Islamic Liberation Party) in Amman in 1953.

Since then, I have met a good number of the victims of the terrible carceralist era upon which the *Jamahiriyya* was founded. In 2014, I went from the office of one of the three NGOs established for former political prisoners to the cells of the terrifying Abu Salim prison in Tripoli's suburbs. In particular, I was able to witness Ali Alakarmi, a former member of the Islamic Liberation Party, recount—his voice choked by tears—the endless ordeal of his three decades in prison. In the same Abu Salim prison compound, in his company and that of several of his former prison companions, I then attended the reenactment of the terrible massacre of 1,270 of their fellow prisoners on the morning of June 29, 1996. I also listened to them describe the comforting way in which the diversity of political opinion among the first generations of prisoners had never managed to shake the togetherness that existed between them—nor the strict discipline they imposed upon themselves. In turn, I brought them to visit the Milles memorial, not far from Aix-en-Provence, that affected them greatly. *In situ*, this stages one of the most shameful carceral episodes of French collaboration with the Nazis, in an area that was in no way under occupation at the time.

Throughout Gaddafi's reign of complete supremacy, access to Libyan opposition activists who had not fled his repression was akin to access to the opposition to the Baathist regimes of Syria or Iraq, that is, infinitely less simple than it was everywhere else in North Africa. A passerby surreptitiously confirmed this to me one day of 1983, as I stood before the storefront of a Tripoli bookshop. The roots of growing tension included encroachment on the religious sphere by the Guide's own "*Jamahiriyyan* revelations," which he attempted to impose as a new social norm. "We live in a country where a book is enthroned that's not even worth the paper it's printed on," the passerby whispered into my ear. He then briskly strode off, without throwing me so much as a glance.

The expression of another divide, expressed more visibly in the rest of North Africa and in Algeria in particular, was confirmed to me in equally fortuitous fashion. A hitchhiker I had picked up a few miles past the border between Tunisia and Libya, at the foot of Djebel Nefoussa, feverishly questioned me: "Is it true that in Paris they have Berber classes?" Aiming to counter the temptation towards Berber identity, Gaddafi had charged unscrupulous academics with establishing the narrative that Berbers were merely Arabs who had long ago come from the south of the peninsula that bore their name—the Barbary Coast—to populate the north of Africa … Gaddafi was an attentive admirer of Nasser. In the face of the threat of Islamism whose danger he had perceived very early on, the Colonel had proactively and skillfully occupied the field of identity politics. This included Arab identity, of course—but also Muslim identity, differing in that respect from his neighbors in Algeria and Tunisia.

Public space had been fully Arabized. The use of Latin characters was purely and simply banned. To reach Libya, I therefore had to call upon a certified translator from the Franco-Libyan Chamber of Commerce to have my passport translated into Arabic. Western musical culture was denounced. Long before ISIS, Western instruments were repeatedly destroyed in public. With little nuance, Pepsi Cola and Coca Cola were condemned for having stolen the ancestral use of the coca leaf from its legitimate owners. According to Gaddafi, the leaf was ... African, and had been corrupted with pork-fat extract. Advertising campaigns even did their best to portray neckties as Crusader symbols. The *Jamahiriyya*'s flag featured the green color of Islam—and nothing else. The Sufi brotherhoods had for a long time—and quite logically—been fought against because they were identified with the social power base of the fallen king, Idris Senussi, whose popularity Gaddafi still feared.[3] From 1986 on, they were suddenly brought out of the woodwork and crassly exploited to counter the disciples of a version of Islam that had ambitions to become the basis of political opposition.[4]

The reactive nature of Islamist self-assertion in Libya could not, however, rely upon the counter-example of a more or less brutal "deculturation" brought about by proactive secularization—such as the process led by Tunisia's "Supreme Combatant," President Habib Bourguiba. Bourguiba, as we have seen, had been ready to bring the long tradition of the prestigious Muslim Zitouna university to a sudden close, and to grant explicit priority to the needs of economic development over those of respect for religion, such as the Ramadan fast. At the fringes of the Arab world, Atatürk and the Shah of Iran, those rulers who would rip off the *tarbush* (i.e. the fez, the men's hats made of red felt that were the historical markers of the Ottoman Empire) from their people's heads and to shave their beards, had blazed the trail for such proactive policies. The boomerang-like reactions that these processes helped to bring about have since become apparent.[5]

Gaddafi embodied a fairly new category in the field of the stance of Arab leaders with respect to religion. His opponents never seriously questioned his faith. It went together, however, with a radical reformism that went as far as brutalizing orthodoxy. In 1978, he thus determined that the entire *Sunna* of the Prophet could be set aside in favor of the text of the Quran alone. More conventionally, he also displayed visceral hostility towards the Muslim Brotherhood stream of thought.

As far as governance was concerned, the core of Gaddafi's political action consisted in forestalling any kind of effective institutionalization of society, with obsessive care. Extreme atomization of society, including within the armed forces, always seemed to him the best protection against any hints of opposition. No expert was therefore ever able to provide too precise an account of the structures of power in the "State of the Masses." These structures were an inextricable, constantly evolving tangle, the product of the rivalry between various nodes of power that the "Guide" kept in permanent competition against one another. The official institutional structure in which "all power" purportedly resided was the Popular Committees. These were closely monitored by militias endowed with fearsome policing powers: the "Revolutionary Committees."

The military establishment was another potential crucible for opposition. Gaddafi's personal guards aside, it was subject to such suspicion that the tracks of the tanks stationed close to the capital Tripoli were kept disassembled, so as to slow down any possible attempt at insurrection. Even the army remained at the mercy of intervention from the Leader's tribal and family networks. Not even the members of the system—those who were best placed to decipher it—were in a position to gauge their degree of autonomy within it. In the 1990s, one member of the opposition in exile in Cairo told me:

> To learn your true place within the system, there is only one method. You call Bab Azizya, Gaddafi's seat of power, and you ask to talk to him. Then you count the minutes, the hours—the days sometimes—before he calls you back. That's how you know if you're still part of the system, and at what level. Or if you're now at the mercy of steps to exclude or even imprison you. If you hear nothing after two days, you know it might be a good idea to think about fleeing the country.

In 2011, the deep turbulence of the Arab Spring confirmed the structural impact on Libyan society of the system that Gaddafi set up and fine-tuned throughout the forty-two years of his one-man show, through the mechanism of the "power of the masses." In order to assess the challenge facing Libyans since the regime collapsed, one must remember how distinctive it was relative to the regimes set up by his Egyptian counterparts Nasser, Sadat, and Mubarak—or, in Tunisia, by Bourguiba and his pale successor Ben Ali. True, the leaders of Egypt and Tunisia had also taken the route of weakening every institution and (especially religious) organization that had existed before they attained power. In order to set up their meticulous control over every component of society, however, they had replaced these institutions and organizations with the powerful apparatus of the modern state. Egypt had an outsized army, a powerful judicial and police apparatus, and a ubiquitous but fully domesticated religious establishment. Tunisia had enormous numbers of police, a "French-style" Jacobin administration, and credible academic institutions. In Libya, there was nothing of the kind. Only the local level of self-administration ever operated with any hint of substance.

It is, therefore, from the local level that Libyan society will have to set out on the long-term development of political institutions liable to have any prospect of truly fulfilling their role. Ideological divides have indeed been reactivated in response to foreign interventions, whether Western (first to support the revolutionary dynamic, then, through the proxy of Egypt and the UAE, to fight it) or radical Sunni ones. These have not, however, determined how the citizen sovereignty recovered through the revolution was first expressed. In the aftermath of the elections of July 7, 2012, to the General National Congress, some rash commentators felt that these could be interpreted as an umpteenth "defeat of Islamism."

Libyan society is more religious yet than its Tunisian neighbor. In 2011, it was good form to proclaim that a liberal in Tripoli would, in Tunisia, be considered a dangerous fundamentalist. In point of fact, what had happened was quite unsurprising. Libyan voters had gravitated towards the only social echelon in which they accepted to invest their trust: the scale of geographical and/or clan closeness. As they emerged from the tunnel of authoritarianism, far more than they voted for a given ideological positioning or a political camp, Libyans voted for the candidates they knew personally, independently of their political affiliation. The overwhelming majority of Muslim Brotherhood candidates had just returned from a long exile that had cut them off from their potential voters. In trying to rally voters on a national, ideological basis, they had overestimated the level of political modernity among their compatriots.[6]

Gaddafi: "I Have to See You Again!"

I have never especially sought out meetings with heads of state. Nor, however, have I refused them on principle. I took part in a brief group meeting with Yasser Arafat in Ramallah in 2002, and spoke, alone, to Omar al-Bashir in Sudan in 1995. These meetings made little impression on me. My only substantive meeting with a head of state, then, took place in April 1987, with Gaddafi, founding father of the "Great Revolution of September 1." It was especially instructive—as is often the case with meetings with political players who, by definition, have a leeway for taking political action and initiative that bears no comparison to that of their counterparts in less autocratic regimes. Granted, it would have been of no interest to ask Gaddafi only indulgent questions, like the visiting courtesans who, year after year, would ask Hassan II, Mubarak, and their ilk to "explain" to them how dangerous their Islamist opposition was. But one was also best advised not to challenge the strongman of the "State of the Masses" too directly. This was probably the mistake made by the Lebanese Shia leader Musa Sadr on August 31, 1978, in the course of a vociferous theological debate. Sadr clearly did not emerge alive. This dug a lasting rift between Gaddafi, Lebanon (where the Libyan leader never set foot again)—and the Shia world as a whole.

Gaddafi received most of his guests inside the barracks at Bab Azizya, under a tent that quickly became famous. This had been set up to replace one of his lodgings that US fighter jets had destroyed during the raid of April 15, 1986, during which one of his adopted daughters was said to have been killed. Our meeting took place a year after that attack, one that had been conducted as reprisal for attacks ascribed to the Libyan regime, in particular for one against a Berlin discotheque. Our interview revealed more than I ever could have dared hope of the extremely confused and obsessive personality of the man who wielded absolute power over a people he repeated several times an hour that he had conferred "all power" upon. The meeting was all striking contrasts. At times, he endlessly went through the verses of the rhetoric that set him up at the heart of a pretentious "Third Universal Theory" of which he was the creator. At others, he took on a puzzled air when, by chance, his interlocutor was impertinent enough to tell him something that didn't quite fit within this framework. At such moments, the Guide lifted his eyes to the heavens, sweated in buckets, and appeared lost. While answering one of his remarks, I found myself sketching out my perception that the rise in Islamist political movements was tied to the context of decolonization. The response was emphatic: "But the Muslim Brotherhood are drunkards, cowards, murderers!"

The interview had lasted an hour and a half. An unexpected verdict was proclaimed. The Colonel blurted out: "*Lazim arâk thâni*" ("I must see you again!"). My plans to return to Marseilles were cancelled. Instead, I was confined to the faded charms of the old Libya's Palace hotel. My Libyan contact (Dr. Mohamed Jarari, Director of the Libyan Studies Center that hosted me) had to join me in waiting two long days for a sign from on high. This came only on the third day.

In this second interview, Gaddafi stared at me at length without really seeming to recognize me. Yet my wardrobe at the time was very limited. I was wearing the very same clothes as I had during our first meeting three days earlier. The Guide, for his part, was sporting a remarkable jet pilot costume. He seemed to struggle to make the connection with the character he had interrogated at length, and had demanded to see again. "Why don't you speak Libyan dialect?" he asked—exactly as he had during our first meeting. The interview was surreal. As we parted, he affected, with an admiring pout, to be seeing for the first time the books of stamps in his effigy that I begged him to sign, along with a few copies of his *Green Book*. I had been so bold as to inquire what might be the response if every Libyan citizen were to be asked how satisfied she or he was with the *Jamahiriyya*'s institutions. His answer was an unexpected commission: "I want you to go everywhere and, like a doctor, write down and tell me what's going well and what isn't." I failed to follow up on this ambitious but somewhat hazy request. I also have every reason to suppose that the Colonel forgot about it all fairly promptly.

Twenty-four years later, this meeting weighed heavily on my mind when—for once—I could not find it in me to criticize NATO and Nicolas Sarkozy's military backing for the opposition that had rallied to oust the Libyan Ben Ali. This was with no illusions whatsoever as to the fact that the goals of such backers were unlikely to be exclusively humanist ones.

Rubbing Shoulders with Tyrants?

Was it right to meet with Gaddafi? Two decades later, I was director of a French research institute in Bashar al-Assad's Syria. Was this compromising one's principles with respect to the dictator? Some polemicists felt they had to level the charge at me in order to lend credibility to their criticism of my citizen's involvement in the conflict, at the side of the Syrian opposition. The answer, it seems to me, is no. No more so than spending time in Algeria meant condoning the methods of its fearsome Military Security agency. In passing, the challenge is more easily raised with respect to the "rebel dictators" than it is towards those who rub shoulders with their "docile" counterparts: the dictators responsible for the Ben Barka affair and Tazmamart prison in Morocco, or who were in charge of Iran when the Shah's fearsome intelligence service Savak held sway there. As far as academics compromising themselves with authoritarian powers is concerned, however, there are actually well-documented examples. One need look no further than the active backing by a number of academics for the Algerian junta's disinformation campaigns (including on film) at the worst stages of its bloody "eradication" of the Islamist opposition during the 1990s. Or, more recently, the endorsement visit to Bashar al-Assad by a group of French MPs on March 27, 2016, when two academics joined the party even while the regime's repression was scaling new and unprecedented heights.

In Libya in 1987, the danger of slipping into "connivance" lay elsewhere than in meetings with the regime's dignitaries. It inhered, rather, in the ways in which more or less realistic—and more or less well-informed—academic observers managed to convey the country's political realities. Here as elsewhere, stumbling blocks—including ideological ones—were in no short supply. For a long time, in Europe, perceptions of Gaddafi oscillated between two conflicting flaws, both of them equally "ideologized." The Colonel seen as icon of the young third-worldist leader prompted both conventional hostility from the right and, from the left, a naïve and idealizing version of "third worldism." Naturally, like most of his Arab counterparts in general, and like Nasser in particular, Gaddafi drew far more spontaneous criticism when he offended Western oil or security interests (or those of the West's Israeli partner) than when he flouted his compatriots' most elementary human rights.

For a considerable time, then, a neoconservative reading led to criminalizing the various markers of Gaddafi's nationalist assertiveness. A strategy that was, in many respects, merely the fairly ordinary, and perfectly legitimate, extension of the political dynamics that had led to independence into the post-independence political field (but also the cultural and economic fields) was portrayed as intolerable "anti-Western acts of aggression." Conversely, part of the Western left's support for liberation movements devolved into more or less unconditional backing for the "revolutionary" regimes that emerged from independence. For many years, convinced that it was "on the right side of history," this strand of the left offered up almost blind support to the third-worldism that Gaddafi embodied. Force of habit has sometimes led to setting up as an idol whatever may sound like the opposite of the colonialist handbook, bowing down to it as a doctrine of its own. Such was clearly the case in Libya.

For a time at least, then, attacks on Gaddafi "from the right" went hand in hand with extreme indulgence towards him "from the left." Certain academics, and certain French ones in particular, as they emerged from the political-academic gatherings that were Gaddafi's longtime stock-in-trade, thought they had found in Libya the revolutionary utopia that the rest of the world insisted on denying them.[7] Thus did the Libyan Colonel's anti-imperialism and his revolutionary façade manage to conceal the vulgar effects of propaganda. Glowing industrial output figures covered up the perverse magic of petrodollars, and the strengthening of national identity masked an atrocious repressive spiral.

For a time (and, in some cases, to this day) Gaddafi's revolutionary virtues were treated reverentially. This was even while, every year, he had several students hanged in front of their own classmates and TV cameras to mark, after his own fashion, the anniversary of the terrible repression visited upon their forebears who demonstrated on April 7, 1976. Gaddafi loudly proclaimed his concern for "emancipating women," thereby drawing the loving gaze of his Western women admirers. Simultaneously, he had dozens of high school students kidnapped to satisfy his sexual whims. Their parents never saw them again. In Libya's prisons, he took revenge for each of his foreign policy debacles upon the political prisoners whom he denounced as "foreign agents" one and all. He even—this, one was to learn only after his regime collapsed—had the frozen corpses of his political opponents preserved in private morgues, the better to deprive them of the eternal rest of the grave, and continue to defy them even in death. Such was the case of the lawyer Mansour Kikhia, who was kidnapped in Cairo in 1993.

The Long Western Tradition of Support for the "Arab Pinochets"

This same deliberate blindness was reprised during the Syrian crisis in 2011. Bashar al-Assad's purported "anti-imperialism" protected him from criticism from a broad swath of Arab opinion. In Europe, it brought him the backing of every "Pavlovian anti-imperialist," as they became dubbed by those who denounced the trap they fell into. For fear of someday finding themselves demonstrating alongside Bernard-Henri Lévy, some preferred to blindly condone the horrendous repressive spiral orchestrated by the Syrian leader and his clan.

Gaddafi's repression eventually legitimated the Western military intervention of 2011. It is too often forgotten that this was called for and approved by an overwhelming majority of Libyan revolutionaries. Earlier, however, at the onset of the 2000s, the Guide basked in a rehabilitation so spectacular that it was matched only by his new friends' appetite for oil. With rare levels of indecency even by their standards, European leaders fought for a place in the line to come pamper Gaddafi in Tripoli. And in December 2007, Nicolas Sarkozy's France welcomed him in Paris with great pomp, against a backdrop of fanciful contracts. This was even while he curiously let part of the government—with the Foreign Ministry at its head—conspicuously boycott his guest, flying in the face of the basic courtesy owed to one who came brandishing an official invitation.

In this case as in others, opposition voices had raised the alarm very early on. They were no more listened to than the voices that rang out from the prisons of many of "our Arab allies." In this respect, the tone of all too *real* French *realpolitik*—unconditional support for Arab dictators—had been set long before. Declarations by President Jacques Chirac in 2003 set a tone starkly lacking in humanism. On a visit to Tunis in December 2003, the president of the "country of the rights of man" had granted the benefit of his expertise to Tunisians crushed under Ben Ali's dictatorship. He explained to them that "The first of the rights of man is to eat, to have medical care, to receive an education and to have a home"—and that "from this point of view, it has to be recognized that Tunisia is far ahead of many countries." In Libya as elsewhere, the United States did try to organize the opposition in exile, in particular by funding a National Front for the Salvation of Libya. But these attempts, by an ally too close to Israel and discredited everywhere in the region, had no practical impact on the opposition's fate.

I met some of these dissidents—especially in the United States, where I caught echoes of the paradoxical dramas of their American exile. A few days after I had been hosted by Gaddafi, in April 1987, I gave a lecture on Libya at Oklahoma University. Several Libyan dissidents attended. One of them was insistent on knowing whether, during my visit to Tripoli, I had visited the French embassy building that had been damaged by US bombs designed to punish the regime. I had indeed gone there. Even though the building was closed, the cultural attaché had allowed me to go inside to gauge how severe was the collateral damage caused by a bomb that had most likely been intended for a building next door, home to one of the regime's many security branches. Heavy typewriters had been flung to the ground; cracks showed in the walls. I was also able to confirm to my questioner that, in this quiet neighborhood, I had indeed come upon the wretched sight of an utterly destroyed villa. The five people who had been killed in this little house, bombed by the army of his temporary hosts, were all members of his close family.

The saga of US–Libyan relations had been inaugurated in 1803 by the capture of the corvette *Philadelphia* off the coast of Tripoli, in the course of the first of the "Barbary Wars." At the time already, business interests hid behind ethical and religious ones. That era was far from over. In September 2011, Christopher Stevens, a humanist and, nonetheless, also a US ambassador, was to suffocate to death in Benghazi in the US consulate on fire. Meanwhile, Libyans were taking Gaddafi's slogan of "power to the people," for so long emptied of its meaning, literally. They set about the endless process of building the institutions that, throughout forty-two years, Gaddafi had carefully "forgotten" to provide them with. Far more so than any new regional interventions, it is these institutions that may allow them to put to rest the specter of extremism.

Popular resistance to ISIS has notched up some victories: in Derna and Sebrata in April 2016; in neighboring Tunisia, in Ben Gardane; and in some Syrian provinces (Idlib in particular). To mention these ISIS setbacks here is no matter of self-indulgently adding to the list of window-dressing victories produced by the West's obsessive and counter-productive propaganda. Nor does it extrapolate to the Libyan context the few advances by Kurdish or Shia militias, harvesting the low-hanging fruit of bombing by the US coalition or their Russian ally in the ruins of the "liberated" towns of Iraq or Syria. Rather, these first setbacks for ISIS in Libya should serve to remind us of a self-evident fact that too often goes ignored. Paradoxically, this fact kindled the West's systematic suspicion towards the political openings that came on the heels of the "Arab Spring"—and was used to justify Western delaying tactics and failures, most obviously in Syria. And yet: in Libya as elsewhere in this part of the world, no society freely chooses the extremes of the political spectrum. Nor, therefore, does any society vote for the *jihadi*s. Much less do they elect the eradicators who produce those *jihadi*s.

Notes

1 Quoted in Isabelle Mandraud, *Du djihad aux urnes. Le parcours singulier d'Abdelhakim Belhadj*, Stock, Paris, 2013.
2 Centre de recherches et d'études sur les sociétés méditerranéennes (CRESM, the forerunner of the IREMAM, Institute for Research and Study of the Arab and Muslim Worlds, Institut de recherches et d'études sur le monde arabe et musulman).
3 This popularity was fought by all means deemed necessary. This included publishing the king's private diaries, which contained allusions to his sexuality. ("In this respect, it'll be twice a month, or once only.") *Watha'iq, souar wa asrar* (Documents, Photographs, and Secrets), al-Manchaa al-Amma, Tripoli, 1983 (in Arabic).
4 Beginning in 1990, the same strategy was used by the Algerian regime when, threatened by the rise of the FIS, it sought to counter it. In Morocco, the throne of the Commander of the Faithful is well endowed in terms of religious resources. Nonetheless, state exploitation of the Sufi brotherhoods gave rise to an especially comical episode twenty years later. In April 2011, in return for payment, thousands of members of the Boutchichiya brotherhood took to the street to counter the Arab Spring tendencies of the March 20 Movement. To that end, and without any hint of irony, they raised up a banner whose slogan was to die for: "No to the Exploitation of Religion for Political Ends!"
5 See, e.g., Jeremy Seal, *A Fez of the Heart: Travels around Turkey in Search of a Hat*, Picador, London, 1995; and Ryszard Kapuscinski, *Shah of Shahs*, Vintage, London, 1992.
6 See François Burgat, "La Libye en 2014: du long *one man show* de Kadhafi aux premiers pas de la société plurielle," *Les Carnets de l'IREMAM*, February 7, 2014, https://iremam.hypotheses.org/4498 (last accessed June 15, 2019). See also the valuable articles by the former French diplomat in Tripoli Patrick Haimzadeh on the *Orient XXI* website, https://orientxxi.info (last accessed June 15, 2019).
7 See Robert Charvin and Jacques Vignet-Zunz, *Le Syndrome Kadhafi*, Albatros, Paris, 1988.

4

Egypt, Arabic, and Grasping Difference

It was in Egypt that, between December 1989 and January 1993, I spent my first period at a French research institute abroad, at the Economic and Legal Documentation Center (CEDEJ) in Cairo. *Masr, Umm al-dunya* (the "mother of the world," according to its Arabic nickname) was an especially important milestone in the development of my approach as a comparatist. The atmosphere in Cairo differed from that in Algeria. Algeria's was of course more familiar, in that it was French speaking. Given the colonial past, it was often also more distant or tense. Egypt provided an essential observation point from which to broaden that horizon. From Cairo, I was able to start seeing North Africa through a new lens: no longer from within it, nor from inside the distorting mirror of France. It was from the symbolic heart of Arabism that my perspective on the Arab world gradually became decentered, and then recomposed. When seen from the scale of Cairo, Algiers, Tunis, and Rabat, notwithstanding their rank as capitals, inevitably became "provincialized." The spectrum of "my" Arab world was slowly taking shape. I soon came to sharpen and fill out its contours in Yemen and the Gulf, then in Syria and Lebanon. Discovering Cairo, then, produced a startling shift in perspective—but also in scale.

The Comparative Imperative, from North Africa to the Levant: Grasping Difference

One of the first expressions of this shift occurred as I set out at the wheel of a rented car into the Cairo traffic, to discover the human density and the infinite urban sprawl of my new environment. It was then that I received one of my first "lessons in being Egyptian." It was powerful and intuitive—"affectionate," even. While driving the three very young children of an Egyptian colleague, I pathetically lost myself amid the muddy alleyways of one of Cairo's popular neighborhoods, where the city successfully challenges the population density record held by a few great Asian metropoles. It was at this moment that my unlikely Fiat decided to give up the ghost. I recall a few dozen anxious seconds as I watched voluble faces press themselves around my windshield. Very quickly, it turned out that *Awlad haratina* (the "children of our neighborhood")[1] were battling only over two things. One was who could seize the honor of setting me up on a chair that spontaneously appeared on the pavement. The other was the pleasure of plying the children with slices of orange and biscuits, while the expert wielder of a screwdriver repaired the electrical contact that had blown. This minuscule episode should have been insignificant. It was quite the opposite.

I experienced a second episode of the same kind in Yemen in 1999. I was then driving a famous French-American couple of Orientalist scholars, whose religion (which was neither my own, nor that of our Yemeni hosts) made them especially nervous in the depths of the land of tribes and "beardies." Our ancient Land Cruiser had given up the ghost in the midst of the majestic stony plateau that leads to the unforgettable citadel of Bokur. And, since Egypt, I had made not the slightest progress as a car mechanic. A pick-up truck stopped at our level. It overflowed with easily a dozen passengers—turbaned, bearded, and armed to the teeth. Their Kalashnikov swang from their backs and their *jambia* (the traditional Yemeni dagger) stuck out indecently above their bare legs beneath their *fouta* (a type of sarong, a wide, vividly colored cloth) hoisted to the waist. They promptly dived into the sleeping engine. Within the space of a minute, the engine had been brought back to life. And in the blink of an eye, the smiling horde set off back on the road.

Already before arriving in Egypt, I had glimpsed the richness of comparatism and the imperious necessity of it, during the stage that I have described as "intuitive accumulation" on the road around the world. In the research field, this had become apparent to me in various ways during my formative years in Algeria. With Algeria as a base, these enlightening perspectives had unveiled themselves during my first language-learning trips to Tunisia on the one hand, and during a few touristic adventures in neighboring Morocco on the other. (This was before disagreements over the question of Western Sahara led to the closure of the border between the two "brother countries" that has stupidly separated them since 1994.)

To the visitor coming from Algeria, the difference of Tunisia and Morocco was blindingly obvious. The two North African neighbors had largely been spared the wishful thinking of assimilation that defined 132 years of French settler colonialism and with it Algeria's fate. This assimilation was of course linguistic—but also architectural. Both Tunisia and Morocco lived through protectorates that were both far shorter (75 and 54 years, respectively) and far less intrusive. A bey in one case, a sultan in the other, were dispossessed of the core of their prerogatives. Nonetheless, they sustained the possibility of identification with an endogenous power that the (sub-)citizens of the three "French provinces" to which Algeria was reduced as early as 1848 had been denied.

In Morocco especially, far more so than in Algeria, public space remains symbolically structured by the countless architectural markers of the "inherited" culture. The monarchy has had to share the dividends of the national structure with the al-Istiqlal (Independence) party. Morocco's accession to independence did not, however, occur amid the same conditions of extreme violence that, in Algeria, forged a generation of nationalist elites who thereby felt themselves to be the lifetime "owners" of the destiny of the entire nation. Finally, neither oil nor gas enabled the governing classes in Tunisia or Morocco to neglect the construction of all and any alternative agricultural or manufacturing sectors. Nor could they indulge the temptation to pour their industrial mistakes into the concrete of an illusory financial prosperity. With respect to the question of the part played by their respective leaders in the religious field, however, Morocco and Tunisia provide two opposite extremes which it is highly instructive to compare. At one extreme lay Bourguiba's determination: unveiling Tunisia's women and proclaiming, while holding a glass of orange juice in his hand in the midst of Ramadan, that the development agenda took primacy over respect for religious norms. At the opposite extreme was the Moroccan monarch's standing as the "Commander of the Faithful," who could profitably allow himself to outbid the religious expectations of his opponents.[2]

Early on in my time in Algeria, one meeting had convinced me of the potential of systematic comparison between very different geographies and experiences. In March 1974 in Constantine, the university administration had requested me to welcome the French agronomist René Dumont (1904–2001) at Aïn El-Bey Airport, at the wheel of a Renault 4L, the worthy successor of the 2CV of my student days. At the time, the work of the author of *False Start in Africa* (1962) had force of authority, if not force of law, over agrarian policies in Africa. My encounter with the great man began in a glacial tone. "The last time I came to this country, it was the president who met me off the gangway," he straightaway announced to me. Ahmed Ben Bella, Algeria's first president, had indeed selected the works of Dumont as his choicest reading in prison. He had then made a point of inviting Dumont to Algiers to provide his views on the launch of the process of redistribution–collectivization of colonial lands.

As we sat in a restaurant in the old city, Dumont had assailed me with simple questions that I had been at a loss to answer. These merely concerned the key socio-economic indicators of a country that he knew very little of—whereas I, armed with my year and a half there, had pretensions to be starting to know it somewhat. To these questions, he added another layer: his burgeoning environmental concerns, at a time when these were all but limited to premonitory articles written by Pierre Fournier in *Charlie Hebdo*. "What is the usual number of skewers? Six? Well then: I'll take only three." Less than ten days later, in Constantine, Dumont delivered a magisterial lecture on ... Algeria.[3] Dumont's analyses concerning the profile of the economy and its hidden contradictions enlightened his audience. They had been checked and cross-checked, measured up against and relativized through his knowledge of several dozen countries on the continent and the world over. That lesson later proved useful to me in several ways. When the scholar is not endowed with the gift of ubiquity, the comparatist approach inevitably requires the relationship with the field to be dynamic. The same proximity with the field cannot be sustained when its scope tends towards expanding indefinitely. It therefore requires learning to be content with brief returns to the already "ploughed" field. This is not necessarily impossible, to the extent that one has previously laid out pertinent analytical categories and meticulously set down one's key markers. It also means learning to trust colleagues, and gradually integrating the use of carefully selected secondary sources. The importance of this lesson was to grow over time, in step with my scholarly ambitions to cover the "Arab world" as a whole.

More structurally, in 1972 I read the political scientist Michel Camau's *Power and Institutions in North Africa*.[4] This enabled me to take the measure of the banal but clarifying the relativeness of each institutional configuration and each national politics—and, when one wishes to grasp their substance, of the imperious necessity of reading these through the prism of other experiences. When I had an opportunity to meet Camau—who was to become a friend—for the first time, I remember phrasing my admiration for his work in these terms: "What impressed me in your book was not the answers that it provided. It was the fact that it addressed questions that I myself had been unable to formulate."

Comparatism is a necessity that comes at a cost, beyond the obligation to adapt one's relationship to each incursion into the field once the range of these fields multiplies. In each new field setting, it requires, starting from scratch or nearly, modestly reconstructing one's legitimacy among those who came before. Those who preceded us often have the natural wariness towards newcomers that we almost all do. Entering a new field requires slowly striving to become accepted. The process takes time, and it must be kept in mind that it will never quite feel complete. Because I have experienced that suspiciousness on several occasions, it tickles me to reencounter the selfsame phrase as I give conferences here and there across the Arab world—even in a country in which I spent a number of years. Colleagues who have never sought to diversify their own geographical fields, and are determined to protect their own "monopoly" exclaim: "But how dare s/he come and meddle here?" Granted, my source for this is highly trustworthy: I myself react in precisely the same way in the *pré carré* that was the subject of my first writing ...

The Country Where "They All Talk like in the Movies"

From December 1989 to January 1993, after my lengthy immersion in Algeria, it was Egypt's turn to provide me with the field for a second major milestone as a comparatist. As previously noted, I had already glimpsed the "mother of the world" as I wandered on my first tour of the Mediterranean, in impressionistic backpacker-mode. In July 1966, as I left King Senussi's Libya, I had discovered Cairo from the back of the Jeep belonging to two British students. One of these, Jack Straw, was probably—I was never able to confirm this—Her Majesty's future Foreign Secretary (from 2001 to 2006). Likely he remembers the gift I made him as we crossed Alexandria: a locally bought bottle of Scotch whisky, magnificently wrapped in its cellophane package—and that revealed itself to contain only tea, perfectly reproducing the color of the anticipated liquid. True, he had himself bought from the same street vendors a magnificent carton of American cigarettes, whose contents were exclusively made up of sawdust ...

In 1984, after I had joined the CNRS in Aix-en-Provence, I visited Cairo a second time, this time for work, with the generous support of an Arabist colleague from Aix, Jean-François Rycx—but very largely at my own expense. Faced with my determination, the cultural attaché at the French embassy remarked that "It's not so often that we see researchers so motivated that they'll pay their own way." Many of the diplomatic mission were at the time performing as extras, playing minor roles as French soldiers alongside Patrice Chéreau and Michel Piccoli in *Adieu Bonaparte* (1985), the film that the great Egyptian director Youssef Chahine (1926–2008) devoted to Napoleon's expedition to Egypt of 1798 to 1801 ... At the time, I admired Chahine unreservedly. It was only much later that I felt the need to distance myself from his 1997 film *Destiny*. Rather than a 70 mm camera, this struck me as having been made with a "105 mm recoilless Howitzer." The film won acclaim at the Cannes Film Festival for providing a Western audience with the compilation of idiotic shortcuts that that audience felt the need for. Back then already, it belabored every obvious cliche tied to the culturalist rejection of the rise of Islamism.

My arrival in the Levant in 1989 was in part, then, a reassuring reunion. It also, however, opened up a major shift in my experience of the Arab world. The Egyptian political imaginary sees Egypt as being the heart of the Arab world—and of the world in general. As such, it differs very significantly from that of Algerians, or of Egypt's neighbors in Libya and Sudan. The immediacy of the colonial footprint is, for instance, less patent in Egypt. On the scale of the Arab world, its cultural standing has endowed Egypt with a strong sense of superiority. One day that I had come to greet him at Cairo Airport, my Moroccan colleague, the great sociologist Mohamed Tozy, provided a shining illustration of Egypt's Arab centrality to North African eyes (and ears): "Well I never! It's the first time I find myself in a country where they all talk like in the movies!"

Reaching the Nile Delta means breaking with the physical geography of North Africa. (There is no Nile to be found in Algiers nor in Tunis—and only a pale imitation in Libya, in the shape of the Great Man-Made River built by Gaddafi.) It also, however, involves breaking with the historical, political, sociological, and religious configuration of North Africa. (There are no Copts to be found in Algeria, either.) Reaching Egypt also means exiting the French colonial paradigm, notwithstanding the many extant traces of the Napoleonic expedition. This has several consequences. The most important is language. For anyone who entered into the Arab world through North Africa (or Lebanon), first and foremost, Egypt embodies a dual shock. French is absent. But its potential substitute, English, is no less absent. The standing of English in Egypt is infinitely less than that of French in North Africa since the independence era. Gone, then, is the startling proximity that the common linguistic denominator of French induces with North African intellectuals. In Egypt, the Other becomes less accessible!

As such, it becomes ever harder to cheat with respect to the imperative of mastering the local language—even if many scholars have long persisted in doing so. The painful (but stimulating) memory sticks in my mind of a joint French–Egyptian symposium in the mid-1980s. Much of the discussion had taken place in Arabic and I had, given the inevitable limits of simultaneous translation, grasped how difficult it was to respond effectively to the "frank" criticism (as the diplomats put it) of some of my Cairene colleagues, while dragging in my wake my hesitant and approximate Arabic. I think it is that very day that I promised myself I would acquire in Arabic at least 30 percent of my eloquence in French.

My discovery of Egypt also involved discovering Arab Christians. These are a small minority there, true, but one central to the Western imaginary of the country, and to Western relations with it. Discovering Arab Christians does not throw off those whose first encounter with the Middle East came through the ... East in general, and Lebanon in particular. It is, however, a real surprise for all those who, as I had, entered into the Arab world through the gate of North-West Africa. I had fleetingly glimpsed this reality in Algeria, when I mixed with a small group of Christian Egyptian, Syrian, and Lebanese teachers. That an Arab could be called Michel or Georges was a new discovery for my Algerian students, and even for their teachers—not to mention for myself. The small number of Algerian Muslims who had accepted giving up Muslim personal status law to take up full French citizenship had been dubbed *m'tourmis* (turncoats). In the "land of the *m'tourmis*," the French consonance of these Arab Christian names prompted both surprise and, sometimes, a certain defiance. One of my colleagues was Egyptian, Christian, and, worse, divorced. She would complain that her condition had painfully "exoticized" her in the eyes of her Algerian students.

In Egypt, this religious divide only very partially reproduced the effects of the language divide in North Africa. In Algeria, far more so than in Tunisia or Morocco, this had both cut off the Francophone elites of North Africa from the use of Arabic, and conferred upon them a near monopoly on communication with Europe. The social status of Coptic elites was in some sense the exception to the prevailing rule in Muslim Egypt: that the banks of the Nile have no substantive equivalent of an isolated *nomenklatura*, along the lines of "Club des Pins Algeria" or "La Marsa Tunisia."[5] From the standpoint of language, such classes are absent: abandoning Arabic for English remains an extremely marginal phenomenon. And from the standpoint of religion, the political class has not taken up the habit of an overly explicit secularism.

In Egypt, the state's management of sectarian tensions between Copts and Muslims, in its role as "protector of minorities," was both pernicious and remarkably cynical. Clashes between the two communities were given much media play. Time and again, they enabled the state to discredit even the least radical Islamist opposition when addressing its own Western partners, who needed no helping hand to believe the regime—then as now. Western (and especially French) diplomacy had the greatest difficulty in setting up cultural bridges with the overwhelming majority of the population. France's foreign development service at the time devoted 80 percent of its funding to institutions run by Christian congregations. Saudi generosity towards the Muslim institutions was highly politically self-interested, and clearly could not compensate for this symbolic disequilibrium.[6] At the time, many foreign companies still preferred to hire Copts in their local branches—or even, in some cases, to hire no Muslims at all. Egypt was overwhelmingly young, Muslim, and Arabic speaking. The practices of the secular French republic thereby contributed to the upkeep of a crowd of aging, French-speaking Christians.

Egypt: Keystone of the Scholarly Construction of Political Islam

It was Egypt (together with Sudan, Jordan, and neighboring Palestine) that enabled me to fill out the hypotheses that I laid out in 1995 in *Face to Face with Political Islam*, which I wrote as soon as I arrived back in France. In this book, before Al-Qaeda appeared on the political stage and in the media, I laid out the core of my analytical framework of the "Islamist question." During this period, the political spectrum of Islamism that I had begun to study in North Africa expanded considerably—and it ranged from Luxor to Alexandria, Minya, and Fayyum. In Egypt, it stretched from the heavyweights of the Muslim Brotherhood to the young "radicals" of the Gamaat Islamiya, via the elusive partisans of *Tanzim al-Jihad*. (In the course of fascinating all-night encounters at the heart of Cairo's urban fabric, I had deconstructed the period in which the Gamaat Islamiya became politicized in opposition to the Sufi circles to which its members had first belonged.)

The wealth of understanding that I gathered in Egypt proved decisive. The intellectual and activist development of the ex-Nasserist Tarek al-Bishri and the ex-Communist Adel Hussein, set against that of Tunisia's Rached Ghannouchi whom I reencountered in 1991 in his London exile, enabled me to set up the foundations of my scholarly "construction" of the Muslim Brotherhood component of the Islamist spectrum.

"I asked myself: can one seriously claim to be nationalist if one is not open to Islam, which is the very identity of this nation?" Adel Hussein had said. He enabled me to pinpoint the common denominator that had allowed the generation of the Nasserist nationalist left to become reconciled with a mode of thinking that they conceived of, less as religious, than as "endogenous." Tarek al-Bishri opened up for me an angle fundamental to understanding the reasons behind the enigmatic fragility of Egypt's state apparatus, and the consequent power of so-called religious discourse.

The authoritarian, purportedly "modern" state was all-powerful with respect to the commanding heights of power. Why, then, was it so ill-represented within the intimate spaces of society's nooks and crannies? Bishri explained it to me thus: fearing competition, the Arab state determined that the network of religious institutions as a whole was incompatible with the state's own authority. In making that choice, it disregarded the powerful intermediary role played by this institutional mesh of micro-forms of belonging that linked the individual with the state, and which the state could have kept within its grasp without endangering itself. Quite the opposite. "I realized that the cement of these different entities, which make up the institutional fabric of society, was religious thought. [...]

When religious membership was attacked, it was this network of associations that was attacked and annihilated rather not improved."[7]

At a later stage, revisiting the evolution(s) of Sayyid Qutb (1906–66), the fundamentalist sentenced and executed by Nasser's regime, and of the "executor of his will," the *jihadi* Ayman Dhawahiri, enabled me to sharpen the fundamental distinction between the Brotherhood and the Salafi movement. At the time, I could not imagine that, nearly a quarter of a century later, Dhawahiri, the *jihadi* who had in 1988 virulently condemned the Brotherhood's compromises, would in turn become the target of the same attacks on the part of the Islamic State generation, who accused him of the same guilty compromises with Western political thought.[8] Above all, my fieldwork in Egypt firmed up a conviction that had long remained latent and that, over a decade later, I would set about reasserting, against the grain of the vast majority of my colleagues. Namely: that the wellsprings of the *jihadi* "theology of war" formulated by Qutb, then implemented by Dhawahiri and, later, by his disciples and competitors in Iraq,[9] are fundamentally political—and fundamentally reactive.

The full scale of the perversity of the state's policy towards the quietist Salafi component of Egypt's Islamist opposition thereby appeared to me, built as it was upon the wholesale criminalization of the Brotherhood. (Egypt was, then as now, France's "great secular partner.") In 1990, the French Senate's President Alain Poher visited, to confer upon Egypt the Senate's Louise Michel Prize for Democracy and Human Rights. Hosni Mubarak condoned and encouraged the disinterest for politics of Salafi preachers of every stripe—but also their extreme conservatism. In doing so, he was fully conscious that he was putting wind in the sails of a far more literalist and far less "modern" intellectual trend than was the Brotherhood—but weakening the Brotherhood was the priority, inasmuch as they alone constituted a political threat.

By heaping praise on "their" Mubarak, Western leaders showed very little concern for their own contribution to nurturing the dynamics of *jihadi* violence. Their gaze was cast no further than Mubarak's idyllic relationship with Israel, their primary ally in the region. As I came to these conclusions, I could not imagine the extent to which, beginning in July 2013, one of Hosni Mubarak's successors, Marshal Sissi, would come to wield this terrible method more radically still—and with Western support no less total than Mubarak enjoyed in his time.

Sudan: From the Brotherhoods to Turabi

Egypt stood at the gates of Palestine. In the shape of the immensity of Sudan, it was also my antechamber to the frontiers of the Arab world.

Sudan was the product of an untypical history, and had not yet been amputated of its southern province that became South Sudan. Had Sudan, after all, not been colonized by Egypt? Sudan too entered into the Islamist movement—that is to say, the politicization of religious belonging in a modern framework, with Hassan Turabi as the key figure in its development.[10] This came into being, more explicitly still than in Egypt, through Islamist players distancing themselves from the framework of the two great rival Sufi brotherhoods, the Mahdia and the Khatmiya, that also invested the political field. Sudan supplied a key illustration of the borderline that had, for a time at least, separated Sufis from Islamists, in both Egypt and Sudan, setting Islamists along a path that was far more modernizing than it was "sectarian" or "radical." "In the countryside, people would ask us Brothers: 'Can we pray with trousers on?' The Sufis said no, whereas we said that these were mere *shakliyyat*, formalist details."[11]

Sudan regularly distinguished itself through Turabi's attempts at syncretism. Aiming to reduce the growing divide in the Arab political scene, he organized highly productive gatherings in which the whole spectrum of Islamist opposition movements (or very nearly) rubbed shoulders with the elite of their "nationalist" competitors and predecessors. These fora later enabled institutionalizing groundbreaking political alliances between certain versions of political Islam that had taken the shape of political parties, and opposition players from outside the Islamist sphere. Such convergences included the Sant'Egidio pact for Algeria (January 13, 1995); in the Yemeni context, the Liqa al-Mushtarak of 2006, in a different sectarian framework; in Lebanon, the alliance between the Aounists and Hezbollah the same year; and, of course, in Tunisia, the October 18, 2005, movement that laid the ground for the relatively consensual configuration of the post-Ben Ali transition.

These great Sudan-inspired gatherings were invariably held under the highly watchful eye of a plethora of Western intelligence services, whose disguises and various identities put on for the occasion were more or less subtle. In 1993, the spy sent by the Direction de la Surveillance du Territoire (DST, the French domestic intelligence service) was clearly not the most hardened professional. During an excursion on a boat on the Nile, he let fall from his pocket his "commission list." This wound up in the wrong hands—mine included. We therefore learned that his mission included acquiring the cell phone numbers of a whole range of activists, Algerian ones especially—including an air force pilot won over to the FIS! He was also tasked with pinpointing the precise nature of the activities and the leadership structure of a given Islamic NGO. A short while later, far from the grand conference hall, in the relative cool of the French ambassador's residence, he fell victim to the diplomatic privilege of access to alcohol. Having lost control of the contents of his pockets, he now lost control of mind and body altogether. Just before passing out dead-drunk in the restroom, he had time to proclaim to his audience, who could not but be moved by such candor, the name of his dispatcher: "Pasqua sent me!"[12]

The next day, one last surprise awaited us, at the dinner given by the president, an event enhanced by a concert given by the artist who long called himself Cat Stevens before he became Yusuf Islam. On the gold-lettered menu, our famous French "crème caramel" was mundanely translated as *caramella*. In Arabic, however, the same *caramel* cream had turned into a "*karam Allah* cream." In Islamist Sudan, even the dessert praised its Creator.

Cairo Airport is historically a stopover or departure-point for flights towards another end of the world—this time the ends of the Arab world: "Yemen al-Saeed." Nasser had long presided over Yemen's political destiny. There, with revolutionary republicans as proxies, he had fought the regional influence of his great rival Saudi Arabia, with none too much care for the sovereignty of his Yemeni protégés.[13] In September 1997 I took flight for this *Arabia Felix*, which still deserved the title then—for six long years, intensely fulfilling ones in scholarly terms.

Notes

1 The title of one of the most celebrated novels by Naghib Mahfouz, winner of the Nobel Prize for Literature (Dar al-Shuruq, Cairo, 2007); English translation *The Children of the Alley*, Anchor, New York, 2016.
2 King Mohammed VI did so, for instance, in 2011, in the context of the drafting of a new constitution, without the vigilant guardians of "secular norms" north of the Mediterranean paying this any mind. With respect to the status granted to *sharia* (the Islamic legal corpus), in this constitution the king adopted a more conservative stance than did his Islamist opponents from the Justice and Spirituality movement (*al-'Adl wa-l-Ihsân*).
3 The next day, April 2, 1974, as we left the university, the death of President Georges Pompidou was announced on the radio. "I have to go home," Dumont exclaimed to his surprised young colleagues: "I have to stand in the presidential election." He was to pick up only 1.32 percent of the vote—but nonetheless contributed to anchoring the Green movement on the political stages of France and Europe.
4 Michel Camau, *Pouvoirs et Institutions au Maghreb*, Cérès, Tunis, 1972.
5 The Club des Pins is a luxurious seaside residential complex a few miles from Algiers. From the turn of the 1990s, it became a "fortified camp in which the Algerian nomenklatura settled, accompanied by its court that, while it was supposed to run the country, perfected its taste for secrecy and political

intrigue" (in the words of the journalist Sid Ahmed Sémiane in his *Au refuge des balles perdues et autres chroniques des deux Algérie*, La Découverte, Paris, 2005). La Marsa is a sprawling residential district east of Tunis that borders the town of Sidi Bou Saïd and where, after the same fashion, Tunisia's governing elites have gathered since independence.

6 François Burgat, *Face to Face with Political Islam*.
7 François Burgat, *Face to Face with Political Islam*, p. 27.
8 In April 2016, issue 14 of *Dabiq*, the ISIS information and propaganda magazine, was devoted wholesale to denouncing the Muslim Brotherhood, to which ISIS's competitor in the *jihadi* field, Al-Qaeda, is related. *Dabiq* took particularly direct exception to the Syrian author of the *Call to Global Islamic Resistance*, Mustapha Ben Abdelkader Setmariam Nasar alias Umar Abd al-Hakim (the name under which he published *Al-thawra al-islamiyya al-jihadiyya fi suriyya* [*The Jihadi Islamic Revolution in Syria*] in 1991). He is now better known to us as Abu Musab al-Suri.
9 See Hassan Abou Haniyeh and Mohamed Abu Roumane, *Tanzîm ad dawla al islamiyya. Al azma al sunniya wal sira' 'ala al jihâdiya al 'alamiyya*, Friedrich Ebert Stiftung, 2017.
10 Hassan Turabi (1932–2016) was a Sudanese politician, the leader of the National Islamic Front, then of the National Congress, and the son-in-law of another major Sudanese political figure, Sadeq al-Mahdi. He was, primarily, a conspicuously influential thinker across the Muslim world. Close to the Muslim Brotherhood stream of thought, he had—by preempting it— wide-ranging influence on the reformist trajectory of the movement founded by Hassan al-Banna.
11 Quoted in François Burgat, *Face to Face with Political Islam*.
12 Pasqua was then interior minister (1993–5) in the government headed by Jacques Chirac (1993–5) under the presidency of François Mitterrand.
13 An unprecedented episode in world diplomatic history illustrates this well— and remains surprisingly little known. In September 1966, Nasser summoned the entire government of the Republic whose painful birth he had midwifed, using the forceps of military intervention. He was wary of the team led by Ahmed Mohammed Nu'man, whom he suspected of indulgence towards his Baathist rivals—so had the entire delegation arrested as soon as they stepped off the plane. For a year and twenty-two days, Nu'man and most of his colleagues were kept in Heliopolis military prison, in especially harsh conditions. The former head of the republican government was freed only due to Egypt's debacle in the June 1967 Six-Day War, which forced Nasser to withdraw his troops from Yemen and to hasten his search for a negotiated solution. (See François Burgat, "Ahmed Mohammed Nu'man et la construction d'une identité nationale yéménite," *Revue des mondes musulmans et de la Méditerranée*, nos. 121–2, 2007, pp. 185–200).

5

Yemen:
Modernization without Colonization

I arrived in Yemen in September 1997, to become Director of the French Center for Yemeni Studies (CFEY). I left the country by road in 2003, via Saudi Arabia, Jordan, Syria, and Turkey, to renew my tenure at the IREMAM in Aix-en-Provence. Yemen both extended my trajectory in comparative politics and diversified it in new and especially stimulating ways. Here was a country that enabled stepping out of both the North African and the Middle Eastern versions of the colonial paradigm. Given how central this variable has been to the scholarly construction of my research object, this was a fundamental change.

I have often described my time in Yemen as the posting that made the greatest mark on me. Travel is often a quest for what is not (or is no longer) under one's nose at home. From that perspective, Yemen is the most gratifying destination possible. After a few days spent in Sanaa, a Lebanese Arabic-teacher friend shared with me this enthralled reaction: "Yemen feels as if I were in my grandfather's house." Encountering Yemen involves a journey through space—but also through time, into the *longue durée* of Arab history. This may seem quite banal to some. To Europeans, Yemen—northern Yemen, at least—is more than just the inheritor of the "Happy Arabia" of the Ancients (mysterious, too), which their successors characterized as pious and wise. ("Al-iman yamaan wa al-hikma yamaani-yya," the Prophet is reported to have pronounced.[1]) It is also—as two more recent visitors dubbed it—the "Tibet of the Red Sea": a region that remained isolated from any foreign (and especially, Western) influence.[2]

Enabling the Research of Others

The French Center for Yemeni Studies was founded in 1982 and built upon a solid foundation by my predecessor, Franck Mermier.[3] Unlike the CEDEJ in Cairo, it devoted itself to the entire disciplinary spectrum, from the social sciences through archaeology to political science. In a country where France had no colonial past, and therefore had fewer exchange networks, a considerable lag in bilateral relations had to be made up in order to benefit from vast opportunities for development. My first task was to institutionalize the center's regional mission—even if this remained for some time embryonic given lack of personnel.[4]

In scholarly terms, the task was in some sense to restore Yemen to its rightful centrality, given its importance within the mythic and symbolic universe of Muslim (but also pre-Islamic) history. French researchers still too often limited their fieldwork in Arab countries to the shores of the Mediterranean and the banks of the Nile, or to *Bilad al-Sham*, the Levant. It was thus incumbent upon me to do everything possible to ensure that the Southern Gulf should become as natural an entry point to scholarly knowledge of the Arab and Muslim worlds as were North Africa or the Middle East.

For historians, Yemen, like Saudi Arabia, is distinctive in hosting a wealth of as yet untapped primary sources. A scholar who wishes to add even the most modest of pages to the book of Algerian history has to contend with dozens of distinguished competitors. A researcher who hopes to do the same in the Arabian Peninsula—and in Yemen especially—has hundreds of manuscripts at his disposal, and every opportunity to comment upon and edit sources that have never before been the subject of scholarly research—or so little. Closer to my own field of contemporary studies, the social science literature on Yemen converges around a key characteristic, the terminology for which varies: "protective," "persistence," "survival," "sustaining" … In the 2000s, one could indeed still witness a very wide range of social practices that had disappeared elsewhere, sometimes long since. Anthropologists and jurists could study *in vivo* the exceptional coexistence of three legal norms: first, traditional tribal law;[5] second, Muslim law; and finally, "modern," Western-inspired legal codes.

The history of contemporary Yemen is defined by a certain dualism, from the outset of the competition between the Ottoman and British empires in 1839 to the country's reunification in May 1990 that formally brought to an end the long and turbulent North/South division. This provided political scientists with a unique laboratory through which to examine the coexistence between how politics expressed itself in the "Afghanistan of the Gulf" in the North, that is, in a region cut off from any direct Western influence—and, in the South, the successor to the only country in the region ever explicitly to adopt the references of a USSR-imported Marxism, wide open to foreign influences. Each of these Yemens also provided scholars of linguistics with a treasure trove of pre-Arabic sources. With respect to contemporary Arabic, it provided a privileged environment in which to study the "language of the *dhad*" (the symbolically defining emphatic consonant of the Arabic alphabet), in a dual country that, unlike those of North Africa and the Middle East, had been infinitely less affected by the incursion of Western languages.[6]

The Historical Alchemy of the Two Yemens

Professionally, Yemen's charms ranged beyond the narrow confines of my semi-bureaucratic prospects as Director of the Centre Français d'Archéologie et de Sciences Sociales. They also ranged beyond Yemen's high plateaux, the scorching fields of the Tihama plains, and the legendary Hadhramaut Valley. It was in Yemen that I produced my third book,[7] *Islamism in the Shadow of al-Qaeda*, integrating to my analysis the specificities of the Gulf—as well as, unavoidably given the political context, the emergence of transnational armed groups.

It was in Yemen that I first realized that the scholarly construction of the local version of Islamism would require in-depth generalist knowledge of the country's very specific configuration—a specificity tied to the dualism of Yemen's contemporary history up until the North–South reunification of 1990. An abundant colonial and post-colonial historiography covers North Africa and the Middle East, but at the time scholarly knowledge of contemporary Yemen remained relatively embryonic. The atypical histories of modernization in Yemen had been partially documented by (among others) a few, primarily Arab, travelers. Their chronicles became my main bedtime reading in Sanaa.[8] My historical quest involved me collecting and documenting a considerable store of iconography. This was published as an expansive volume in 2003; difficulties in distributing it (*publish locally*, etc.) failed to prevent it from becoming something of a success—and, more so, from teaching the team of scholars who worked on it an enormous amount.[9] My research in countless private collections was guided by my invaluable Tunisian colleague Mohamed Sbitli, who often called upon the inexhaustible fount of knowledge of Qadi Isma'il al-Akwa (1920–2008), the first Director of the Yemen Antiquities Service, and a historian of great repute.

Welcome surprises punctuated this quest. In the French director René Clément's film *Forbidden Arabia*, Rémy Audouin, the first Director of the French Center for Yemeni Studies, (re-)discovered the only photographs (actually, a film clip) of Imam Yahya Hamideddin. Clément had taken these from the window of his residence in 1936, while visiting Sanaa. Another major surprise awaited us in the home of a descendant of the famed Mahmoud Zubeiry, one of the two leaders of the Free Yemeni Movement. Abandoned in the back of a cupboard since its owner had been assassinated in 1964 lay a satchel overflowing with several hundred unpublished photographs. By some miracle, in Casablanca, seated at the table of the founder of the JDP,[10] I made the acquaintance of the son of Omar Baha'uddin al-Amiri, Syria's ambassador to Pakistan and future foreign minister, who welcomed Zubeiry in exile in 1948. In Paris (and in Sanaa) I met the son of Antonin Besse, the Franco-British businessman tied to the economic fate of Aden, the foundation of Oxford's Saint Antony's College, and whole swaths of Yemen's history. On the shores of the Red Sea, one of my fellow attendees at the World Economic Forum recounted to me his landing in Aden in September 1962, flying his little single-engined airplane. He also shared with me his startling photographs of the lynching of the royalists, taken soon afterwards on the "Square of Sparks," during the very first hours of the revolution. When we exchanged business cards, I was the more startled of the two: I learned that I had just made the acquaintance of Winston Churchill, the eponymous grandson of his celebrated grandfather. In Jeddah, Saudi Arabia, it was with no little emotion that I met one of the descendants of Imam Ahmed, whose private possessions I had been authorized to photograph in his palace-cum-museum in Taiz. He, too, opened up the doors to the family collection.

A "Party of God" to Struggle against Theocracy?

In terms of my own research, Yemen was primarily an entry point into the distinctive political problematic associated with the Gulf. In Yemen, in the absence of a direct conduit for colonial norms, political "modernization" and the reactive alchemy of Islamism have operated in a very different context from the remainder of the Arab world. This distinctive political geography allows analysts to step over the colonial fracture and the many scars it left behind, which remain so potent in North Africa. This enables seeing how, in the case of Saudi Arabia for instance, "colonized" as it was by Aramco,[11] distance from the West developed without popular representation of the Western world ever being directly associated with the colonial mold. In Sanaa, modernizing Otherness was long identified with the Ottoman masters of the Sublime Porte. Granted, these were "foreigners," sometimes derided as "trouser-wearing." They remained, however, Muslims—and were, as such, less exogenous than Westerners.

The Ottomans mounted a first excursion into Yemen between 1538 and 1635. They resettled there in 1872, on the territory of the Zaidi Imamate that had ruled over Yemen for nearly a thousand years. (The Imamate arose from a split within Twelver Shiism, and was imported to Yemen at the end of the 9th century.) The British remained in Yemen from 1839 to 1967—that is, nearly as long as the French in Algeria, but with far less intrusive methods. They then gave way to the People's Democratic Republic of Yemen (1967–90). South Yemen enters into the classic framework of a modernization process that more or less correlates with the colonial presence. In the North, a different scenario operated. In 1911, at the end of their second occupation of Yemen, the political space left by the Ottomans' departure was not filled by a new colonizer, nor a Western power taking up a League of Nations Mandate. It was, therefore, Turkish intellectuals, and later, in the main, Arab nationalists, who became the conduit for modernizing ideas. This included the stillborn idea of setting up a constitutional framework to limit the all-but-absolute theocratic power of the Zaidi Imam, the local version of the "Commander of the Faithful."

The lessons to be drawn from this atypical configuration are all the more instructive. As against received wisdom concerning political modernization, in North Yemen it was Muslim Brothers who took the initiative of sowing constitutionalist ideas. They saw Yemen as a haven of "Muslim virginity," which had remained out of reach of Western appetites—as opposed to demanding to "introduce Islam into the constitution," along the lines of their counterparts in the region. This was something that the late Mohamed Qahtan,[12] one of the leaders of the Islamist Tagamu al-Islah party (the Congregation for Reform, often abbreviated as "al-Islah" or "Islah") proudly recalled to me. In 1948, the Sacred National Pact was nearly put into practice. This consisted of a charter to limit the absolutism of the Imam's theocratic power, defended by an Algerian emissary of Hassan al-Banna. But, like the constitutional revolution, this charter was short-lived. The assassination of Imam Yahya Hamideddin had already set it off on the wrong foot. What followed was a terrible counter-revolution that put an end to all hopes of political modernization in the kingdom for nearly fifteen years.

The ease with which the absolutist Imam was able to rally "his" tribes against the modernizing urban elites is especially instructive. The Free Yemeni Movement was accused of nothing less than planning to "abridge the Quran." Even while they were inspired by the Muslim Brotherhood, the Free Yemenis fell prey to a real deficit of empathy with the local popular—that is to say, religious—culture of the rural masses that made up the overwhelming majority of the population. The same mistake was recurrent among Arab modernizers as is so well deconstructed by the Egyptian Tarek al-Bishri (see Chapter 11, p. 170). Namely: underestimating the functional nature of the relationship between the elites of religious thought and those of the political imagination and with it political action—including revolutionary political action. It nearly recurred in 1964. The republican revolution was clumsily supported by Nasser's Egypt,[13] which showed no hesitation in short-circuiting the leaders of the 1948 revolution. When the revolution seemed on the cusp of being rejected, what saved it, *in extremis*, was the setting up of a proactive linkage with religious thought. Yemen's two great reformist intellectuals, Ahmed Mohammed Nu'man and Mahmoud Zubeiry, sought to anchor the tribes within the republican revolution. These had long remained the "armed wings of the Imamate"; the quip went that to them, *dimuqratiyya* (democracy) sounded more like the name of one of Egypt's President Abdel Nasser's possible wives than it did like their own political future. To this end, Nu'man and Zubeiry thought to create a more effective institutional framework than the abstruse reference to the Republic. They chose to found the first Hezbollah in the region's history. And so it came to pass that in Yemen it was a "Party of God" that shored up the revolution that brought the political reign of religious doctrine to a lasting end.

"Civil Society in Arms"

During my time there before September 11, 2001, Yemen was also an excellent perch from which to witness the many consequences of US petro-diplomacy.

Yemen became among the prime crucibles for the development of Sunni radical groups. Even earlier in the 1990s it was already considered an unstable and dangerous territory. The kidnapping of foreign tourists had become routine. The practice testified more to the unfinished nature of state-building than it did to any (remarkably absent) animosity on the part of Yemenis towards their Western visitors, and it had been contained within humanly acceptable limits. The victims generally emerged safe and sound. Sometimes, as in the case of several groups of French tourists, they even emerged all but delighted by their extra adventure. Nor was the CEFAS team spared. In August 1998, two of our colleagues were visiting an archaeological site at the heart of the Jawf region, known for being dangerous, and bore the brunt of the kidnapping phenomenon.

In this instance, they were distinctly not overcome by Stockholm syndrome. Their fortnight's captivity felt interminable to them. The army shot at the group to intimidate their kidnappers. So did the gunmen of their guide's tribe, who were similarly upset at seeing the rules of hospitality that had been extended to one of their own be so flouted. Contact remained possible between the two sides via the guide's tribe; the kidnappees' friends sent them ambitious food packages, with little prior coordination. Alas! The mountains of *foie gras* and *camembert* swiftly melted in the heat, and were of no comfort whatsoever to them. Rather, they interpreted these as evidence that we expected their detention to last a long while yet. Nor did a fotonovela shot in their apartment, starring their forsaken cat, give them any more reason to smile. The scenario, however, was well practiced. The trick is to not cave in too early, in order not to encourage more kidnappings, even while making the kidnappers feel growing military pressure. Thankfully, contacts at the highest level eventually bore fruit (including between presidents Jacques Chirac and Ali Abdallah Saleh).

Kidnappings were not the only moments that gave life in Sanaa's warlike tinges. These were quite new to me. The kidnapping of our colleagues had led the Foreign Affairs Ministry to cut short the new ambassador's vacation. The first night the ambassador spent in his residence was interrupted by a terrifying explosion. A disagreement, which was most likely merely business related, had led the wronged party to take justice into his own hands by blowing up one of his rival's crown jewels: the city's largest mall. Unfortunately for the neighbors, the wide variety of goods sold by the City Market included a considerable store of cooking gas. For what seemed an eternity, a slow, soft, colorful rain, made up of the debris of every kind of food packaging, including a supply of American breakfast cereal, fell upon the gardens of the ambassador's residence. At an impressive distance from the explosion, a window there had been shattered.

A few days later was the evening on which our two colleagues had been freed. We were raising a glass in their honor in the company of the new ambassador. Automatic rifle fire crackled in the night. The regulars opined that it was most likely a wedding. The choppy rhythm of a large 12.7 mm machine gun did make them raise their eyebrows a little: the gun-carriage of such a beast is generally set up in the back of a pick-up truck. More alarming news came in. This confirmed that the shots had indeed come from a wedding. The party had, however, gone rather sour. In order to make his punitive entrance into his host's villa, one of the guests had borrowed a tank. This set off an impressive pitched battle throughout the neighborhood. It was now out of the question to cross town; we had to find a lengthy bypass route.

In the "great open-air museum" that is Yemen, some archaeologists fall prey to the fragility of state institutions. On one occasion, the members of a successful archaeological mission allowed themselves to be filmed in front of the funerary pottery which they had excavated in the Mareb region's intriguing tombs. (The mission had encountered success beyond the mere fact that its head had allowed me to take my first, modest but fruitful steps as a tomb excavator.) They were as yet unaware that these pictures were not designed to celebrate the scientific importance of their discoveries—but only to raise their market price. The video artists returned a few hours later, brandishing this time not a camera but a Kalashnikov, to convince the scientists to hand over the results of their excavations. These amiable visitors were unambiguously identified. They nonetheless remained unpunished.

As Center Director, I received countless offers to purchase pillaged archaeological objects—offers that I imperturbably declined. This was not the case of every member of every diplomatic mission, including those none too distant from us. When the objects stood out as being exceptional, some of my colleagues tried to have the National Museum acquire them instead. At the close of a lengthy process begun in 1999 by my friend the epigraphist Mounir Arbach, in my company at the home of the Prime Minister Abdul Karim al-Iryani, Arbach managed (in return for 100,000 dollars to its owners) to provide an impressive bronze lion with a home in the National Museum. The prime minister was fascinated by the work of the Catalan archaeologists who spent time at CEFAS. Had the name of his village, Iryane, which has a namesake in Spain, been (plausibly) carried over in the luggage of the tribes that had set off to people Andalusia? Or, conversely, had the Iryanis of Andalusia brought the name back with them on being expelled from Andalusia in 1492?

The miscellaneous news rubric of untypical events was a lengthy one—even while this is very far from being exclusively a Yemen-specific phenomenon. A sample: a few attacks, in particular against the British embassy; the kidnapping of the German ambassador's twelve bodyguards; the kidnapping of the parents of my colleague, the Director of the American Center (who desperately strove to acquire a home for the center that would be as magical as her friendly French competitor's); a grenade exploding in the Bab al-Yemen souk; but also the public executions during which the condemned are thrown facedown to the ground and riddled with bullets.

True, weapons are an inseparable part of the most ordinary everyday life of the region. Nor are they merely folkloric. Yemenis are fond of their weapons in ways not unlike Americans are. These are inscribed within a fairly similar political and "democratic" symbolic universe. This "civil society in arms" is part of the regulatory mechanisms of a still-embryonic central political system. The basic rights of Yemen's citizens are not to be infringed upon lightly. Their (tribal) group has kept hold of the means to have those rights be respected: cutting off roads, kidnappings, and so on. Political players outside the circles of state power have retained the privilege of limiting the excesses inherent to the ruler's monopoly of legitimate violence. They draw their weapons—for worse, but also, very often, for better, too. Unlike most of their counterparts in the Arab world, from Ben Ali's Tunisia to Mubarak's Egypt, the poor in Yemen did not let themselves be dispossessed.

Foreigners often take themselves to be invited to "integrate" this societal feature of Yemen. For a few days I became the caretaker of an impressive light machine-gun that a minor sheikh from Khawlan dropped off at my place in my absence, hoping that it might act as a deposit for a sizeable financial loan. With a heavy heart, a French colleague entrusted me with the most modest of 9 mm revolvers, which he had lovingly taken care of during his time in Yemen. I did not take the time to improve my training. (To this day, this is a field in which I have much to learn.) I handed it over when I left in turn. The Lebanese entrepreneur friend to whom I entrusted it did not exactly find supplying himself a struggle. I dined at his table in the company of his compatriot of Armenian descent Sarkis Soghanalian (1929–2011), one of the century's most notorious arms dealers, and especially famous for having been the CIA's intermediary in not a few of its "dirty wars" in the four corners of the globe. Soghanalian was, for instance, involved in arming Saddam Hussein against Khomeini's Iran—and again, this time without the help of his American HQ, in delivering to Argentina murderous French Exocet missiles during the Falklands War of 1982.

From Yemeni Folklore to Regional Authoritarianism

For several decades, instability in Yemen was more of the order of folklore than it was a real danger. I did, however, hear the sound of these weapons being used in more dramatic circumstances at least once. It was December 28, 2002, amid the rows of the gigantic hall in which the opposition party al-Islah held its Congress, to which I had been invited along with a British anthropologist colleague, Paul Dresch. At the time, Yemen's opposition had set out on the unifying turn that eventually led it to test out the ambitious Liqa al-Mushtaraq (the "Joint Meeting Parties" coalition) in the 2006 elections. The coalition sealed the fate of al-Islah's Islamists, and of the socialists who had for a time held power in South Yemen. President Ali Abdallah Saleh had always sought to divide his opponents. He looked upon this alliance as a threat. That day Jarallah Omar, the Socialist Party's second-in-command, had just made a highly unifying speech—and as such, a highly alarming one for the "veteran" president. As Jarallah came down from the podium and weaved his way up one of the hall's corridors to give an interview to Al-Jazeera, two deadly shots rang out.

It later emerged that the backdrop to this drama was especially unsettling. The young killer's identity fooled no one. He was a *salafi* (but of course!), supposedly motivated by hostility to any rapprochement with the "Communist" Jarallah. But he also happened to be an army officer. His commander-in-chief was none other than Ali Abdallah Saleh. For several months, Jarallah had been subjected to systematic harassment from the president's inner circle, who had made him their favorite whipping boy. Regularly, a few seconds after he entered his home, his phone would ring. He was sarcastically wished a "Welcome home!" designed to remind him that he was under close surveillance. On one of these occasions, he was asked: "Do you have any idea how long you have left to live?"

In the wake of Jarallah Omar's assassination, a recent event at CEFAS retrospectively took on a more sinister quality. A few weeks earlier, the Socialist leader had done us the honor of participating in a colloquium we had co-organized with our Yemeni partners, entitled "Yemen and the World."[14] On the day the colloquium was inaugurated, another prestigious attendee was present: Prince Turki al-Faisal, former head of the Saudi intelligence services, who was later to become the ambassador to the United Kingdom, then to the United States. He also directed the King Faisal Center for Research and Islamic Studies in Riyadh, which was also the first Saudi institution to host French researchers. "Sahib al-Sumou al-Maliki" (His Royal Highness), as I learned to pronounce without too much stumbling, was a remarkably open and cultured character. I had been the discussant of his World Economic Forum panel of 2002, moved from New York to Davos in the wake of September 11. He had forgiven me when, with a certain impertinence, I had inquired of him why, given the principles of regional cooperation that he preached, the contrast remained so absolute between the two sides of the Saudi–Yemeni border. On one side, shanty towns; on the other, a cyber-society and air-conditioning. He then invited me to Riyadh and, more surprisingly, took up my invitation to visit CEFAS in Sanaa.

Jarallah Omar was in the audience and asked him a question. The prince jokingly replied, prompting hilarity from the audience: "Oh, but I recognize you, Mr. Jarallah: you filled my briefings for years." That same evening, there was a reception at CEFAS, in the little salon that adjoined the *birkeh* (pool). Turki al-Faisal gestured towards Jarallah to invite him to come sit by his side. They talked for several minutes in the most friendly manner. The next day, in Aden, Prince Turki met with President Abdallah Saleh, with whom he had stayed in Sanaa. A few weeks later, a witness to that meeting passed on a sample of their exchanges, which took on the fullest meaning only in retrospect. Turki al-Faisal had told Abdallah Saleh "You know, I met your enemy Jarallah Omar. [...] He's a thoroughly pleasant character, and I plan to invite him to come to Riyadh." Yemen's president was unable to conceal his displeasure. For his fiercest rival to become his competitor for the good graces of the Saudis was a terrible offence. It takes no great stretch of the imagination to imagine the next episode ...

Close scrutiny of the uses of "Yemeni" armed violence was therefore highly instructive regarding the favored methods of those in power and their regional allies—at least as much so as was observing the "tribes and the beardies" who supposedly stood up to them. A member of the French embassy's military delegation was similarly exposed to the uses of violence by the powers that be. Like many of his colleagues, he had acquired a thoroughly respectable standard in the study of Arabic language and culture. He often professed to me his admiration for his teacher, an Egyptian Islamist in exile, who had been close to the *Takfir wal-Hijra* group, and who had fled Mubarak's repression. One day, as Friday prayers came to an end at the mosque the teacher attended, an altercation broke out. Almost at once, he fell to the ground. A bullet had struck him directly in the head. The Egyptian intelligence services were fond of such set-ups: taking advantage of a vague scuffle organized by one of their agents from start to finish. Another Egyptian intelligence agent, posted in a tower a few dozen meters away, would then take out the target whom it had been decided should be "discreetly neutralized." When he learned the circumstances in which his friend had died, the military attaché at the French embassy became more convinced than ever that the political uses of violence in Yemen were hardly the monopoly of the "Islamist" camp to which the prevailing Western media and political orthodoxy of the time ascribed it.

"Sectarianize and Rule," Yemeni Style

For all its turbulence, and despite the range of religious identities to be found there, Yemen remained a country in which sectarian tensions were more a matter of the past than the present state of political dynamics. At the time of the Imamate, the highest echelons of power had been reserved for members of the Zaidi community alone. Among the most revealing illustrations of this fact was that Cheikh Abdallah Hussein al-Ahmar, who had founded the Tagamu al-Islah party and was considered a direct disciple of the Sunni Muslim Brotherhood's school of thought, was, like many of his fellow party leaders, of Zaidi (i.e. Shia) "origin." Having struggled to abolish the religious Imamate as the expression of Zaidi political absolutism, these political players had left their doctrinal belonging entirely behind them.

During the 2000s, however, the first, lethal signs of the sectarian degeneration that was to strike the Spring 2011 protest movement were already becoming apparent on the Yemeni political stage. Today's analysts invoke the violence of local "Shia rebels." Very few of them deign to recall that it was the regime itself that initiated the sectarianization of national debate, which republican Yemen had for several decades successfully avoided. In the wake of September 11, Ali Abdallah Saleh faced the risk of being moved from the list of US allies to that of targets of the US "War on Terror," and found himself compelled into humiliating concessions with respect to national sovereignty. Predictably, at the turn of 2004, this incurred the virulent recriminations of one of his former protégés, Hussein Badr Eddin al-Houthi. A few years prior, Saleh had suggested to the very same Hussein al-Houthi that he create a religious movement (the Believing Youth). He doubtless hoped that this would divide the "religious" opposition on a sectarian basis. To reprove President Saleh for his submissiveness towards Washington and its Israeli ally, al-Houthi loudly reminded him of the movement's anti-imperialist (anti-American and anti-Israeli) basis.[15]

How could so popular a stance be challenged? Clearly encouraged by the US, Saleh chose the route of brutally repressing the Houthi clan. In order to justify this reaction, he accused it—thoroughly implausibly—of undermining the foundational values of the nation, or the "Republic," by seeking to restore the "Shia" Imamate that the Republic had abolished in 1962.[16] Worse yet: of doing so with the help of Iran and its Lebanese Hezbollah surrogates. And so it was the head of state, and not his "radical" Islamist opponents, who reopened the Pandora's Box of sectarian division. Over a decade on, the box had, alas, not yet been closed again—far from it. In the category of the most shameless political exploitation of religious discourse, Ali Abdallah Saleh beat off much of the regional competition. A few of his key steps are especially instructive.

In 2004, Saleh set out to discredit mundanely political demands. He took the risk of denaturing these by characterizing these as a sectarian challenge—even while, given Yemen's history, it was precisely the Shia Zaidi identity that he could have laid claim to.[17] On this occasion, however, the weapon of sectarianization proved counter-productive. So Saleh found himself compelled to use it again. Two years on, in the autumn of 2006, Saleh realized that the opponents he had selected for "Shia-tization" were drawing the benefits of the (Shia) Lebanese Hezbollah's exceptional popularity, in the wake of its military success faced with Israel's latest campaign against it. At the outset of 2007, he therefore launched a campaign to strip some of this nationalist aura from his newly inconvenient rivals. Saddam Hussein had just been put to death in Iraq under US occupation (on December 30, 2006, coinciding with Eid al-Adha). A poster campaign was therefore timed to remind Yemenis tempted by the nationalism of Hezbollah and its putative Houthi allies that these were of the same (Shia) confession as Saddam's executioners, that is, servants of the "American" decision to hang the Baathist leader, who was renamed the "Lion of the Sunnis" for the occasion.

Five years later, Saleh had been let go of by his internal and regional allies. In January 2012, he was compelled (even while remaining president of his party) to hand over the presidency of the Republic to his feeble second-in-command from Aden, Abdelhadi Mansour al-Hadi. Saleh then set about taking revenge over his former allies, the Islamists of al-Islah, and reconquering the power he had lost through the Spring of "Taghir"

Square.[18] To lend strength to his counter-revolutionary offensive, Saleh had no hesitation. He took command of a counter-revolutionary alliance with the very same Houthis who, for nearly a decade, he had accused of seeking to destroy the unity of the nation through sectarian division ... Saleh and the Houthis were careful to leave their doctrinal identity well in the background. Their opponents had no such compunction. The day after the Houthis in arms entered Sanaa in January 2015, for instance, and before even she took refuge in Riyadh, the young feminist journalist Tawakkul Karman,[19] a member of al-Islah, put out a resounding call to "free Yemen, occupied by Iran" ...

The Saudi princes played a major role in this trying (and tragic) Yemeni role-play, made up of shifting alliances and side-switching among local actors, which outside observers struggled to interpret. Within this role-play, the main political goal of these princes was, however, quite clear. It was no longer, as in the past, a case of "exporting" their Wahhabism (the ultraconservative religious doctrine from which the Saudi kingdom was founded), as so many commentators repeated a little too straightforwardly. It was now strictly a case of holding on to their throne. Before their about-face of March 2015, when they launched the deadly aerial bombing campaign "Decisive Storm" against the Houthi rebellion (to be followed a month later by Operation "Restore Hope"), neither Saudi leaders nor those of the other Gulf oil monarchies had lifted a finger to slow the march of the "Shia" Houthis on Sanaa. Rather, they saw the rebellion as having the advantage of weakening the power of the Muslim Brotherhood—albeit to the benefit of their traditional Shia rivals.[20] The Brotherhood, as embodied in Yemen's al-Islah party, had more often been opponents than partners of the Saudis' traditional ally Ali Abdallah Saleh. Since the outset of the Arab Springs, they had become (along with the radicals of the Islamic State organization (ISIS)), one of the two main regional threats to the Saudi and other Gulf thrones.

These hugely rich princes were concerned to sustain their religious legitimacy. This was even while, in the fight against the Sunnis of ISIS, they found themselves, more or less shamefacedly, in the allied camp, alongside not only the Western powers—but also, *de facto*, alongside Iran. Targeting a "Shia" political player enabled them to water down the dangerously negative symbolic fallout of the anti-ISIS alliance at home. Launching a campaign against the "Shia" Houthi enemy, while simultaneously lining up with Yemen's revolutionary movement, also had another distinct benefit. It muddied the fact that the "democratic threat" had long been far more worrisome to the Saudis than any sectarian threat posed by the Houthis.

The "anti-democratic" priority of Saudi strategy is very clear in Tunisia—just as it has been in Egypt both before and since the counter-revolution of Marshal Sissi. It made concessions in Syria and in Yemen only because these conflicts risked affecting the balance of power between Saudi Arabia and Iran—to the benefit of Iran. Last but not least, the rivalries that ran through the coalition of convenience between Houthi revolutionaries and the counter-revolutionary ex-president Ali Abdallah Saleh led to his spectacular demise on December 4, 2017, after—with no regard for doctrinal solidarity—he had betrayed his (Shia) Houthi allies for the (Sunni) Saudis.

The two members of this coalition were constantly at odds over the allocation of ministries. On several occasions, they had felt the need to display their respective strength, mobilizing their supporters in gigantic meetings organized in two distinct areas of Sanaa. Unsurprisingly, these disputes over power-sharing degenerated. On December 2, following armed clashes over control of the Sanaa Great Mosque that bore his name, they led Saleh to call on his supporters to fight the Houthis and to turn a new page with the coalition if it stopped its embargo. His fleeting Houthi partners were not in the least destabilized. Two days later, they managed to corner and kill him.

This indeed turned a "new page": one yet more filled with uncertainties. These were both with respect to the precise military capacity of Saleh's supporters—but also with respect to Iran's reaction were its Houthi ally to become excessively weakened.

Radicalization in Yemen and the Common Denominator of Foreign Interventions

As my research trajectory developed, Yemen struck me for the remarkable diversity of the dual historical matrix of its Islamist movement. Also, for the North's extraordinary ability to integrate the reformist version of the Islamist movement, even while it harnessed its armed fringe.[21] Yemen enabled me to decipher the fascinating way in which Saleh associated the al-Islah party and the tribes that supported it, gathered around the figure of Cheikh Abdallah Hussein al-Ahmar, to his own power. His political system also, however, enabled me to understand one of the birthplaces of Al-Qaeda—even while Yemen was less famed in that regard than was Afghanistan under the Taliban. For a time, some analysts (most likely mistakenly) flirted with the notion that Al-Qaeda's name came from the village of the same name, a few kilometers north of Yemen's Taiz, where Ben Laden found his fourth wife. To this day, one comes across fascinating carpets there adorned with Bin Laden's exploits.

Even if the genealogy is less direct, it was in many ways in Yemen that, on the scale of the 20th century, Sunni political radicalism first crystallized at the national level—before it became transnational. The Yemeni context lent itself especially well to the process. Soon after the British left South Yemen in 1967, the People's Democratic Republic had witnessed a unique experiment. This was the only one of its kind in the Arab world, directly influenced by the materialist ideology of its Soviet sponsors.[22] Unsurprisingly, part of a society whose religiosity had been so brutally stymied by foreign intervention developed an "Islamist" response. The first *jihadi*s were therefore above all radical "anti-socialists" or anti-Marxists, concerned with countering Soviet influence in the region. Soon after he came to power in North Yemen, Ali Abdallah Saleh moved to exploit them against his rivals in the South. Yemeni *jihadi*s thus appeared on the scene before the conflict in Afghanistan. The US and its Arab allies had supported those who fought the Soviet occupation under the banner of Islam. That war then provided them with what has since become notorious as their springboard in Afghanistan, first on a regional scale, later on a global one—even while nothing lends substance to the claim that it was the CIA that "created" Al-Qaeda.[23]

After the Soviet intervention, successive US interventions, first in distant Afghanistan, then in neighboring Saudi Arabia and Iraq, perfected the Yemeni production line of subscribers to (Islamist) armed struggle. The drivers of September 11 or, rather, the shortcomings that had "manufactured" the perpetrators of those attacks, were clearly to be discerned from Sanaa in 2001. Yemen had already experienced a "dress rehearsal" for 9/11 in the shape of the attack of October 20, 2000, against the *USS Cole* destroyer in Aden port. The attacks followed those of 1998 against two US embassies in the Horn of Africa, which had killed more Kenyans and Tanzanians than they had American citizens.[24] The deaths of seventeen *USS Cole* sailors (and the many injured) could have been a warning to the US as to how widely rejected their policies in the region were. During the victims' funerals President Bill Clinton had, however, pronounced—in tones of terrible sincerity—words that were as inept as they were terrifying. America's new enemies were hostile to it because, it was said, they hated American citizens for their love of freedom. In so doing Clinton laid the "foundation stone"—foundational in every respect—for Western blindness in the coming fight against "terrorism."

From the carpet-bombing of Afghanistan triggered barely a month after September 11, to the invasion of Iraq in March 2003, through the Patriot Act of October 2011, US reactions to the attack on the *Cole* and its terrible aftershocks in New York and Washington, DC, have been governed by the prisms of "security" and repression, and the all-but-exclusive recourse to hard power. Granted, no one had foreseen the exceptional scale of those attacks—nor their targets. But the mechanisms that produced such violence had long since been apparent. To take their measure, it was enough to understand how an overwhelming majority of the citizens of the Middle East felt towards US strategy in their region. In the wake of the attacks of September 11, a (more or less discreet) empathy for the blows struck at what was a (or *the*) superpower clearly identified as hostile was apparent on the part of large swaths of the peoples of the Middle East. In Sanaa, the US embassy had to intervene to stop young street vendors from selling tapes of "Sheikh Osama's" speeches at major intersections.

On September 13, 2001, two days after the attacks on New York that I had witnessed from Sanaa, I published my first impressions on the website of Radio France Internationale (RFI) under the headline: "Bush, Good, Evil, and Respect for the Dead." It ran as follows:

> Consciously or otherwise, US diplomacy leads to making the men and women of an entire region of the world as violent and aggressive towards the US as the US accuses them of being in the first place. In a blaze of self-fulfilling prophecy, the US denounces "Islamic terrorism," in tune with certain European countries. In the same breath, however, it dedicates itself with obsessive care to ensuring that the very blindest violence should, here and there in the Muslim world, appear as the one and only means available to resist the abuses of US hegemony. From the Algerian War to the Vietnam War, via the resistance to Nazism or … the Israeli struggle for independence from the British, anyone in good faith can fathom this. What is dubbed terrorism, sometimes wrongly (in Aden,) sometimes rightly (in New York,) has very often merely been the weapon of the weak. But the weak have not held any monopoly on violence—very far from it!
>
> In Palestine, the American machine for mass-producing hatred and political despair operates through the proxy of Israeli intransigence. In Iraq, it acts more directly, through force of arms, year after year, through recurrent airstrikes but also—and more so—through an embargo whose murderousness is matched only by its seeming eternal. The hundreds of thousands of children who die in Iraq far from CNN's cameras are, at the very least, no less innocent than were the employees at the WTC—if not more innocent still than were the officers at the Pentagon, or the sailors of the *USS Cole*. In the Gulf, as in a number of other states across the region, American violence also operates under the protective umbrella of tired oil dictatorships.
>
> Those regimes are as repressive as they are corrupt. They purchase the protection of the US "cradle of democracy," whether through enormous weapons contracts or through keeping the price of their oil artificially low. The politics of double standards; the willingness to confess only to "collateral" damage produced by "smart" strikes; terribly selective uses of the UN veto, and terribly selective emotion when faced with the victims violence produces; the slanderous conflation involved in pointing at "Islamic networks" in every case of "terrorism": all these fine-tune the terrible engine that constantly reproduces the causes of violence. Concerning this murderous apparatus, which already has new victims in its crosshairs, the

overwhelming majority of commentators on the tragedy of September 11th have not thought to say a word. That it might usefully be condemned seems not even to have crossed their minds.[25]

Fifteen years on, and after the patent failure of a decade of the "War on Terror," it was the turn of the French state —borne on the wings of the same fraudulent media experts and the same electioneering ambitions. It explained, without batting an eyelid, that the violence inflicted upon Parisians during the terrible attacks of January and November 2015 had one sole target. This was ... "our freedoms," and our naughty obsession with drinking fine wine at the terraces of our *bistrots*. These shortcuts came at the cost of clear-headed but more demanding policies—very far removed from an especially hateful shortcut: the proposal to strip French citizenship from those convincted of terrorist offenses, amid one-upmanship in the war against ISIS. They came, that is, at the cost of any policies that might have some hope of actually cutting down the number of "bomb makers"—policies that would, as such, be equal to the threat they pose.

Could such clear-sighted policies still have been entertained by French leaders in 2019? My decades of "participant observation" of French policy in Palestine provide every cause for skepticism.

Notes

1 Faith is Yemeni, as is wisdom.
2 Claude Deffarge and Gordian Troeller, *Yémen 62–69. De la révolution sauvage à la trêve des guerriers*, Robert Laffont, Paris, 1969.
3 See Franck Mermier, *Le Cheikh de la nuit. Sanaa: organisation des souks et société citadine*, Sindbad/Actes Sud, Arles, 1999; *Récits de villes, d'Aden à Beyrouth*, Sindbad/Actes Sud, Arles, 2015.
4 In 2000, in order to expunge the reference to Yemeni-only studies from its name (something the neighboring countries would very reasonably have regarded with suspicion), the CFEY became the French Center for Archaeology and Social Sciences in Sanaa (Centre français d'archéologie et de sciences sociales de Sanaa, CEFAS). Its remit was thus extended to encompass the Sultanate of Oman and Saudi Arabia—but also to Eritrea, since the Ethiopian Studies Center (Maison des études éthiopiennes) in Addis Ababa could not coordinate field research in the former dissident province of Ethiopia. In 2015, after having for a time been run out of Jeddah, the CEFAS was transferred to Kuwait City, to what is likely one of the countries of the region where public debate is most open.
5 See Paul Dresch, *The Rules of Barat: Tribal Documents from Yemen*, CEFAS/ Deutsche Archaeologiches Institut, Sanaa, 2006.
6 During my time in Yemen, poetry and literature remained understudied: both of the popular kind and of the very official kind indeed. Studies of musicol-

ogy (which the work of Jean Lambert, one of my successors, made brilliantly accessible to a French-reading audience) had a complex and diversified corpus from which to draw (Hadhramaut, Sanaa, and Tihama) that was involved with sophisticated regional influences from Africa, the Arab-Persian Gulf, and India (see Jean Lambert, *La Médecine de l'âme*, Société d'ethnologie, Paris, 1997).

7 After *The Islamic Movement in North Africa* and *Face to Face with Political Islam*.

8 To name a few: the famous *Muluk al 'arab* (The Kings of the Arabs) by the Lebanese-American author Amin Rihani, who visited Imam Yahya as early as 1922; *Al rihla al yamaniya* (The Journey to Yemen), the chronicle of the Tunisian founder of the Destour party Abdelaziz Thaalbi (1876–1944), who came to Yemen in 1924 to convince Imam Yahya of the virtues of Arab nationalism; and the Syrian nationalist Nazih Mu'ayyad al-'Azm's fascinating *Rihla fi bilâd al 'arabiya al sa'îda* (Journey to Happy Arabia). Al-'Azm was twice sentenced to death, first by the Ottomans, then by the French. I would later encounter his family in Damascus—but, unfortunately, not his archives.

9 François Burgat (ed.), *Le Yémen vers la République. Iconographie historique 1900–1970*, CEFAS, Sanaa, 2003. With the help of Eric Vallet, a brilliant historian of Yemen's epochal Rasulid dynasty, a much-expanded second edition was published in 2011 and is now available online: CEFAS, 2012, https://books.openedition.org/cefas/92?lang=fr (last accessed June 15, 2019).

10 The Justice and Development Party was founded in the 1960s by Abdelkrim al-Khatib, and relaunched itself in 1996 by taking in the Islamists from the Unity and Reform Movement, who themselves emerged out of the Shebiba Islamiya.

11 See Robert Vitalis, *America's Kingdom Mythmaking on the Saudi Oil Frontier*, Stanford University Press, Redwood City, 2007. On Saudi Arabia, see also Pascal Ménoret, *The Saudi Enigma: A History*, Zed Books, Chicago, 2005, as well as the brilliant methodological rethinking that Ménoret provides in the fields of urbanism and urban deviance: *Joyriding in Riyadh: Oil, Urbanism, and Road Revolt*, Cambridge University Press, Cambridge, 2014.

12 Qahtan was arrested by the Houthis in April 2015, and may have been killed by bombing from his Saudi allies.

13 The revolutionaries of 1962 reportedly only agreed to launch their attack against Imam Badr's palace after they received formal notice that the Egyptian troops that were supposed to come to support them had left Port Said.

14 François Burgat *et al.*, *Al Yemen wal 'alam*, Madbouli/CEFAS/CYES, Sanaa, 2002 (in Arabic).

15 "God is Great, Death to America, Death to Israel, A Curse upon the Jews, Victory to Islam." The extent to which this Houthi slogan recalls the phraseology in Iran has been used by some to prove Iran's involvement in the launching of the movement—an involvement for the most part greatly overestimated.

16 When Saleh faced the complaints of army officers from Aden whose pension payments were late, he used the same irresponsible rhetoric. He labeled them

"Southerners." They, too, were said to undermine the nation's foundations. In their case, this was by questioning the renewed unity between South and North Yemen achieved through reunification in 1990.

17 In tandem, in 2011, in order to prompt a sectarian reflex of support from Iran and the Lebanese Hezbollah among others, Bashar al-Assad chose to "Sunnify" his political opponents.

18 See Laurent Bonnefoy, Franck Mermier, and Marine Poirier, *Yémen, le tournant révolutionnaire*, Karthala, Paris, 2012. In 2011, to prevent a repeat of the events of Cairo's Liberation (Tahrir) Square, Yemeni authorities had preemptively occupied the square of the same name in Sanaa. The opposition was forced to set up instead near the university, on a square that was renamed "Taghir" ("Change") Square for the occasion. See also Laurent Bonnefoy, *Yemen and the World: Beyond Insecurity*, Hurst, New York, 2018, and Helen Lackner, *Yemen in Crisis: Autocracy, Neo-Liberalism and the Disintegration of a State*, Saqi, London, 2017.

19 With the precious help of my friend Laurent Bonnefoy, it was for the very same Tawakkul Karman that I wrote (at the Norwegian Nobel Prize Committee's request) a modest but convincing reference to the Committee, that may have made some small contribution to her taking the 2011 Nobel Peace Prize.

20 Courtney Freer, *Rentier Islamism: The Influence of the Muslim Brotherhood in Gulf Monarchies*, Oxford University Press, Oxford, 2018.

21 See François Burgat, "Le Yémen islamiste entre universalisme et insularité," in Rémy Leveau, Franck Mermier, and Udo Steinbach (eds), *Le Yémen contemporain*, Karthala, Paris, 1999; and *Islamism in the Shadow of al-Qaeda*.

22 The carriers of Soviet ideology in Yemen included the dockers of Aden port, whom their British counterparts had helped politicize (see Vitaly Naumkin, *Red Wolves of Yemen: The Struggle for Independence*, The Oleander Press, Cambridge, 2004).

23 See Mustapha Hamid and Leah Farall, *The Arabs at War in Afghanistan*.

24 These attacks came before another on October 6, 2002, off the Yemeni port of Al-Moukalla (480 km east of Aden), targeting a French tanker, the *Limburg*. We hosted the crew at CEFAS, where they told of the traumatic circumstances in which they had been evacuated. One of their colleagues was killed when jumping into the sea from a height of nearly 20 meters.

25 RFI, September 13, 2001.

6

"Beneath Israel, Palestine[1]"

> Palestinians are sometimes called cowards because, it is said, they send their children to be killed in their stead. What I actually see here is children who talk granny and grandpa out of going all the way.
>
> Régis Debray, 2008[2]

Palestine and Israel hold an important place in my research trajectory. Their importance is in keeping with the political role played by a territory that has become the extension of the US and Europe in the Middle East. I had traveled to Israel to encounter the Christian "Holy Land" at a very young age. At the time, I had not been in a position to separate out the two, almost contradictory realities that attach to the existence of a state that is barely older than I am. The first of these realities is Israeli society. This is complex—and, of course, shifting.[3] It includes a significant, majority-Muslim Arab component—even if, unsurprisingly and like elsewhere in the region, its Christian minority wields substantial political weight. It is also affected by the trend towards re-Islamization. Even while I have not carried out truly systematic field research there, I have been able to visit and move within Israel-Palestine very frequently. I have also, however, quite often had to wrestle with Israel as a regional and international political player. In that capacity, Israel has been a powerful catalyst of the most reactionary stances towards political Islam throughout the region—as well as a highly influential player within French media discourse.

Like the other geographies of the region, Israel has been another panel in the comparative tapestry that enabled me to hone in on the diversity of the Islamist phenomenon as a whole, through the particularities of each of its national components. My first task there was to gather comparative reference points among so-called "Israeli Arabs": those Palestinians who did not leave or were not expelled from their lands in 1948 during the *Nakba*.[4] The period from 1948 to 1967 is especially instructive. In those decades, the nascent Islamist movement—in particular the branch associated with Sheikh Raed Salah, which was banned in 2015 by Benjamin Netanyahu—

was built up without interaction with the rest of Palestine or the Arab world, from which it was cut off. Beyond this, examining the rise of an Arab political movement within Israeli political society—and especially of an Islamist movement—enables one to draw enlightening analogies. First, of course, with the situation of Palestinians in the Occupied Territories. Second, and more broadly, with the situation of Muslim minorities living in Western societies. Third, with the situation of other "minorities" within the Arab and Muslim worlds that cannot lay claim to monopolize the key symbolic reference point for identity politics—for instance, Hezbollah in its Lebanese context. What meaning attaches to political mobilization based on identity politics when it takes place in an environment in which the dream of becoming a majority is not an option? When seizing power cannot determine a movement's agenda, inasmuch as it implies allying with political forces that wield other political identities?

Islamism on Shabbat

Very quickly, it became clear that my relationship with Israelis was less tense than it was with some members of the French Jewish community. The behavior of the latter often struck me as being more radical, sometimes to the point of sectarianism—as I was later to learn to my own cost (see Chapter 11, pp. 183–4). Unwittingly, I shared in this the informed stance of Alain Finkielkraut, who wielded an infinitely greater reputation on the matter than I did. In 1980, he wrote: "Absolute support for all Israeli policies is the symptom of a malaise. The diaspora, beset by diffuse guilt-feelings, makes up for these by an especially vehement loyalty. Out of sight but ever-in-mind, Jews in exile set aside their historical situation by sticking to the official Zionist narrative—or even by outbidding its orthodox pretensions."[5]

I have of course developed firm friendships among French citizens of Jewish culture—and not only among the ranks of the brave activists of the French Jewish Union for Peace (Union Juive Française Pour la Paix, UJFP). Most often, by chance; sometimes, by seeking them out. In the wake of Hamas's election victory, I despaired at seeing the movement caught up in the vice-grip of the repression orchestrated by the occupying power and its local and international backers. Before scribbling yet another op-ed, I attempted to give it a resonance that would outstrip little me. I thus had to have my call to put an end to the boycott of Hamas cosigned by someone as different from me as possible. I determined to seek out a woman (since Hamas purportedly persecuted women) and, if possible, if not an Israeli woman, then a Jewish one. A friend well acquainted with the political labyrinths of the French Jewish "community" to which she refuses to be circumscribed proffered advice: "No, this one is too marginalized by her activism; this one will never accept," and so on.

I eventually made contact with Esther Benbassa, who would later become a senator for the Greens. She accepted at once. Having made the piece her own by adding a few paragraphs, she cosigned the op-ed in the daily *Libération*. By chance, the SMS she sent me to announce the article had been published arrived while I was at the Erez checkpoint between Israel and the Gaza Strip, where I had for several hours been failing to enter the Strip, there to honor an invitation to give some conferences. "It's awful, François," she wrote, "the responses are terribly violent. And the blows are coming from within my own community!"

I later came to join those among my colleagues who had cut their links with the academic institutions of the Jewish state. Previously, I had participated in several colloquia in Israel, including at Jerusalem's Bar-Ilan University. I arrived there in 1994 from Cairo via the Sinai desert, a fascinating journey during which the feeling was of moving from one world to another in just a few hours on the road. In Jerusalem I had visited the Shasha Institute and, at Tel Aviv University, the Moshe Dayan Center. Back in Jerusalem in 1995, I gave an unlikely public lecture at the Center for Zionist Organizations. The audience's reactions were highly instructive. I had expected greater reservation in response to my analysis of the cultural aspects of colonial domination, as I laid these out in my *The Islamic Movement in North Africa*. After warmly congratulating me, one audience member told me: "Very interesting, this lecture of yours. I have only one comment: you seemed to take it for granted that the audience should be hostile towards your thesis." Another: "I'm Libyan!" Given my surprised reaction, he added:

> A Libyan Jew. You know, I'm the one who tried to organize with colonel Gadhafi for two buses of Libyan pilgrims to come to Jerusalem.[6] What interested me most in your lecture was that I know European cultural imperialism all too well! I'm married to an Ashkenazi from New York, who came from Central Europe. Well: it's been thirty years that I, the Libyan, have been trying to explain to her that her symbolic and cultural universe isn't the only one—and, moreover, that it isn't superior to mine.

Israel provided other clarifying encounters. In 1995, I was part of an official French cultural and academic delegation (that also featured Olivier Roy). Our Israeli hosts had rather explicitly expressed their aim to influence our perception of their actions in the region. To convince us of the soundness of their policy in Lebanon, they brought us into occupied Lebanese territory. We were the lunch guests of General Antoine Lahad, the head of the South Lebanon Army,[7] the auxiliary militia founded in

1976 in an attempt to contain Lebanese popular resistance. In the course of this adventure, they also introduced us to the mayor of Metula, one of the Israeli towns bordering Lebanon, who was of Central European origin. In an impassioned address, he invited us to follow him through the vast transnational geographies of his Jewish identity. Then, as a frontline player in the politics of the Lebanese–Israeli border, he moved on without a beat to his territorial understanding of the Israeli–Arab conflict. "The problem," he told us from a terrace overlooking Lebanon,

> has nothing to do with the neighborhood! You see that farm 200 meters away. Very often in the past, sheep got lost on our side of the border. Well, believe me: we brought them back to their owner! I'm telling you, the problem isn't with our neighbors. The ones who fight us live at least ten kilometers away from here, if not further! Those are the ones who come and stir up trouble. With our actual neighbors, we get on very well!

In the minibus that took us back to Tel Aviv, a retired colleague from Tel Aviv University, whom I had known in Aix-en-Provence, asked me what I had got out of the meeting. "But what I heard is terrible!" I replied.

> This kind of talk is exactly what French settlers in Algeria said when they explained that they never had the slightest problem with their agricultural workers, and that the *fellaga*s who stirred up trouble came from very far away. In order to legitimize his presence in the land of Israel, the mayor of Metula thinks himself quite entitled to lay claim to an ancient transnational identity. He came to the ends of the world to defend his little plot of land! But as he sees it, that right is his alone. How the Lebanese peasant who lives ten kilometers away from the Israeli border may feel about the cost to himself of his neighbor's state's policies is irrelevant. He lives "much too far away" …

My colleague's reply was taking some time. I leaned in toward him and realized that my words had hurt him. He was weeping. The strange and touching fragility of Israelis.

During a period I spent at the Shasha Institute in the mid-1990s, two young journalists from a French-language Jerusalem radio station were left similarly vexed by remarks that I had not in any way intended to be aggressive. They had expected me to become enthused about a cultural program that meant to bring together Israeli and Palestinian children around the songs and dances of both cultures. I told them very frankly why I remained distinctly unseduced by the prospect of a culturalist treatment of a divide that I (and all those who daily pay the price of it) consider to be political above all else. "I rather fear that the violence upon which your country is built—the violence that its territorial expansion nurtures and exacerbates—that violence scarcely strikes me as amenable to being dissolved in a cultural *rapprochement*," I insisted—before cutting short my reply faced with their consternation.

Ever since 1964, I had acquired the first markers of my political consciousness through facing up to Palestine. In 1973, it was from Algeria that I lived through the fleeting reconquest of the Suez Canal and part of Sinai. I had every opportunity then to grasp how emotional this had made my colleagues at the University of Constantine. I next gazed in Israel's direction from Cairo, where the ambivalent status accorded to Israel need not be spelt out. The Camp David peace of September 17, 1978, had made its mark. Israel's flag floated over the great Arab capital. More precisely, it floated very high above it indeed—atop a building on the Nile Corniche. This was not for it to be as visible as possible. Quite the contrary: it was for it to remain as discreet as possible, out of reach of any demonstrators. So far removed did the cold peace appear to me from the room "temperature" of the Egyptian street.

Palestine: Next Year Will Be Worse than the Last

As in Israel, I took my first steps in Palestine to supplement the framework of my scholarly construction of Islamism, by introducing myself to new variants of it. But entering into the intimate spaces of the oppositional dynamics tied to Islamist self-assertion first required taking into account the Israeli domination endured by Palestinian society as a whole.

In the course of my time in the country, my direct encounters with the various expressions of the violence of occupation have built up a series of cognitive strata. Each of these is covered over by the next, yet darker encounter. In the 1990s, we often ended meetings with our hosts in the Occupied Territories with "God willing, things will be better next year." We did our best to believe it. But by the turn of the 2000s, an unavoidable conclusion had to be faced up to. Not only had nothing been resolved: everything had got even worse. In 2007, when I searched for a title for a section I was writing on the question of Palestine, the answer seemed obvious: "Next year will be worse than the last."[8] Quite how obvious this was became further apparent to me over the course of a never-ending series of observations and direct testimonies, each of them more striking than the last. These fashioned my perception of this conflict, whose deep dissymmetry the "politically correct" gaze persists in denying to this day.

When a foreigner visiting Ramallah is minded to visit another celebrated, iconic West Bank town, Bethlehem, the day's agenda will depend entirely on whether she chooses to travel alone or in the company of a Palestinian. One choice is 15 miles or so of the swift and comfortable highway reserved for Israelis or their foreign visitors. The other is at least double the journey time, driving along unplanned narrow and sinuous back roads that cross countless *wadi*s. Welcome to occupied Palestine! The experience is more eloquent than any lengthy theoretical expose on the Israeli grip upon space in the West Bank.

Nablus, April 2004, close to midnight. A ticker appears along the bottom of the TV screen tuned to Al-Jazeera: Israeli commandos are conducting one of their usual, brutal visits to the heart of the Old City. We soon learned that they were often accompanied by their colleagues from United States Special Forces, who trained in Palestine before going on to export their expertise to Iraq. I was told that the previous day a driver, driven to distraction by police harassment and blocked at a checkpoint one too many times, had decided to set fire to his vehicle. Entering Gaza, where I was to meet the future Hamas Foreign Minister Mahmoud al-Zahar, police dogs paddled through shipments of loose flour. In Jerusalem, soldiers broke through the iron frontage of a shop with a battering ram. From the terrace of the magical Austrian Hospice, Israeli settlers' flags floated arrogantly over the most sacred recesses of the Arab Old City—including the flag of Ariel Sharon, first among the settlers.[9] In Hebron, tomatoes inevitably rotted in trucks in the blazing heat, trucks detained for no reason at one of the countless roadblocks that turn the supposedly "autonomous" territories into derisory confetti.

"Why did I try to commit an attack?" a Nablus preadolescent told a reporter from *Le Figaro*. He was one of those young men who know that the sea is within touching distance—but have strictly no hope of ever seeing it. "Well, you know—prison is good. You get to see people from all over Palestine; you really feel like you're travelling!" A colleague from Bir Zeit University gestured towards the horizon: "See, over there, in the distance, behind Ramallah: that's Jerusalem. That's where my parents were born. Well—I haven't had a permit to take Leila, my 12-year-old daughter, there since she was born. Not once." "Before the Wall (i.e. 2002)," the mayor of Tulkarem explained to me, "we just crossed the road to go and sell our products. Everything ground to a halt from one day to the next. Today, what can we do?" The list of acts of violence is interminable, ranging from the physical to the symbolic, and from the military to everyday civilian life.

In 1996, on the road that leads from Jerusalem to Allenby Bridge, I took my seat in the back of a taxi, next to a young and striking Palestinian-American mother who was traveling with her 7-year-old daughter. An impromptu checkpoint thrust our fate into the hands of a young man who had clearly only very recently arrived from the United States to do his military service (or perhaps even a stint as an activist volunteer) in the ranks of the Israeli Army, the so-called Israeli "Defense" Forces. From behind his little golden round spectacles, he carefully examined my travel companion's documents. Either the mother or the daughter was "illegal": on this particular road, only some Palestinians have the right to board taxis. The only option legally available to them was the jam-packed bus of Palestinian laborers transiting to Jordan. What was the young mother to do? Well: she had to get off, with her luggage and daughter, and wait at the side of the road for the workers' bus to pass: in a few minutes—or a few hours. Thankfully, it was wintertime. The sun burned less harshly than did my impotent rage—and my shame.

In 2003, the setting for a group interview with Yasser Arafat was especially striking—more so than the rather conventional content of the interview. Never before had the scale of the failure of the Oslo Agreements, and of the international deception that persisted in considering it a "peace process," been so resoundingly apparent to me. The treaty that was supposed to enable the exchange of "land for peace" had granted its Palestinian signatory only a few confetti of land. This was a fact that it took considerable effort to remain blind to. A visit to the Palestinian signatory of the Accords made the truth of the matter ... blindingly obvious. The confetti plot of land of the Muqataa, the headquarters of the Palestinian Authority's president in Ramallah, should have been the symbol of Palestinian national sovereignty achieved at long last. One building after another, it had been razed with maniacal meticulousness—by the very occupier who was purported to have yielded up these fragments of Palestine by freeing them of his presence.

The aging leader was confined to the narrow slab of a building that had remained standing at the center of a vast field of ruins, strewn with burned-out cars and eviscerated by tanks. The effect was devastating to any visitor, struck dumb with shame at knowing that his own country—and so many others—let such things happen! In fact, as I was often to repeat later to those who sought out my analysis of the Palestinian condition, conferences and colloquia are of little use. It is enough to give anyone the opportunity to see the routine violence of the occupation on the ground, and to confront this with the picture of the situation provided by the "politically correct" media of one's own country. The violence is multifarious—and, most often, it knows no bounds.

At least once, I saw the jailers of Palestine inadvertently blurt out irrefutable testimony of their most unacceptable practices. This was in the very formal setting of a European conference in Oslo in June 2003, one of countless gatherings organized by Norway to exorcize the guilt that some of them feel at the outcome of the Oslo Agreements.[10] One of the Palestinian participants was blind. As he came to the lectern, he begged the audience's indulgence for the extra difficulty that he would have in giving his presentation. His expensive braille-enabled computer was broken. At the Allenby Bridge, on his way to Amman Airport, the Israeli security services had briefly confiscated it. "Is it still working?" they had asked him as they gave it back. "Yes," he answered. "Oh—do excuse us for a moment." They then took it away again before restoring it a few minutes later, quite out of order this time. One of the participants in the conference was a senior Israeli civil servant. He could do no more than mumble pitiful apologies in front of the appalled audience.

Truth be told, the perpetrators of this very commonplace "blunder" deserved our thanks. They had just spectacularly concentrated the minds of the conference participants. These had been laboriously striving to identify the "root causes of terrorism." They were on the verge of indulging in the culturalist reading of some Quranic *sura*s. A celebrated "Muslim participant" had expressly come from Germany to enlighten us about the key motivations of resistance on the part of "the fundamentalists of Hamas," funneling the rhetoric spread far and wide from Bernard Lewis to Bernard-Henri Lévy. If a few participants were still hoping to be enlightened as to these root causes, what a precious opportunity they had just been granted to identify the true components of the dread engine of radicalization!

The Lessons of Palestine

From an internal perspective, the key originality of the question of political Islam in Palestine is the unfinished quality of Palestinian para-statal structures, deprived to this day of the greater share of the prerogatives of a state. This explains the relatively late emergence of Hamas in 1987. How and why could one fight a "state" that did not really exist—and that was itself supposed to be part of the "resistance" to the nation's shared enemy? Who should be the primary target of the resistance to a twofold domination: the internal foe—or the external one? In the field of resistance, the Muslim Brotherhood thus remained for a considerable time in the shadow of Yasser Arafat's PLO, which had itself emerged from within the Muslim Brotherhood in the 1950s. This remained the case even though the Egyptian Brotherhood, like their Palestinian counterparts, had been on the front lines of armed mobilization against the nascent Jewish state.

For some decades, however, the subtleties of internal oppositional dynamics remained concealed from public view, given the strong propensity of the outside gaze to focus exclusively on the international conflict in which the entire society was involved. The oppositional self-assertion of the Islamist generation became visible only later, superimposed upon the dichotomy of the old nationalist conflict and the ruins of a largely discredited Palestinian "state" power. But one does not make a bonfire of what one has worshipped for so long: a Palestinian Authority (PA) born of several decades of national liberation struggle. It took considerable time before scholarly research began to address head-on the obvious democratic deficit of the new Palestinian political institutions.[11] Inevitably, Islamist self-assertion in Palestine was at first subject to the same lazy and conspiracist analyses as it was elsewhere in the region. Hastier Western and Arab analysts long stuck to the analysis that Hamas was a product, not in this case of a nationalist establishment aiming to weaken its leftist opposition—but, rather, an Israeli creation designed to weaken Fatah.

Concerning the question of resistance, Palestine provided the discourse on Islam as a "religion of violence" with an essential (and a too often underestimated) perspective. The militarization of the political struggle had no need whatsoever to wait for its "Islamization" by Hamas. The Popular Front for the Liberation of Palestine (which emerged from the Arab Nationalists Movement), for instance, one of the first groups to move to armed struggle, had no defined religious basis. Its founder, George Habash, had a Christian upbringing. The history of Palestinian resistance also reminds us of the routine flexibility of the Muslim vocabulary, and its ability to adapt to a wide range of modes of political action. Palestinian "state" institutions have deployed that vocabulary on a regular basis, regardless of whether those institutions have been run by Fatah or by its Hamas opponents.[12] The Palestinian Islamic Jihad movement pioneered the "nationalist" use of the Islamic lexicon even while it sustained subtle differences with Hamas, in particular with respect to the increasingly burning question of how to relate to the Shia world.[13]

The contemporary history of Palestine—more precisely, that of the occupation and colonization of the "1967 territories"—is filled with testimonies that ground an absolutely essential claim, central to my research. It illustrates the fact that when the most ordinary political conditions of radicalization are brought together, the root causes of extreme violence have no need whatsoever of any ideological contamination from Salafism or any other quarter. This includes when they manifest themselves in self-destructive jihadist form. Further, they can affect any component of the oppressed society in question, regardless of age bracket, gender, social conditions, or religious affiliation. One testimony, provided to a self-professedly highly "innocent" traveler to the Holy Land, illustrates the all-but-universal drivers of the recourse to (counter-)violence more eloquently perhaps than the academic register of the social sciences ever could:

> In a single episode of bombing, my host had lost his two daughters, his wife, his father, his grandmother, his sister-in-law, his brother, his sister, and his

mother-in-law. "I was never a terrorist, like they say over there. Now—I can't guarantee anything," he hissed at me. My translator, a primary school teacher in the town, reproved him, then whispered into my ear: "They destroyed our society. We no longer believe in anything. They've turned us into monsters." A few days later, a grandmother from the neighborhood blew herself up as an Israeli patrol passed by. The patrol suffered only three injuries. She was aged 67, and had left plenty of candy for her 73 grandchildren, prominently displayed on the kitchen table for the day of her funeral. By all accounts, it was a festive one. One of her sons had been killed in the street shortly before. Two others were imprisoned, accused of being Fatah militants. Her house had been destroyed by bulldozers as punishment. She had had enough of living in fear. She donned a green Hamas headband, recorded her last will on camera, took a shower, and stuffed some sticks of TNT into her dress. She became the heroine of the neighborhood. But apparently not everyone approved. Palestinians are sometimes called cowards because, it is said, they send their children to be killed in their stead. What I actually see here is children who talk granny and grandpa out of going all the way.[14]

Hamas and the "Triple Domination"

Seen from the outside, the configuration of Islamism in Palestine provides observers with an endless supply of examples of the double standard of Western claims to ethical and political universality. Under the impassive gaze of Western political players, Israel has been authorized to sink into the most absolutely anachronistic practices. It "colonizes" in the most literal sense. Not only does it take over land and conquer it; it moves settlers to it. Year after year and betrayal upon betrayal, Israel's backers display their desire to conceal the reality of a relationship of domination to which they are very directly linked. The Palestinian crisis thereby provides an eloquent example of the American and European West's ethical contradictions with respect to authoritarianism, which they profess to fight in the name of their "attachment to democratic values" (as, indeed, they profess to have turned the page of colonialism). This double standard has heavy symbolic and political repercussions. As opposed to what has been very imprudently argued by my colleague and (nonetheless!) friend Olivier Roy (see Chapter 13, pp. 222–3), this never-ending ethical felony provides enormous dividends to the rejectionist dynamic that threads through the political imaginaries of (but not only) the world's "Islamist" camp.

Finally, on the regional scale, Palestine enables us to verify the universality of the historical divide between the "nationalists" (of Fatah) and the "Islamists" (of Hamas). In 2006–7, the process by which Fatah, suddenly won over to its Arab counterparts' eradicatory affinities, elected to confiscate Hamas's electoral victory[15] through setting up a coup is especially instructive. In Palestine, beyond colonial domination, another type of violence—one that is infinitely less covered in the media—is tightly linked to my subject here. In this highly specific "national" context, Israeli and Palestinian state apparatuses, however grossly mismatched and supposedly in conflict with one another they may be, forged a union to wield this mode of violence against Hamas.

The occupying power had unremittingly criticized Palestinian governance. In 2006, with renewed vigor, it demanded to select the representatives of the people it occupied. The usual suspects relentlessly went after those who had been anointed by the ballot box, jailing newly elected Hamas parliamentarians en masse.[16] For once, they were joined in this not only by their powerful lifelong Western allies—but also by a new and unexpected partner: Fatah itself.

This setup was not without recalling the trap laid for the FIS in Algeria in January 1992—forerunner of the trap into which the Egyptian Muslim Brotherhood would fall in 2013. Instead of setting up Hamas as the "enemy of democracy," this powerful coalition raised it to the status of "enemy of peace." The Palestinian proto-state apparatus remained embryonic as far as sovereignty was concerned. Thanks to European financing, however, its repressive abilities were overdeveloped. It therefore pooled its resources with those of the Israeli occupying power. This powerful local tandem received unwavering support from the international community, led by the US, in its task of confiscating the choice that had been so clearly expressed by the electorate. The European Union, having exhausted any capacity for shame, perjured its pledges to promote competitive elections. It took up the challenge of financially asphyxiating the election's victors. Hamas was thus caught in three crosshairs at once: those of the Israeli occupier; of the EU, Israel's ally, shamelessly playing on the same team; and of the Palestinian Authority's very own "eradicators." The latter were rarely willing to acknowledge their position openly. But they were ready to ally with the devil in order to keep hold of the reins of their derisory power over the "Authority."

In the days after this power play by the PA and its Israeli–European allies, the tension was palpable in Hamas offices. In her attempts to get her message out, the minister for the rights of women probably didn't fully realize that her claims to feminism were falling on deaf ears with her foreign visitors, fixated as they were on her full *niqab*. Two days before our visit, a Hamas leader had been freed at last, after seven years in prison. The very next day an Israeli commando entered the area in which Palestinians supposedly exercise "sovereignty" to arrest him once again, together with two other militants, kidnapped from the building site where they worked. At the party's headquarters, the commando had seized the opportunity to rip all the hard drives from the computers. Needless to say, no international press headline reported this routine violence. It had already been drowned out by a new layer of "Palestinian violence" perpetrated by Hamas, the impertinent victor at the ballot box.

Doctor Said and Mister Edward: When the Dominated Turn Dominant

As in the other countries of the region, the divide produced by the self-assertion of Islamist movements has threaded through Palestinian society for many years. The banishment of Hamas by the PA's Western sponsors is embedded in an intellectual background of still older vintage.

The Palestinian Edward Said's rejection of the intellectual normalization of Islamism is among the most emblematic examples. The author of *Orientalism* was among those who most rationally deconstructed the mechanisms and the cultural component of colonial domination in general, and of the Israeli occupation of Palestine in particular, laying them out explicitly with the greatest efficacy. And yet: the feebleness of Western support for elected Palestinian representatives after Hamas's victory in the parliamentary elections of January 2006 is not unrelated to the fact that neither Said in his time, nor more of his "secular Arab nationalist" counterparts in his wake, were willing to take part in the intellectual normalization of their Islamist challengers. As members of a dominated (Palestinian and Arab) elite, Said and others had contributed to the production of one of the sharpest analytical frameworks of political domination. As part of a dominant (secular and Westernized) elite, however, the author of the memoir *Out of Place* did not always write or direct his activism "against the grain."[17] Faced with an Islamist generation that called into question the hegemony of the political family that he identified with most intuitively, Said kept in line with the overwhelming majority of the intellectuals of his age.

In *Out of Place*, Said offers up some of the more intimate elements of this very ordinary difficulty in overcoming the obstacles of essentializing the "Other" and the pitfalls of Othering, whose roots go back to his Egyptian childhood. Unsurprisingly, the Muslim Brotherhood's presence is here alluded to only briefly—and without much nuance, as the social illness that agitated his family environment. Most revealing perhaps of Said's inability to bridge the yawning gap with the Islamist generation was the metaphor he used towards the end of his life to describe his understanding of the Islamist phenomenon—even though this embodiment of Islamism came in the person, not only of a woman, but of a school principal.

Said had had to leave Egypt at the outset of Nasser's reign, accused, along with his father and the family business, of having broken foreign trade regulations. When he returned for the first time, in 1989, one of his first acts of pilgrimage took him to Maadi, to the British school from which the colonial occupier had expelled him. On the Friday he visited, the school was closed. Said nonetheless prevailed upon the guard to let him enter briefly. During his visit, however, the school principal appeared and, in a firm tone, enjoined him to leave. It so happened that she wore "an Islamic robe and veil." "The very British Eton of Egypt had turned into a sort of elite Islamic sanctuary from which, 38 years on, I was again to be expelled," Said concluded. For Said, thus, the occupation of the land of his childhood by the British had come to an end only to give way to something that clearly resembled a further occupation—this time, an "Islamic" one.[18]

Yet Edward Said was very far indeed from being a fervent supporter of the Oslo Accords. He had (perhaps a little excessively) dubbed Yasser Arafat "the Pétain of the Palestinians." That description seems entirely appropriate today, to refer to Arafat's successor, Mahmoud Abbas.[19] Then again: Pétain had a country to lead. Abbas cannot lay claim to even that. "They manufactured Abbas when Arafat was alive, before killing off the 'Old Man,'" the taxi driver taking me to Bir Zeit University in October 2013 summed up.

> If they'd assassinated Arafat before setting up Abbas and letting him take over everything, the PA wouldn't have survived Arafat's death. It would have collapsed at once. The PA was invented by America and Israel to stop us from resisting, no other reason! So that it would be Palestinians who would stop Palestinians from resisting! Before all this, we conducted regular military operations, we attacked, we went into Israel! Look at Gaza, a tiny strip of land completely strangled economically. Israel can keep crushing it with bombing, with missiles, every day, from all sides: it can't take control. Why not? Because in Gaza, they make rockets, missiles, bombs! They resist! Just like we used to do! I used to be with Fatah. I spent six years in an Israeli jail. When I came out, pfft! I joined Hamas immediately. Only Hamas will free this country!

On December 6, 2017, Donald Trump formalized the Congressional decision to recognize Jerusalem as the capital of Israel, which had been frozen since 1995. The Palestinian side logically condemned the decision. It is, however, unclear that the Trump declaration truly undermined Palestinian interests. Indeed, it put an end to the lengthy hypocrisy of the professed neutrality beneath which the US sought to conceal an extremely one-sided commitment to the Israeli side. More structurally, the decision put an end to US pretentions to embrace, and thus to guarantee, a multilateral world order based on something more than the most cynical wielding of hard power by its dominant players.

Notes

1 The title of this chapter is borrowed from a book whose author's great lucidity and vision concerning the "Israeli–Palestinian conflict" were also precocious: Ilan Halévi, *Sous Israël, la Palestine*, Le Sycomore, Paris, 1979. Ilan Halévi (1943–2013) was a journalist and Palestinian-Jewish political figure who held important positions within the Palestine Liberation Organization (PLO).
2 Régis Debray, *Un candide en Terre sainte*, Gallimard, Paris, 2008, p. 74.
3 See Alain Dieckhoff, *Israël, une identité nationale en crise*, La Documentation française, Paris, 2001; *L'Invention d'une nation. Israël et la modernité politique*, Gallimard, Paris, 1993.
4 The "catastrophe," the name given to the expulsion in 1948 of 700,000 to 900,000 Palestinians, which the Israeli "New Historians" helped bring back into the spotlight (see especially Ilan Pappe, *The Ethnic Cleansing of Palestine*, Oneworld, London/New York, 2006; and Benny Morris, *The Birth of the Palestinian Refugees Problem Revisited*, Cambridge University Press, Cambridge, 2003).
5 Alain Finkielkraut, *Le Juif imaginaire*, Seuil, Paris, 1983; quoted by Nicole Lapierre in the *Journal du Dimanche* of 30 August 2015, who commented: "[Alain Finkielkraut] refused [at the time] to be held hostage to the politics of the Israeli government and called upon readers not to wrap themselves in the victim-centered heritage of Jewish history. At the time, this required considerable audacity. He would no longer write such things today."
6 On May 31, 1993, Israeli authorities had granted permission for a group of 192 Libyan pilgrims to visit al-Aqsa Mosque, for Eid al-Adha. Palestinians had swiftly denounced this attempt at a rapprochement. It fell apart when the Libyan delegation called for the "liberation of the Holy Places."
7 On November 17, 1988, Antoine Lahad had been the target of an attempted assassination by Souha Bechara, an activist who was then 21 years old, and who later spent ten years in Khiam prison. I went to visit her tiny cell. This was before the Israeli Air Force decided to bomb it in order to wipe out one of the darker pages of its role in the region. Parts of Souha Bechara's life in prison are recounted in the film *Incendies* and in Souha Bechara and Cosette Ibrahim, *La Fenêtre. Camp de Khiam*, Elizad, Tunis, 2014.
8 François Burgat, *L'Islamisme en face*, updated edition 2007, p. xviii.
9 Al-Wad Street runs from Damascus Gate to the Haram al-Sharif. At no. 35, Israeli soldiers protect the house of the former prime minister (1928–2014). The house was purchased in 1987 from an Israeli settler, to remind Palestinians that Jews have given themselves the right to live wherever they see fit— including in the heart of the Muslim quarter of the occupied part of Jerusalem.
10 These feelings of guilt are not entirely misplaced. The brave research of the Norwegian scholar Hilde Henriksen Waage shows that Norway's supposed neutrality actually gave way to the most absolute surrender to the strongest (Israeli) party. (See Hilde Henriksen Waage, "Postscript to Oslo: The Mystery

of Norway's Missing Files," *Journal of Palestine Studies*, no. 38, 2007–8, pp. 54–65.)

11 For a promising breakthrough, see Xavier Guignard, "Un autoritarisme discret? Les élections municipales de 2012 en Cisjordanie," *Noria*, January 12, 2016, www.noria-research.com/fr/un-autoritarisme-discret-les-elections-municipales-de-2012-en-cisjordanie/ (last accessed June 15, 2019). This research angle is being more broadly developed through an ongoing program at the Institut Français du Proche-Orient, "Authoritaranism without a State? Origins and Practices of Kurdish and Palestinian Political Power" (directed by Xavier Guignard, Robin Beaumont, and Arthur Quesnay).

12 Bjorn Brenner, *Gaza Under Hamas: From Islamic Democracy to Islamist Governance*, I.B. Tauris, London, 2016. Jean-François Legrain reminds us that the secular circles close to Mohammed Dahlan produced proclamations of *takfir* towards Hamas and its partisans. For more detail, see the original French version of his contribution to the International Conference on Sunni-Shia Contemporary Relations, Brussels, 2009, www.historiae.org/documents/Brussel.pdf (last accessed June 15, 2019).

13 Bjorn Brenner, *Gaza Under Hamas*. See also the work of Wissam Alhaj, Nicolas Dot-Pouillard, and Eugénie Rebillard, *De la théologie à la libération. Histoire du Jihad islamique palestinien*, La Découverte, Paris, 2015.

14 Régis Debray, *Un candide en Terre sainte*, Gallimard, Paris, 2008, p. 74.

15 In the immediate wake of Hamas's victory in the 2006 elections, Fatah, Israel, and their Western allies removed from the newly elected prime minister, Ismail Haniyeh of Hamas, the prerogatives which they had conferred in 2003 on then-Prime Minister Mahmoud Abbas. At the time, in 2003, this had been to strip those prerogatives from President Yasser Arafat, in the name of "good governance." See, in particular, Eduardo Emilio Dabed, "A Constitution for a Non-State: The False Hopes of the Palestinian Constitutional Process, 1988–2007" (PhD thesis in Political Science, directed by François Burgat, Institut d'études politiques d'Aix-En-Provence, 2012).

16 The Israeli army had "preventively" arrested 450 Hamas members and candidates before the 2006 election. On June 29, 2006, alone, 8 ministers and 26 parliamentarians were detained—the overwhelming majority of them belonging to Hamas.

17 The title of the French translation of Said's memoir, Edward Said, *Out of Place*, Vintage Books, New York, 1999.

18 See François Burgat, "Double Extradition: What Edward Said Has to Tell Us Thirty Years On from *Orientalism*," *Review of Middle East Studies*, vol. 43, no. 1, 2009, pp. 11–17, www.jstor.org/stable/41888550?seq=1#page_scan_tab_contents (last accessed June 15, 2019).

19 Mahmoud Abbas's security forces have increasingly become referred to as the "South Lebanon Army," Israel's proxy in South Lebanon. See, e.g., Thomas W. Hill, "From the Small Zinzana to the Bigger Zinzana. Israeli Prisons Palestinian Prisons," *Journal of Palestine Studies*, vol. 45, no. 3, 2016, pp. 7–23.

7

Syria and *Bilad al-Sham*[1]

> They locked us up like dogs for about ten days, naked. [...] Ten days later, [...] they locked us up in individual cages hung from the ceiling. Every day, the officers insulted us and threatened to execute us. At that moment, naked and reduced to an animal state, shitting and pissing on ourselves, I had no other desire than to be executed as soon as possible.
>
> Ali al-Hawrani, deserter from the Syrian Arab Army[2]

Syria was to be the last (to date) of my forays into comparative politics in the field. It was also the most dramatic. Dramatic not, of course, for the highly privileged expatriate I never forgot that I was—but for all those whose lives I shared in Damascus, the "bride of the world," the "rival of paradise."[3] In the final months of my time there, I would slowly but inexorably realize that the "Spring" of March 2011 was leading those towards the darkest of hells.

I will certainly not pretend here to have foreseen the scale of what was to come. At most, a comparative framework provided me with the means to bring out how the nature of Bashar al-Assad's political base set the odds in his favor relative to his Egyptian and Tunisian counterparts. He was younger, less timeworn—but also with more "anti-imperialist" capital, given his involvement in the Israeli–Arab conflict alongside the Lebanese Hezbollah. Just as obvious, however, was the list of reasons accumulated by a majority of Syrians to want to breathe in the Spring air that was spreading across the region. Nothing, however, could have foreseen the tenacity which the regime's Russian and Iranian backers deployed to keep Bashar al-Assad on his throne come hell or high water. Nor could anything have predicted the speed with which the false "Friends of Syria,"[4] after having loudly proclaimed their support for the revolution, would one by one come to betray their promises.

In the midst of the Syrian uprising, legalist Islamists winning at the polls in Tunisia and Egypt also came to deeply transform—and not for the better—the Western imaginary concerning the Arab Spring that it had briefly idealized.

Syria before the Storm

I began to gain an understanding of Syria starting in May 2008. It gradually took up a central position in my writings for at least two reasons. First, I aimed to capitalize on what I learned during a long period in Damascus. While management responsibilities meant that I could not devote myself to research as systematically as I would have wished, these few years nonetheless enabled me once more to broaden my trajectory in comparative politics. From Damascus, the French Middle East Institute (IFPO, « the Institute »),[5] whose director I became in May 2008, provided access not only to Syria, that was in the midst of a euphoric reconciliation with France under Nicolas Sarkozy—but also to the regional environment as a whole. This included Lebanon and Jordan, where the Institute had long had a presence in its various guises—but also the Palestinian territories and Iraqi Kurdistan, since I moved to open two new branches, in Jerusalem and Erbil. In Damascus, the Institute very cautiously provided a space for some of the needs of leftist intellectuals deprived of freedom of speech to express themselves. (Shortly after my arrival, the French ambassador semi-publicly advised me: "Burgat: Your Institute must be *dull*. You hear me? *Dull*.")

Brought together by the talented Hassan Abbas and his exceptional colleagues, Maher Chérif, Jamal Chehayed, and the late Souhayl Chbat, an impassioned audience was regularly able to encounter authors—who were sometimes not exactly to the taste of officialdom (in the "IFPO Literary Mondays" series)—and to view banned films.[6] One evening we hosted Rami Farah, director of *Samat* (*Silence*), a film that questions, among other keystones of the official political creed, the level of national resistance encountered by the Israeli incursion of 1967 into the Golan. He thanked IFPO for having allowed him to "show his film in Syria for the first time." I feared the Institute's final hour had come. On that occasion, we dodged the lightning strike. A project for a dictionary of Syrian dialect presented in public by two linguists from the Institute, Jérôme Lentin and Claude Salamé, however, triggered outraged protests from the authorities, which spread as far as the pages of newspapers in the Gulf. The project was perceived as an infringement upon the status of classical Arabic, the only version of Arabic deemed worthy of study by the prestigious Arab Academy of Damascus. An explanation, in the form of an apology, had to be provided to Syria's Vice-President Najah al-Attar,[7] one of the Institute's prestigious neighbors in the neighborhood of Abou Romaneh.

The first "Syrian Psychoanalysis Society," barely tolerated by the government, had found a home at the Institute. Its founder, Dr. Rafah Nached, now a refugee in Paris, was among the first targets of the wave of detentions in 2011: she organized interfaith workshops that the regime swiftly considered especially harmful to its strategy of sectarian division. The leading lights of the leftist opposition sometimes came together in the Poets' Circle (Bayt al-Qassid) run by a historian, Roula Rokbi, who initiated me into the world of the prison generation that Yassin al-Haj Saleh[8] describes so well: "See: at this table, the four of them put together embody nearly eighty years of prison!"

In 2014, I was granted further—albeit unsurprising—evidence that the day-and-night attentiveness of the various security services towards me was not confined to the four walls of the Institute. Senior regime officials were holidaying a few miles away from my French home in Aix-en-Provence. They met a friend of mine they had encountered in a Damascus club, and shared this surprising confession with her: "You know Burgat, the director of the Institute, right? What an idiot his cleaning lady is! In Damascus, all she ever told us was 'He's very nice, Mr. Burgat. You can't move in his flat for portraits of the president.'" And it was true: my love of political iconography had become channeled into a superb collection of fridge magnets devoted to the whole al-Assad family. This confession of the level of surveillance that I was under was nonetheless, in retrospect, worrying.

During my time in Damascus, this same unreasonable passion of mine for iconography had earned me another demonstration of the efficiency of Syria's security services. Even at the very break of dawn, it was a reckless endeavor to photograph the immense frescoes that decorated the façade of the Civil Aviation Directorate. I was given to witness with what speed a squad of *mukhabarat* (intelligence services) agents could spring out of nowhere at any moment: on foot, in cars, and on motorbikes whose use in Damascus had for some considerable time been the sole preserve of government officials, for fear of terrorist attacks.[9] On another occasion, the scale of the regime's concern for security became more apparent still when, as I brought some plants to my home in the al-Malki neighborhood at the wheel of a modest delivery tricycle, I tried to drive into a street that passed one side of one of the president's residences—and that was, unbeknownst to me, banned to all utility vehicles.

The complexity of Syria's history did not fit into the boxes that had been familiar to me—far from it. The gaps filled in gradually. Was Yarmouk just a Palestinian "camp"? Not only. It was also a peripheral neighborhood of Damascus like any other, a little adorned with the posters of the Palestinian groups which the regime had taken under its wing.[10] True, Syria had also taken in some of the hundreds of thousands of Iraqi refugees who had fled their country after the invasion of 2003, especially in the Damascus neighborhood of Jaramana. At the time, it took them in en masse, just as a few years later Lebanese, Jordanians, and Turks would take in Syrian refugees in turn. They were to do so without screaming bloody murder—unlike French politicians in unison when, faced with the wave of migration that followed the Arab Springs, they came to throw themselves body and soul into a nationalist bidding-war with the National Front.

The history of the regime's relationship with Palestinian refugees, however, which lies at the heart of the complex Syrian–Palestinian and Syrian–Lebanese experiences, contained the very darkest episodes.[11] As we sat one day in the al-Siddiq restaurant, off the beaten tourist track, in the neighborhood of Bab al-Seghir where some episodes of the famous TV series *Bab al-Hara* were filmed, a colleague discreetly directed my gaze towards another customer. "You see the guy sitting behind me? That's Ali al-Madani. He has several thousand Palestinian dead on his conscience. He's the one who led the assault on [the Palestinian refugee camp of] Tel al-Zaatar [in Lebanon]." In Tyre in 2016, doctors who had escaped that massacre, in which 2,000 were killed in 1976, told me that, as children at the time, they had fled through Christian areas in a garbage truck. As they drove by, the locals coolly kept throwing their trash into the truck; militiamen occasionally stopped it to execute one of their fellows. In Ayn al-Hilweh camp in Lebanon, where they live today, these survivors are forbidden by Lebanese labor laws from practicing outside the camp. Those same laws are duly approved by the same Hezbollah that purports to be the vanguard of military support for the Palestinians.

Deep Fractures and Not Only Social Ones

During my time in Damascus, the signs of an exceptionally intricate conflict did show through here and there. In September 2009, as I accompanied to the airport a friend from the French Foreign Affairs ministry who had come to take a language course at IFPO, I decided to let him greet the great capital one last time from the heights of Mount Qassioun. This delayed us slightly. When we drove past the neighborhood of Jaramana, the car bomb parked behind an army barracks had already exploded before we passed by, turning the motorway we were driving on into the stage of a terrible panic. The attack remained a mystery. Perhaps it was already part of the score-settling between the regime and the *jihadi* groups that— already—it manipulated in the framework of its policies in Lebanon? The crass handling of the incident by state TV was a harbinger of the methods that would become widespread over the course of the Spring of 2011 to travesty reality with the help of a highly professional cohort of PR specialists, both Syrian and foreign.

The question of Islamism, whether in its local or transnational forms, held little prominence in the public spaces of Damascus. At Abou Nour, an important Arabic language-learning center, the son of the religious dignitary Sheikh Ahmed Kuftaru played host to hundreds of young foreigners—who were very conscientiously tracked by the French intelligence services and their Western counterparts. It was to close from the first months of the Spring protests. Finally, and above all, Syria took up so central a place in my concerns because, by moving to Damascus as the last stop in my comparative trajectory, I had "saved the best for last"—as some of my interlocutors (and not only Syrian ones) sometimes suggested to me, without gauging the tragic weight that the phrase was to acquire. The country's slow disintegration was to go in step with the exceptionally complex transformations that the Spring of 2011 initiated or accelerated in Syria, the symbolic heart of the Arab world.

Prior to the crisis, the tone was set by the euphoria of Nicolas Sarkozy's reestablishing Franco–Syrian relations that had been frozen by his predecessor after the 2005 assassination of "his friend Rafiq Hariri." In the whirlwind of ministerial visits, Syria's most strikingly "Middle Eastern" distinctive features—that I had only glimpsed during my first brief periods in the country—would fast become apparent. Beneath the sheen of a secular ecumenism celebrated in tandem by the regime and its hastier analysts, deep divides had persisted, delaying the construction of a truly citizenship-based social fabric. These divides were economic and social, given how unequally the benefits of development had been distributed. They were also, however, ethnic—and, perhaps even more so, sectarian ones.

Shortly after arriving in Damascus, I hailed one of my colleagues from the Institute with a *"Salaam Aleikum"* that struck me as appropriate. The speed with which he corrected me ("No! Not *salaam*, not *salaam*, I'm a Christian") left me speechless.[12] Countless confirmations of this deeply ingrained suspicion finally enlightened me on the subject. Another of my new colleagues struck an indignant tone: "Come on, Mr. Burgat, 'those people' are all ... Muslims." Yet another explained to me: "Out of my whole cohort at the Christian college, I'm pretty sure that I'm the only one who's kept Sunni friends to this day." As for the priest who approached this foreign visitor to Damascus, his main concern was to passionately rail against the threat of the "Satanic" laws that a Sunni government would inevitably put into practice.[13]

Beneath the perfectly honed discourse of the Baath party's secularist discourse, in Syria the mechanisms upon which citizenship—all the more so equal citizenship—is built were very far from having so much as got off the ground. Such was the primary distinctiveness of Syrian society, and of the Lebanese and Middle Eastern political fabrics, which stood out in the light of my previous experiences, including those in Yemen. Ethnic and sectarian divides in Syria were both more numerous and more starkly asserted than they were in, for example, Libya, or Tunisia under Ben Ali—notwithstanding the regional separatist identity-claims in both countries, or their Berber populations.[14] Ethnic and religious identities also had more provenly transnational potential in Syria than did, for instance, those of Copts in Mubarak's Egypt with respect to their fellow Middle Eastern Christians who followed other denominations. In Syria, by contrast, the effects of the regime's extreme authoritarianism had led to these divides losing the visibility that they had recovered in neighboring Lebanon or Iraq in the wake of those countries' respective traumas.

Before the protests of March 2011, religious and ethnic diversity was, in Syria, a merely latent political variable. While its persistence was palpable, it did not translate directly into the political sphere. Its discreet presence within the public sphere was deployed only to celebrate, in wisely unanimous fashion, consensual support for the regime on the part of the various religious and ethnic components of society. These components were, however, never promoted to the level of political players, interlocutors, or potential ingredients of civic or political life. The regime's authoritarian framework had succeeded in shackling the expression of sub-state identities. It nonetheless integrated this diversity into its strategies of domination. Showing no fear of disproving its secularist pretensions, the regime allowed itself a discreet form of "state fundamentalism."[15] In particular, it paraded its own conviction that, no matter how secular the state may be, "God protected Syria"—and, of course, its president.

The aim of these incursions into the religious field was to preempt any inclinations on the part of the demographic majority—i.e. on the part of Sunnis—to lay claim to any monopoly of the religious field. More broadly, the status of religious or ethnic belonging was circumscribed by a few principles that were scrupulously respected. The Kurds, for instance, had under the Baath party been subjected to three successive types of political status—with the exception of a few figures who had been very symbolically promoted to the highest ranks of the state's political or religious apparatus.[16]

In the time of triumphant Arab nationalism, they had been seen as so many grains of sand potentially jamming the mechanism designed to promote the ethnic Arab bond with which they refused to identify themselves. In the face of the first Islamist-related political tensions, the Kurds were then—notwithstanding their being Sunnis—raised to the rank of plausible useful allies within the corporation of "minorities" that the regime aimed to unite against the Sunni Arab majority. As Iraqi Kurdistan underwent its push towards separatism, the Kurds reacquired the status of potential dangers for national unity, and consequently endured the brutal repression of demonstrations organized in Qamishli. By the Spring of 2011, the regime once again ascribed to at least part of the Kurdish political field the second of their two historical roles. From the first months of the rebellion they were—rather willingly for many of them, under the influence of the highly "convincing" PYD[17]—to play the role of dividers of the Sunni majority. This role they have performed to this day.

On the religious front, the division of power was as follows. Firstly, the religion of the dominant political group, the Alawites, who had once upon a time been the whipping boys of the Syrian political community[18] and whom Hafez al-Assad then brought to power, was never mentioned. This was in order to preserve the façade of secularism—but also, and especially, because to mention it would have risked emphasizing the regime's isolation in the field of religious orthodoxy.[19] Beyond this, every time the links of religious community threatened to enter into competition with the loyalty owed to the single party, or to provide individuals with a form of protection that would limit the state's hold upon them, these were obfuscated, fought, or denied.

No one was safe from state violence specifically directed against their community whenever this was deemed necessary: Christians no more so than Druze—and Kurds no more so than, of course, the Sunni majority since the Hama uprising of 1982. Most often, these communities therefore lived side by side without really mixing. This framework provided every opportunity for manipulation. Among the paradoxes of the revolutionary moment was that, at first, it lowered the barriers that separated these communities from one another, providing their members with the opportunity to come to know and recognize one another. For many of the new revolutionaries, the first Spring demonstrations had the hitherto unknown flavor of an intercommunal mix. The regime's discourse of imposed unanimity had never in fact brought this into social practice. The first months of protests thus perhaps did more to put into practice the regime's ecumenical or supra-sectarian pretensions than the regime itself had done throughout its forty years in power.[20]

"No Spring for Syria"[21]

True, the crisis that has wracked Syria since 2011 is indeed "terribly complex," as most commentators have correctly pronounced it to be. "Correctly," that is—if they said no more than that. Much if not most of the time, however, that proclamation is followed up by their favorite narrative, no matter how simplifying and reductive it may be: "Indeed, yes, quite, absolutely; but nonetheless, Assad is a lesser evil than ..."[22] The Syrian crisis has invaded the daily life of so many of our contemporaries, and outstripped the reasoning abilities of so many minds (including the "greatest"), that it feels essential to provide a pared-down narrative. To this day, I have remained convinced that one can make the Syrian crisis legible as the product of a few major processes which the social sciences are eminently able to render in all their concreteness.

Granted: hindsight is always easier than prediction. But I do believe that the structure of my initial reading of the crisis has not changed.[23] When attempting to illustrate my understanding—which remained that of a foreign analyst—by letting one of the players of the crisis speak, I very often quoted the Syrian producer of a film directed by Talal Derki, *Return to Homs*. Released in 2014, this told the emblematic story of the siege of Homs, the great metropolis north of Damascus,[24] and the political trajectory of the national youth football team's popular goalkeeper Abdelbasset Sarout. The film's producer, Orwa Nyrabia, has said that he made the film "so that the world should know that, as opposed to what so many commentators and experts tell us, the Syrian crisis is a 'simple' crisis: it is a people's rebellion against a dictator." This has remained my conviction to this day. It remains the framework of the crisis, no matter how deeply it has been transformed by the internationalization of the cast of characters and political dynamics in the field, ranging from the Kurdish camp(s) to the *jihadi* one. It matters that this should be restated, when faced with all those who would forget the chronology and the division of responsibilities in the rise to power of the Islamic State—a sectarian political player that has come to make the crisis illegible to many, and to reconfigure dominant perceptions of the crisis as a whole.

Unquestionably, the Syrian revolt was encouraged by the optimistic scenes beamed from Tunisia and Egypt by Qatar's Al-Jazeera. But it was not "imported" by commandos shipped in from Qatar, Saudi Arabia, France, or Hariri's Lebanon. Nor was it funded by any of them. With or without the help of Bernard-Henri Lévy, popular protest was well and truly "home-made." Protest dynamics were initially non-sectarian, peaceful, and pluralistic. As time went by, the nature of these dynamics partly—but only partly—changed character and lost their initial revolutionary innocence, as the militarization of protest came onto the stage. This was the result of a highly selective policy of repression and of the intervention of a very wide range of international actors.

Understanding that process requires reminding ourselves of the most fundamental trigger of the militarization of the uprising. As a young Syrian colleague recounted it to me when he arrived in Beirut in September 2012:

Among my most striking memories is a civilian screaming into the camera of a foreign TV station, and who was I think from Tartus. As he emerged from a peaceful demonstration in which several participants had been massacred, he kept repeating: "We are not animals, we are not animals, we are not animals!" Well—a few weeks later, I saw him again, on the very same channel. He had taken up arms. He was the leader of a *katiba* (brigade).

The moment one steps out from under the rhetoric of the regime and its allies, countless testimonies bear witness to the fact that the rise of sectarian dynamics within the uprising was the result of regime strategies directed at the Sunni majority—and at the minorities that it aimed to cut off from the majority. The specific political leanings of members of the Sunni majority were a far less relevant variable in escalating these dynamics.[25] In every one of the more clearsighted assessments, each successive step by which the regime escalated its use of force came long before a consequent escalation on the part of the opposition's various components. At first, Kalashnikovs killed unarmed protestors. Next, RPGs became the weapon of choice to crush the first bearers of Kalashnikovs who had come to protect the initial protestors. Tanks and fighter jets then took over to deal with the first bearers of RPGs on the opposition side. "The idea of liberating territory was wrong. Weapons began to kill the revolution, and so did the regional interventions. But worst of all was the regime's constantly escalating violence. We must criticize the revolution—but we must also remember the primary cause of all this."[26]

On July 9, 2011, I accompanied the French journalist Alain Gresh to the city of Hama, which had been temporarily "liberated" from any police presence. It was here in 1982, in a city that has acquired mythical status for so many Syrians, that a bloodbath put an end to what, in this age of counter-revolution, increasingly takes on the appearance of having been the first of the Arab Springs. I had already come to Hama with a colleague, who had recounted her family's painful memories to me. Before the city was finally crushed with heavy weapons, Rifaat al-Assad's troops had executed all young men aged over fifteen in her apartment block. Their bodies were piled up in a shop on the ground floor.

Her uncle had been found alive three days later, buried under the pile of bodies. A few months later, however, having needed his leg amputated, he had been struck down by a nervous depression. A neighbor, Wardeh, had lost her seven sons. Nearly three decades later, she remained convinced that they had been incarcerated, and still begged for news of them wherever her steps led her.

It was from Hama, too, that a key lesson emerged from Syria with respect to the drivers of jihadism. For it was in the wake of the terrible agony endured by Hama that Mustapha Ben Abdelkader Setmariam Nasar broke with the Muslim Brotherhood, which was accused of excessive hesitation when faced with the crushing of Hama. It was then that he made his choice: the choice of *jihadi* violence—or was it perhaps counter-violence? No foreign scholar had yet made him famous under the name of Abu Musab al-Suri ("The Syrian").[27]

I had thought I was well acquainted with the reality of the regime's repressive practices. In 2011, in "liberated" Hama, these broke out into the open, live, through the testimonies of the survivors of a demonstration that, on July 1, had just witnessed the killing of dozens. As one of these survivors thrust the atrocious pictures in his mobile phone into my hands, he exclaimed to me: "I swear to you, believe me, we were all carrying a rose in our hand. *Wallahi*, believe me, roses are expensive!" In early 2014, in Amman, I met with general Ahmed Tlass, who had been the commander of the security forces that carried out the massacre that day, before he defected in July 2012.[28] He mentioned commandos ("Alawi Kurds, all of them chief warrant officers, brought over from the town of al-Yaroubieh") as being responsible for the massacre, directed by a cell outside of the formal hierarchy of the security forces. The result was the same. At the outset of the uprising, in Hama and elsewhere in Sunni-majority areas,[29] the regime's answer to the roses carried in popular protests was above all else written in letters of blood.

That answer was not just limited to the massive use of armed force, which came long before each of the steps by which the opposition gradually became militarized, and "encouraged" that militarization every step of the way. More perversely still, this highly selective violence was complemented by a pernicious divide-and-rule strategy. A few months later, in Yemen, Ali Abdallah Saleh experimented the same tactics to regain power. In the same manner, Bashar al-Assad was to have massive recourse to a weapon which neither Mubarak in Egypt (despite some attempts to exploit the Coptic question) nor Zine al-Abidine Ben Ali in Tunisia had at their disposal: dividing his democratic opponents by sectarianizing their ranks. This divide-and-conquer strategy was to become a key weapon across the region, and, later, the world. Since, gradually, the whole world was to involve itself in Syria, each country striving to bring to fruition its own goals or those of its allies, its own fears, or—as in France—the electioneering interests of its politicians. These being motivated at least as much by the prospect of appearing more "virile" as they were by the protection of their own citizens.

Therein lies the second distinctiveness of the Syrian crisis. First its internationalization, far swifter and more consequential than it was in the case of the Tunisian or Egyptian Springs—since it was not only diplomatic, but also military. Second, the fact that the results of the U-turn in Western diplomacy, from supporting the authoritarian regime in Tunisia and Egypt to leaning towards the Libyan and Syrian revolutionaries, were not spectacular, as in Libya—but, rather, terribly fleeting.

Before they gave way to less conventional concerns (concerns that were doubtless also less noble ones and, as such, less amenable to being articulated), foreign interventions in Syria at first portrayed themselves as being in the service of routinely political strategies. The dividing line between the two sides of the initial conflict (i.e. before the Kurds and Islamic State entered into the conflict between the regime and the Free Syrian Army, FSA) for a time appeared to be analogous to the dividing line between the former "Rejectionist Front," made up of powers aligned with the Palestinian cause on the one hand, and their rivals on the other. This deceptive equivalence came to obscure the true structure of the crisis to a large part of the Arab and Western lefts.

In the face of the slow agony of the Syrian democratic opposition, the "pro-Palestinian" rhetoric of the Syrian regime and its regional allies led much of the left to sink into old "anti-imperialist" mantras. This was worsened by the fact that these mantras were simultaneously being whispered into the left's ears and onto their screens by the media performers hired by the regime to leverage its messaging. In the name of this Pavlovian "anti-imperialism," the various lefts came to refuse to condemn a regime that had, in their conception of things, the virtue of being fought by their own Western opponents from time immemorial. Stances with respect to Russia's strategies in the conflict were governed first and foremost by highly reactionary anti-Western considerations. In Syria, Vladimir Putin decided above all else to make the West pay for its excessive interventionism in the Libyan crisis and, worse yet, along Russia's borders—in Ukraine in particular.

Upon this framework that was broadly inherited from the Cold War, first state alliances, then (as the Lebanese Hezbollah, Iraqi Shia militias, and Afghan mercenaries entered the conflict) sub-state ones gradually took on a more or less explicitly "sectarian" resonance, for all the opposition's attempts to preserve the uprising's democratic agenda.[30] The political resources of tribal and clan-based identity-structures, which had been the first to make up for the weakened national fabric, ran out. Within each of the warring sides and on the international stage alike, military alliances unstoppably took on increasingly sectarian overtones, rather than, as in the case of the Kurds, an ethnic one. The Alawis (who had long been ostracized by the Shia community[31]) and their Lebanese and Iranian allies lined up against the Sunnis. In the first instance, this was along the lines of the divide between Iran, Hezbollah's Lebanon, and the Alawi minority on the one hand, and Turkey and the oil monarchies on the other, with

Saudi Arabia and Qatar playing the leading roles. But the sectarian divide also widened beyond the Muslim world alone—albeit less explicitly. Little by little, it came to exacerbate the old mistrusts between on the one hand Russia and the Christian Western world, with "secular" France at the forefront, and, on the other, nothing less than the (Sunni) majority of the Muslim world.

From Asymetrical Internationalization to the *Jihadis'* "Revolution Apart"

Beyond the diversity of the political and ideological variables that motivated it, the most important structural component of the internationalization of the Syrian crisis came to be its increasingly *asymmetrical* nature. The disequilibrium that defined the crisis came about firstly from the fact that those who (for various and evolving reasons) took the regime's side did so with a coordination and a constancy that vastly outstripped those of the opposite camp. Bashar al-Assad's backers were all wise enough to go straight for the heart of the matter. They granted him diplomatic backing. But also, and more importantly, they sustained their champion's military superiority by any means necessary, be it men or military hardware. It was at first Iran, via Hezbollah, that played this key role from the end of 2012, enabling the key victory of Qusayr in August 2013. Come the autumn of 2015, it was Russia that stepped in to substitute for them, after having made consistent use of its veto power in the UN Security Council and kept the regime's air and land forces in action. Taking advantage of the hesitations and division of the Western camp, it then intervened very directly to rescue the regime.

In the opposite camp stood those who in March 2011, for varying reasons and with differing ambitions, decided to support the protestors. They did so from their respective capitals (Washington, Paris, Ankara, and, until the military coup that toppled Morsi, Cairo; Tunis, until the governing "troika" there fell; and Doha and Riyadh), often in the most disorderly fashion, bearing agendas and political demands that differed to the point of sometimes turning contradictory. Crucially, they also did so with ever-diminishing conviction, led first by the United Kingdom, then by the United States, with France increasingly being merely dragged in their wake. Growing suspicion with respect to the Free Syrian Army would eventually become devastating to its cohesion and morale. The FSA quickly splintered into hundreds of armed groups that were sometimes partners and sometimes rivals, inevitably undermining its military efficacy and political credibility.[32] This failure on the part of the opposition's backers was first displayed by French efforts to manufacture from Paris an opposition to its own taste. That is to say, in a French image: one that would be as "secular" as possible, in the "counterfeit" and excessive sense of the term. This was heedless of the risk of seeing such an opposition become cut off from the political and military fabric rapidly being reconstructed inside Syria itself.

The West's failure to put its resources where its mouth was was next displayed by the Obama administration's early and persistent refusal to provide the Free Syrian Army with the means to defend itself. Or to allow any of its allies to provide them—including, crucially, anti-aircraft weapons—on a scale equivalent to that mustered by the regime's allies.[33] At the core of this failure of the opposition's Western backers lay the question of "Islamist Otherness" that also lies at the core of this book. Given how central this question is, it must be restated that it was the self-contradictory management of the Islamist variable that prevented the opposition's Western backers from being able to realistically define which forces they could support. As Tunisian and Egyptian ballot boxes displayed the ability of the Islamist parties—so widely underestimated by mainstream commentators—to reap the rewards of the opening-up of the political sphere, the debasement of the currency of the Syrian opposition intensified and accelerated. Nothing helped. Not the democratically reassuring tune sung by the leadership and supporters of Ennahda a few thousand kilometers away; nor the similar tune sung by the elected president of Egypt. Both were drowned out or denatured beneath the waves of the propaganda of their opponents of all stripes, from the various shades of "eradicatory" left defeated at the polls to the collective of "Arab dictators without borders."

The Syrian opposition's backers determined that this opposition was insufficiently "secular." They swiftly abandoned it to its fate, on the basis of startlingly fragile criteria that were to feed the deep distress of those who were henceforth decreed "beyond the pale." At the end of 2013, Mohamed Arar, a captain who defected from the Republican Guard, laid this out bluntly:

> Our main problem is that weapons, ammunition and money are distributed at a rate that isn't fast enough—and also, for some of it, to more or less anyone. [...] Our foreign contacts, those who take the decisions, are from the intelligence services and have little idea what they're doing. [...] It's a little as if a beautiful lady walked into this room where a group of friends are sitting together, and gave a rose to just one of us. The others would ask themselves: "But whatever did we do to deserve that?" [...] Jabhat al-Nusra's funders are more faithful and consistent than ours. America and Europe help us ... sometimes. Once, we went four months without seeing any aid whatsoever.[34]

In August 2013, the United States betrayed its vows to prevent Bashar al-Assad from using his chemical weapons with impunity. This was the point of no return in the slow process of the opposition's discrediting and weakening. (Incidentally, it was rarely emphasized that, aside from Bashar al-Assad, the main beneficiary of the abandonment of the option of military strikes in favor of dismantling Syria's chemical arsenal was Israel.) The opposition was left more and more systematically ghettoized, starved, and, for months already, everywhere that it had chased away regime troops, crushed under bombs and barrels filled with explosives ("barrel bombs").[35] At the beginning of 2014, it was from the mouth of a survivor of one of these terrible machines of death, now a refugee in Jordan, that I would grasp the scale of this dimension of the crisis, which had remained out of reach of so many analysts of "Islamic radicalization."

As he recounted to me the story of the deadly bombing of his town, Jassem, in December 2013, he added:

> Do you know the difference between a bomb dropped from a MiG or a Sukhoi and a barrel of TNT? A bomb destroys a house. A barrel-bomb flattens the whole block. A barrel can contain up to 800kg of TNT. I saw one of those that didn't explode. The one they dropped that day killed 37 people! I saw everything with my own eyes. They were in pieces. [...] Children mainly, but also women, men, old people, young people who were walking in the street. 37 people. They were in pieces. Heads, feet. Those of children and adults, women and men. We picked them up and we buried them. We didn't know who was who. They all went into a mass grave. In Jassem, we got hit by 26 barrel-bombs in seven days. 26 in seven days! And that's not counting the four that didn't explode. And that's not counting the bombs dropped from MiGs or the Grad missiles! No tanks, no heavy artillery. Over 30 air raids in eight days and Grad missiles, Grads, Grads and more Grads![36]

After the symbolic regime victory at Qusayr six months later, this decisive desertion on the part of the opposition's backers became the turning point of the crisis. Both internally and across the region, American disinterest in the crisis accelerated a shift in the balance of power, first in favor of the regime, then, within the opposition, in favor of its most radical fringe. This swing helped confer upon the crisis the third of its successive identities: the partisans of a revolutionary "counter-project" basked in a spike in world interest and took over the center stage of media attention, if not of actual power. This project differed from both the FSA's and from that of the Kurds—though it would join the latter in its ambition to lead a "revolution apart." The mobilizing capacity of the newly arrived *jihadi* players lay in a triple secret. First, they picked up FSA fighters abandoned by their Western backers. Next, they benefited from special treatment from the regime and its allies, to whose strategy of criminalization of the opposition the *jihadi*s were the greatest boon. Finally, they emancipated themselves from any regional or international backing, by leaning on large swaths of the outcasts of, first, the Iraqi Sunni community, then their Syrian counterparts—and, finally, on a global scale.

This alternative revolutionary project in Syria and Iraq was, of course, that of the Islamic State, which was soon embodied by Abu Bakr al-Baghdadi. Both transnational and sectarian, it came to add a second level of internationalization to the conflict, this time at the sub-state level. And it capitalized on the support of thousands of "*jihadi*s without borders" who arrived from nearly eighty countries—including, to the great misfortune of the Syrian opposition, from … France. The mobilizing utopia of the Islamic State was broader than that of overthrowing Bashar al-Assad, a goal that became secondary. Rather, the Islamic State sought to create a proto-state space in which Sunnis could emancipate themselves from any intervention, be it Western or Shia: a kind of free "Sunnistan."

The transnational armed groups that emerged from the Afghan context of the 1990s, then from the Iraqi stage on which Al-Qaeda deployed itself in the 2000s, had long been in search of a territorial base. They found, first in Iraq, then in Syria, the opportunity to advance a partly renewed strategy: an alliance between their transnational project and the demands of regional irredentist movements. First Al-Qaeda, then ISIS, provided Sunnis abandoned and ostracized by their respective governments in Iraq, then in Syria, with one kind of answer to their felt needs: the hope of a precious territorial haven. Before the Touareg in Mali, the "Southerners" in Yemen or the "Northerners" of Nigeria, then, Iraqi and Syrian Sunnis appeared—to those Sunnis who supported them—to be the first to have at least partly succeeded. This was in conferring a territorial basis upon the proto-state utopia of a "Free Sunnistan," free of any Western or Shia presence—and free, therefore, of the fetters that came with those.

The Trap of "ISIS First"

The first Paris attacks of January 2015 changed the international status of the crisis raging in Syria. Henceforth, the territory in dispute was no longer just the stage on which highly diverse foreign interests played out. To many European countries, with France at the forefront, it came to be seen as a plausible danger to their own security. Syria was no longer merely the stage for an internationalized civil war. It had become the spring from which flowed, first, refugees, but also, and very swiftly, battalions of potential *jihadi*s. Such was the interpretation that gradually became dominant, and that came to monopolize the representation and the management of a crisis whose far greater intricacy was swiftly forgotten.

In December 2015, I asked a young Syrian woman, a student who had escaped from Raqqa, to describe for me life under ISIS rule. Her answer was: "Oh, but you know, ISIS kill much less than the regime did." This fundamental variable escaped the attention of the members of the coalition in which France joined enthusiastically. One-upmanship by ISIS in the field of provocative violence, directed more towards Westerners than towards the regime, led all of these players, in their attempt to get some grip on the Syrian crisis, to take up the strategy of "everyone against ISIS—and only against ISIS." This was about as thought through—and as effective—as the strategy of the bull faced with a red cape. The strategy obfuscated the core of the conflict: the repressiveness of a regime that, through barrel-bombs dropped on residential neighborhoods, was given almost unlimited license to kill or to create refugees. It did so in far greater numbers than did that fringe of the opposition to the regime that the regime itself had played the lion's share in radicalizing.

In August 2015, then, four months before regional elections in which a new breakthrough for the National Front was forecast, France militarized its Syrian diplomacy and went to war. But France's weapons were not rolled out to weaken the actor of the crisis that was the most adept at killing. The agenda of decision-makers was increasingly filled with strictly electioneering considerations. They caved in to the easy option of mobilizing their forces only against those whom the convergence of regime propaganda and ISIS's own had identified as absolute evil—and at the expense of opposition hopes. From September 2015 onwards, this one-sided military commitment against the wrong target deeply transformed the configuration of the crisis by creating an extremely paradoxical situation. The dictatorial regime was responsible for infinitely greater human casualties, including tens of thousands of refugees fleeing the country. Yet it benefited from the support not only of several key states (Russia and Iran)—but also of either silent indulgence or indirect armed support from more or less the rest of the globe put together.

By contrast, ISIS was in large part born of the leeway granted by the international community to the regime to continue its practice of physically eliminating its opponents, whether armed or otherwise. Almost all states around the globe now target Islamic State, in word or military deed (even while those words and deeds may differ from the opinion of some of their citizens). The scrum of foreign players intervening in the conflict, as it made that conflict increasingly complex, had made it seem impenetrable. By 2016, this confusion gradually gave way to a lethal simplicity. Foreign state players now lined up in only two categories. On the one hand were those (Iran, Russia, and various Shia militias) who took a very active part in the indiscriminate crushing of any armed resistance to the regime's repressive madness. On the other were those who looked on, and more or less entirely let matters take their course—led by the United States, with France and the United Kingdom playing the part of more or less docile followers.

The Syrian opposition were not merely gradually abandoned as Europe and the US came to focus on the *jihadi* variable of the conflict, to the exclusion of all others. They were no less abandoned as Erdogan chose to focus Turkey's involvement on the Kurdish question—and as this option was exacerbated by the US strategy of arming his Kurdish opponents or even, in 2016, others among those opponents.[37] In July 2016, Erdogan convinced himself that his US ally was de facto aligned with his opponents. Not only had the US possessed prior knowledge of the coup attempt; it had quite plausibly encouraged it. The worst was yet to come, as the Kurdish militias close to the PKK, Erdogan's most sworn enemy, became Washington's preferred military partner in its struggle against ISIS.

Come September 2018, the military outcome of the crisis scarcely left room for doubt. As telegraphed by the "liberation" of Aleppo—in this case, following the Mosul model—a catalogue of "victories" followed, from Raqqa through Ghouta, then Deraa, with the fate of Idlib remaining unresolved for now, partly protected by its proximity to Turkey. To speed up the process of seizing their property, the regime has begun to publish the names of thousands of its citizens, claiming that they all died in its jails from the selfsame "heart attack." On the basis of these "victories," some hasty commentators now glimpse the "end" of the Syrian crisis. These "victories," however, were not the victories of one part of Syrian society over another. They were made possible only by the combination of foreign support for the regime, first from Iran and the Shia world, then from Russia. This was out of all proportion to any support which the opposition received from Western or Arab sources. The part played by blind Western passivity completed the equation.

The ultimate "victory" of Bashar al-Assad that is taking shape was imported from Moscow. It thus appears as the "victory" of a fallen political minority, artificially propped up by a massive, double intervention, over a majority that was abandoned by everyone. In December 2016, it was not the Russians or the Iranians who left Aleppo. It was, instead, Aleppo's most legitimate inhabitants who were exiled. The goal that Russia and Iran granted themselves the means to achieve, on the regime's behalf, is simple. It involves destroying any resistance to the longevity of their Syrian pawn. With a single exception: a *jihadi* scarecrow that they skilfully allowed to prosper. This was all the more deliberately so that the entire planet was willing to delay any pressure on Bashar al-Assad in order to fight the scarecrow—and, to that end, to delay any pressure on the regime's backers. This "victory" is therefore the victory of a minority carried on the shoulders of foreign authoritarian regimes, over a majority that was abandoned by all the purported "defenders of democracy." Needless to say, this triumph of "hard power"—this victory of the weaponry of the authoritarian Winter over the hopes of the democratic Spring—can provide no genuine resolution to the crisis.

In fact, in Syria—as elsewhere—the most plausible outcome is that the triumph of force will lead to a mere *reconfiguration* of the crisis. The players of the defeated camp have every reason to remain mobilized, even from the new territorial base that they have been expelled to. In no way does this "triumph" of brute force push in the direction of the "reconciliation at the center" that is the precondition for reconstructing the political fabric. A reconstruction on that basis would have required that, those who were defeated on the battlefield, and who managed to survive the destruction of Aleppo, Raqqa, and Deraa, to join the millions of refugees who preceded them, might have some prospect of being made to feel truly included in the reconstruction process.

Needless to say, nothing of the kind is on the horizon. The explicitly sectarian tone of Iran's presence in Syria is expressed at the highest levels of the Syrian state. Both this and Iran's military interventions in various parts of Syria—"to be close to the Israeli enemy's borders," as Khamenei, the Supreme Guide, has put it—bodes ill for any healing of the sectarian divide. It also, of course, sustains the risk of an escalation with Israel. Inevitably, this triumph of injustice will feed the rise of extremism, if not accelerate it. Moreover, after the fact, it will also finally discredit, not only the West with its repeated retreats—but also all those Syrians who believed in the promises made by the West, and who provided it with the guarantees of "moderation" that it demanded. In practice, therefore, this result will rule in favor of the most radical player: the *jihadi*s. Notwithstanding the scale of their military defeat, outnumbered a hundred to one, they are the only opponents to Bashar al-Assad who are now able to claim that they were not betrayed.

On the scale of the contemporary history of the part of the world in which I have invested my research efforts, the Syrian crisis has contributed to producing the very worst of what conflicts breed—and then exported it, across the Middle East and to the rest of the world. First came the normalization of the most extreme uses of violence. Next, the weakening of national social links in favor of a variety of sub- or supra-national identities that were necessarily more polarizing, and whose reactivation swiftly came to irradiate the entire globe.

As against a widely held (mis-)representation, waves of extremist violence cannot be explained merely by a rise in religious radicalism—which itself is not limited to the Sunni world, nor even to the Muslim one. Nor can instances of extreme violence be correlated with only one of the parties to the conflict. The conflict has witnessed every variety of torture, from mass sectarian killings through burying alive, systematic rape, deliberate starvation, and the use of chemical and ballistic weapons of mass destruction against civilians. These have been carried out primarily by a state actor, in the name of the "rule of law" and the defense of order, of minorities—or even of "secularism." As concerns increasing counter-violence, this has largely been exercised in the name of a broad ideological spectrum, whose basis long remained that of the protection (or the defense) of an absolutely universal ambition: full citizenship.

In parallel, and going against the difficult construction of a universalist political field, the crisis has witnessed the assertion on every side of a more or less explicit tendency towards falling back onto sectarian ties—self-consciously for some parties, more latently so for others. This drift towards sectarian ties took place, first within (and to the detriment of) the Syrian national fabric, then, more broadly, on the regional scale as a whole. In a fundamental "nuance," the resurgence of, first, clan-based ties, then sectarian ones, was not limited to the Muslim components of these societies. Behind the façade of the rival political creeds of each camp and their respective supporters (in particular their Russian and Western ones), forms of social solidarity that may be considered in large part tied to religious identity became unstoppably widespread.

For at least some of the players involved, the Syrian crisis did indeed nurture a genuine withdrawal into sectarian ties and identities. This was as true on the regime side as it was among those who challenged state authority (or, for some, who challenged the very existence of the state within its current borders and institutional structure). Within the ranks of the "secular" regime, the conflict witnessed the birth of a double sectarianization: initially Alawi, then more broadly Shia, it became Christian, or at least "anti-Muslim." It thereby affected both the regime's Syrian backers—and, more unexpectedly, its Russian and Western supporters. Within the camp of those who set about the task of freeing themselves from the grasp of the Syrian state, or taking advantage of its weakening, the Kurds mobilized politically more on ethnic than religious lines. They thus provided evidence that, when national ties begin to come undone, the religious touchstone is not the only substitute. For all the other players, however, when the bonds forged by the construction of the opposition's institutions failed to reinvent the national link shattered by the civil war, it was indeed sectarian modes of belonging that came to substitute for the national fabric: for Muslims, Shia as well as Sunni—but no less so for Christians.

Sectarianization ... It's the Other Who Started It![38]

Of course, the Syrian democratic opposition, and Syrian society as a whole, paid the highest price of the ethical setback produced by the sectarian fragmentation of their national belonging.

But Europe, and France in particular, is already among the collateral victims of the Syrian conflict's having become exported abroad. On both left and right of the political spectrum, electioneering one-upmanship moved into battle mode to reap the benefits of rallying against the extremism of French *"jihadis."* But all those who make electioneering hay from the fear that this new scourge arouses are in many ways the very same who have most actively contributed to creating it, consciously or otherwise. Before the *jihadi* offshoot of Muslim politics came onto the stage, expressions of sympathy by French Muslims towards the Syrian opposition triggered the old French inability to manage the French relationship to Muslim Otherness on the basis of equal citizenship: the French Republic's Achilles' heel since its darkest colonial days. France's blustering entry into the war to defend ... "endangered minorities" compounded the ruin of its secular and universal pretensions.

There is a simple way to take the measure of the ways in which the political class nurtures the process of religion-based communitarianization that it purports to fight. One need only take note of one of the most flagrant double standards that it has allowed to set in. Transnational religion-based solidarity is portrayed as being banal when it concerns Jewish citizens and is exercised in favor of the Israeli army (despite the recognized illegality of that army's missions in occupying Palestinian territories). When such solidarity concerns their Muslim "counterparts"—when, say, it is exercised in favor of Palestinian or Syrian rebels—it is immediately criminalized. An overwhelming majority of the French political class, left and right put together, actually whips up the pernicious confessionalization that it purports to condemn. By wielding the weapons of suspicion, exclusion, and stigmatization towards the Muslim component of the national fabric alone, with great selectiveness. Or by locking up "Muslim" political speech within the ghetto of cynically prefabricated spokespersons—of whom the "imam" Hassen Chalghoumi is the most pathetic symbol. That political class contributes to the reactive slide of hundreds of individuals into the *"jihadi"* behaviors of refusal and breach with the social order that follow from their politicians' discourse and actions. And that allow those to "justify" *ex post facto* their reticence in the face of any "Muslim" solidarity towards Syria.

Never, since the Syrian crisis began, have France's pretensions to fight the sectarianization that it arrogantly condemns everywhere except at home been caught out so explicitly—or so dangerously.

Notes

1 See François Burgat, "La crise syrienne au prisme de la variable religieuse (2012–2014)," in Pierre-Jean Luizard and Anna Bozzo (eds), *Polarisations politiques et confessionnelles. La place de l'islam dans les "transitions" arabes*, Roma Tre-Press, Rome, 2015 (revised and expanded in this chapter).
2 Testimony taken by François Burgat in Amman in October 2013, published on the blog "Un œil sur la Syrie," November 30, 2013, http://syrie.blog.lemonde.fr/2014/03/31/syrie-temoignage-du-general-ahmed-tlass-sur-le-systeme-et-la-repression-44/ (last accessed June 15, 2019).
3 But also, according to an unconfirmed etymology, Damascus the "watered by blood" (See Myriam Harry, *Damas, jardin de l'islam*, J. Ferenczi & fils, Paris, 1948).
4 Named after the international conference that for a time brought together governments and representatives of civil society in various Arab or European capitals, but came to be defined by its inertness.
5 IFPO was created from the merger in 2003 of the French Institute for Arab Studies in Damascus (Institut Français d'Etudes Arabes à Damas, IFEAD), the French Middle East Archaeological Institute (Institut Français d'Archéologie au Proche-Orient, IFAPO), and the Center for Studies and Research on the Contemporary Middle East (Centre d'Etudes et de Recherche sur le Moyen-Orient Contemporain, CERMOC). IFAPO and IFEAD had been founded in 1922 in the Azm Palace. See Renaud Avez, *L'Institut français de Damas au palais Azem (1922–1946) à travers les archives*, Institut français d'études arabes de Damas, Damascus, 1993, https://books.openedition.org/ifpo/7405?lang=fr (last accessed June 15, 2019); Eliseeff *et al.*, *Soixante-dix ans de coopération scientifique à l'Institut français de Damas. Actes du colloque (novembre 1992)*, Institut français d'études arabes de Damas, Damascus, 1995.
6 See Cécile Boëx, *Cinéma et politique en Syrie. Écritures cinématographiques de la contestation en régime autoritaire (1970–2010)*, L'Harmattan, Paris, 2014.
7 Najah al-Attar, a linguist and former minister of culture, is the sister of Issam al-Attar, one of the founders of the Syrian Muslim Brotherhood, who settled in Aachen in Germany in 1978. In 1994, he welcomed me into his home, where his wife had been killed by the regime.
8 Yassin al-Haj Saleh, *Récits d'une Syrie oubliée. Sortir la mémoire des prisons*, Les Prairies ordinaires, Paris, 2015. On the long decades of practices in the regime's prison archipelago, see Moustapha Khalife, *The Shell: Memoirs of a Hidden Observer*, Interlink Books, Northampton, MA, 2007; and Aram Karabet, *Treize ans dans les prisons syriennes. Voyage vers l'inconnu*, Actes Sud, Arles, 2013.
9 In neighboring Lebanon, my passion for photography, a commonplace hobby in other countries, earned me a spectacular arrest. I had succumbed to the temptation to photograph one of the giant posters of Hezbollah's "martyrs" in the southern Bekaa valley where, close to the border with Israel, it is assumed some of Hezbollah's newest-generation missiles are buried. Shortly after-

wards, a tractor and its long trailer suddenly blocked my way while another car screeched to a halt at my level. Only a swift call made by my Lebanese host ("François Burgat has always defended Hezbollah") allowed me to get back on my way to my Damascus home and to keep my escapade as discreet as I had wished.

10 See Khadija Fadhel, "Recompositions sociales d'un camp de réfugiés à Damas: le cas de Yarmouk," in Jalal Al Husseini and Aude Signoles (eds), *Les Palestiniens, entre État et diaspora, le temps des incertitudes*, Karthala, Paris, 2011.

11 See Élizabeth Picard, *Liban-Syrie, intimes étrangers. Un siècle d'interactions sociopolitiques*, Sindbad/Actes Sud, Arles, 2016.

12 It takes a very sketchy familiarity indeed with the Gospels in Arabic to be ignorant of the fact that Jesus frequently punctuates his addresses with a very Christian "*Salaam Aleikum*" (Peace Be Upon You).

13 See, in particular, François Burgat, "La stratégie al-Assad: diviser pour survivre"; and François Burgat and Romain Caillet, "Une guérilla "islamiste"? Les composantes idéologiques de la résistance armée," in François Burgat and Bruno Paoli (eds), *Pas de printemps pour la Syrie. Les clés pour comprendre les acteurs et les défis de la crise (2011–2013)*, La Découverte, Paris, 2013.

14 Élizabeth Picard, *Liban-Syrie, intimes étrangers*.

15 On this point, see Thomas Pierret's remarkably subtle study: Thomas Pierret, *Religion and State in Syria: The Sunni Ulama from Coup to Revolution*, Cambridge University Press, Cambridge, 2013. Among its other virtues, this book lays out a further distinctiveness of the variables of Islamism in Syria. This is the subtle game of "hide-and-seek" that Sunni religiosity, in its various organizational and other forms, played with the regime, in a field undermined by the regime's strict ban on any oppositional political mobilization.

16 For instance, Sheikh Ramadan al-Bouti, who was assassinated on March 21, 2013, in his own mosque, most likely at the hands of his state patron.

17 The Partiya Yekîtiya Demokrat (Democratic Union Party), Syrian twin of the Partiya Karkeren Kurdistan (PKK, Kurdistan Workers' Party), gradually hijacked majority political representation among Syrian Kurds.

18 Sectarian tensions were especially exacerbated in Syria by the fact that the Alawites, before being tightly linked to the Assad clan's regime, had long been ostracized by the Sunni bourgeoisie, whom they provided with housekeepers and security forces rather than with intellectual or political elites.

19 Cf., in particular, Bruno Paoli, "Et maintenant, on va où? Les alaouites à la croisée des destins," in François Burgat and Bruno Paoli (eds), *Pas de printemps pour la Syrie*.

20 See, e.g., the testimony of a leftist activist related by Abir: "It's maybe the first time that we talk with the beardies and respect one another. We have something in common!" (quoted in "Laïcs et islamistes en Syrie, un front uni," Oumma.com, July 5, 2012, https://oumma.com/laics-et-islamistes-en-syrie-un-front-uni/ (last accessed June 15, 2019)).

21 See François Burgat and Bruno Paoli (eds), *Pas de printemps pour la Syrie*, for the multiple facets of this crisis. At the beginning of 2013, together with

François Gèze, editor of that collection, we took the decision to remove the question mark that initially made the title a question.

22 Marie Peltier has laid out with great skill the discursive rites that ultimately let the regime off the hook: Marie Peltier, "Syrie: la propagande assadienne facile pour briller en société," Lexpress.fr, July 10, 2016, www.lexpress.fr/actualite/la-propagande-assadienne-facile-pour-briller-en-societe-partie-1_1810985.html (last accessed June 15, 2019).

23 See, in particular, the study I published under the pseudonym "Jean-Marie Cléry," "L'impasse syrienne," *Algérie Network*, November 2011, http://algerie-network.com/algerie/136-2/ (last accessed June 15, 2019).

24 Magnificently documented by Jonathan Littell, *Carnets de Homs*, Gallimard, Paris, 2012; see also Édith Bouvier, *Chambre avec vue sur la guerre*, Flammarion, Paris, 2012. Adam Baczko, Gilles Dorronsoro, and Arthur Quesnay have put forward several convincing approaches towards the processes by which institutions have been established in the areas held by the opposition and by the Islamic State, based on two research trips to opposition-held territory: Adam Backzo, Gilles Dorronsoro, and Arthur Quesnay, *Civil War in Syria: Mobilization and Competing Social Orders*, Cambridge University Press, Cambridge, 2018; and "Vers un nouvel État syrien? Les institutions du gouvernorat d'Alep," in François Burgat and Bruno Paoli (eds), *Pas de printemps pour la Syrie*. Majd al-Dik (with Nathalie Bontemps) provides an especially enlightening description of repressive methods in opposition-held territories—Majd al-Dik (with Nathalie Bontemps), *A l'Est de Damas, au bout du monde, Témoignage d'un révolutionnaire syrien*, Don Quichotte Editions, 2016, preface and chronology by Thomas Pierret. See also Yassin al-Haj Saleh, *The Impossible Revolution: Making Sense of the Syrian Tragedy*, Hurst, London, 2017.

25 See, e.g., the testimony of Basel al-Junaidi: "As far as we were concerned, this was a Syrian revolution, not the rebellion of any sect. Sunnis didn't really identify as Sunnis – the Sunnis of Aleppo were different from those of Damascus; the Sunnis of the countryside weren't like those of the city. But sectarianism grew when people saw 90% of Alawis stayed loyal [to the regime]" (quoted in Robin Yassin-Kassab and Leila al-Shami, *Burning Country: Syrians in Revolution and War*, Pluto Press, London, 2016, p. 113). Or that of Nahed Badawi: "The most important thing is to fully understand that, faced with a democratic protest movement that outstripped all and any sectarian divisions, the regime knew that its only hope of winning was to reimpose these divisions and to confer on the revolt the character of a sectarian conflict" (quoted in François Burgat, "La stratégie al-Assad: diviser pour survivre").

26 Robin Yassin-Kassab and Leila al-Shami, *Burning Country*.

27 See Umar Abd al-Hakim (*alias* Abu Musab al-Suri), *Al-thawra al-islamiyya al-jihadiyya fi suriyya* [The *jihadi* Islamic Revolution in Syria].

28 François Burgat, "Témoignage du général Ahmed Tlass sur le système et la repression," *Un œil sur la Syrie*, March 29, 2014, http://syrie.blog.lemonde.fr/2014/03/31/syrie-temoignage-du-general-ahmed-tlass-sur-le-systeme-et-la-repression-44/ (last accessed June 15, 2019).

29 See, e.g., the testimony that I collected in Zaatari camp (Jordan) in November

2013. Mohamed Arar was a captain in the Republican Guard—"A great position," he told me, "We had many benefits." He explained to me why he had deserted: "At the beginning of the revolution, we were sent to monitor a demonstration in Duma, in the suburbs of Damascus. We were armed only with batons: there couldn't have been more than one rifle between a hundred of us. That day, we were all shot at, just like the demonstrators, from a rooftop, by guys dressed as civilians. The Friday after that, we came back armed. That time, there was a violent clash with the same shooters. Eight of them had holed themselves up in a building and were killed. They were still dressed in civilian clothes. We were stunned to discover that they were members of the State Security service led by Hafez Makhlouf. Clearly, their mission had been to shoot at both the demonstrators and the security forces. It was that day that I realized exactly what the regime was up to." (François Burgat, "Syrie. Témoignage d'un déserteur, capitaine dans la Garde républicaine," *Un œil sur la Syrie*, December 3, 2013, http://syrie.blog.lemonde.fr/2013/12/03/syrie-te-moignage-dun-deserteur-capitaine-dans-la-garde-republicaine/ (last accessed June 15, 2019).)

30 This included the Muslim Brotherhood, who made a series of explicitly secularist proclamations promoting coexistence, in particular with respect to the Alawi community. (See François Burgat, "Les frères musulmans syriens et la communauté alaouite," *Carnets de l'Ifpo*, https://ifpo.hypotheses.org/3825 (last accessed June 15, 2019).)

31 It was only in 1973 that Shia *ulama'* (religious scholars), including Musa Sadr, conferred their support for legitimating Alawis (thus the Assad family) within the Shia religious field, at a time when Bashar al-Assad's father was exposed to a sharp Sunni challenge.

32 These developments are meticulously documented in Aron Lund's reports for the Carnegie Endowment for Democracy.

33 See Ziad Majed, *La Révolution orpheline*, Actes Sud/Sindbad, Arles, 2014. See also Salam Kawakibi's valuable contributions to our understanding of the crisis: among the most recent, for example, the interview with him published in "Partis et partisans dans le monde arabe post-2011," *Confluences Méditerranée*, no. 98, 2016 (edited by Xavier Guignard and Robin Beaumont).

34 François Burgat, "Syrie. Témoignage d'un déserteur."

35 See, in particular, Majd al-Dik (with Nathalie Bontemps), *À l'est de Damas*.

36 Abu Bashar, a refugee in Zaatari camp (Jordan), narrating the five months of hell that pushed him into exile. (François Burgat, "La véritable histoire de Marwan, quatre ans, 'perdu dans le désert,'" *L'Express*, February 22, 2014, www.lexpress.fr/actualite/monde/proche-moyen-orient/la-veritable-histoire-de-marwan-4-ans-perdu-dans-le-desert_1494345.html (last accessed June 15, 2019).)

37 Cf. Hakan Yavuz and Bayram Balci (eds), *Turkey's July 15th Coup: What Happened and Why*, The University of Utah Press, Salt Lake City, 2018.

38 François Burgat, "La crise syrienne au prisme de la variable religieuse (2012–2014)."

8

The Other "at Home," or: Islam in France

The Other "at home." The recentering of the relation with the Other, who was once distant and is now so near, is unquestionably the most important transformation that I have lived through in the course of my career. Gradually, the question of our relationship to the Muslim Other came in from the exotic lands of the South or of the Orient, where, for so long, one had to travel in order to document it. And it landed at my doorstep: in France, and in Europe. It knocked at the door, insistently.[1] I have never made the question of European Islam the primary focus of my research. Ineluctably, however, it came to incorporate itself to my research themes, to the point that today it is central to them—inevitably, given the phenomenon of "French jihadism."

The scholarly construction of Islamism as a research object has to my mind been inseparably tied to the representation of French Muslims by their compatriots steeped in Christian, Jewish, or agnostic religious culture. Granted, the width of the Mediterranean is incompressible. It makes the conditions in which a Muslim in France becomes politically integrated necessarily different from those of their co-religionists living in Algeria. But the caesura of the Mediterranean is, at the same time, entirely relative. With respect to all but the small number of converts, one cannot truly think through the imaginary of French Muslims independently of the links that tie them to the land that they, or their forebears, left.

Thinking through this imaginary therefore requires paying attention to what happens there—and, more especially, to what French authorities do there. The imaginary of French non-Muslims is equally tied to their representations of political dynamics on the other side of the Mediterranean. Often, during the Algerian "Civil War" of the 1990s for instance, the Mediterranean border disappeared; the Algerian conflict was exported to France, and France took an active part in it—on both sides of the Mediterranean. Authorities on both sides, from the generals in Algiers to France's Interior Minister Charles Pasqua, united against a common enemy—the Islamists who had won at the ballot box—and found a common interest in doing so. The contours of Islamism as a research object became clearer, then, when one examined both sides of the Mediterranean simultaneously.

He Doesn't Come Down the Pub with Us. Can He Be One of Us?

Deconstructing the French intellectual milieu's attitude towards Muslims in France enables us to trace the outline of the divide that contributes to isolating a great majority of them. It also underscores the more or less conscious means by which, through stigmatization, defiance, and one-sidedness, this intelligentsia has played its part in opening up the terrible jihadist breach between the Republic and some of its children. From very early on, it appeared to me that the only kind of Muslim who could become acceptable to the upholders of the "fraudulent" version of secularism (*laïcité*)[2] was a Muslim ... who was no longer Muslim! The only one eligible to become "one of us" was, as it were, he who goes down the pub with us (who "drinks with (and like) us," "qui boit son verre comme les autres," as the French song has it). At nightfall, when the time comes for the *maghrib* prayer, those for whom religious ritual takes priority over socializing over an *aperitif* are instantly—even if not explicitly—inscribed as being on the wrong side of the dynamic of "integration." As such, in recent times, they are deemed on the brink of "radicalization."

"French Islam" opened up to me a new facet of my research object—and a new opportunity to broaden my comparative approach. My initial bearings came mainly through meetings on the fringes of talks organized by Muslim organizations in several dozen French towns, from Marseille to Lille, via the Institute for the Training of Imams in Château-Chinon. In July 2004, Tariq Ramadan and the Muslims of the International Colloquium of Muslims of the Francophone World[3] invited me to the banks of the Niger River for a fascinating series of events featuring a very wide variety of Francophone Muslims from two dozen countries in Africa and Asia, as well as Canada. This was especially stimulating—like all such comparative introductions to Francophone and African Islam I had encountered in very diverse political contexts. If only because for those who, like me, have become familiar with the Muslim variable only in its Arab environment, it matters to hear it articulated in the language of one's *own* inherited culture.

Of course, my analysis of the stakes of the self-assertion of North African immigration to France and to Europe also drew on the little capital that I had acquired while living there. But even before then, I had already set down a few markers from which to begin to fill out that imposing subject, the "Muslim problem."[4] In the mid-1960s, my father had worked in the human resources department of a steelworks that had come to the Alps to seek out hydroelectric resources. "You see these buses?" he had explained to me, "Not so long ago, we sent them to Morocco, to the Rif, empty. And we found ways to bring them back full. Again, and again. That's what allowed the company to become what it is today." He was, in passing, granting me access to an essential historical perspective on the "problem" in question. It is this perspective that today's polemical commentators on the evergreen issues of "immigration" and the "Great Replacement," from Zemmour to Houellebecq,[5] never took the trouble to learn. Or that they have preferred to forget.

Reception of my arguments during even occasional meetings with a wide social and generational spectrum of Muslims in France has always brought me useful feedback—as well as extras both humanly comforting and academically enlightening. I met "Georges" at the end of a lecture I gave in 1995, in a southern French town in which the National Front had already firmly asserted its hold. The exchange between us illustrates the state of the society within which "French Islam" was then trying to find its bearings, better than any long description. "Until now," he explained to me, "before your lecture tonight, I had always chosen to say that I was called Georges and that I was a Middle Eastern Christian. From now on, thanks to you, I'll dare to say my real name. I'll dare to say that my name is Mohammed, and I am Muslim."

The contours of "Islam in France" as a research object came into focus to me as the various ways in which it was articulated in the collective imagination of the French interlocutors who questioned or criticized me became clearer.[6] Fitting inside one another like Russian dolls (non-Muslim) French representations of Islam in France gradually appeared to me as tied above all to the identity-based problematic of how Otherness is constructed. For an overwhelming majority of French people, myself included, "Islam in France" refers to the resounding intrusion into the national fabric of the very symbol of the Other's culture. In order to acquire their full meaning, however, the terms, the context, and the temporality of this initial definition require important clarifications. Things get "worse" when one grasps the measure of the fact that "the Other's culture" is not just any culture. "Worse" still: this Other is not just any Other. The encounter with this particular Other occurs within a territorial framework, and a temporal context. Each of these carries specific meaning. There were the English of the Hundred Years War. There were the Germans of the great conflicts of the 19th and 20th centuries. In a different register, there were also the Italian and Spanish immigrants, and their East Asian counterparts (including the Vietnamese, whom France had also colonized). Today, in this alchemy of identity-construction, the figure of the "Muslim"—who was, until recently, still an "Arab"—has come to fill the central position taken up by he who tells us who we are: the Other.

Above all, the culture of the Muslim, first among French "Others," is not just any culture. Mainstream French thought asserts that it has achieved a secularizing detachment from the religious idea. Yet is this not mere fantasy? This specific Other culture is still approached through the prism of religious Otherness. And the encounter with this Muslim Otherness unfolds in a historical moment when a long period of hegemony of the one over the Other is coming to an end. The unstoppable "revenge of the South" is planting its economic, financial, cultural, and symbolic flags in the four corners of the Western imagination. Last but not least, the site of this encounter foregrounds the most disturbing dimension of this "return of the South." Muslim culture had long remained in the home of the Other: the colonized subject whose homeland we built cathedrals in. It is now "among us," at the very heart of France. This Other's prayer halls had long remained discreetly in the depths of our cellars. S/he now has the impertinence to claim to emerge into the full light of day, into the "national" public sphere—our very own public sphere, over which we had always imagined that we held an absolute monopoly.[7]

Might not our unease, then, be prompted by this intruder? S/he who so insistently reminds us of the closing of our imperial dream and, more troubling yet, of our fleeting but intoxicating monopoly of the universal?

Reforming Islam?

When we are overcome with melancholy faced with the myriad ways in which this disturbing proximity of the "Other's culture" is expressed, we very often dream of reforming that culture—in order to compensate for the destabilizing effects of difference. To ease our anxieties at home, we prefer to search for the roots of this turbulence, to which we are so intimately linked, as far away from ourselves as possible. We focus our attention on the Other's Islam. We dream of modeling it in our image. Hence a recurrent temptation: to remodel to our advantage the reference points of this Other culture, that we have set up as the "ideological" opponent and spoilsport to our "modernizing" urges.

Reformation of the normative codes of Muslim doctrine has been widely embarked upon, as how that doctrine is expressed adapted to certain societal developments. Such reformation can scarcely be remote-controlled from Paris, on French radio and TV, by prefabricated "reformers." Nor can it be directed by the very same figures who mean to benefit from the political "domestication" of how Islam is expressed. Reform will not be channeled through the voice of those men—more often still: of those women—whom we have selected primarily for them to tell us what we want to hear, in a language that we understand. What is it that we want to hear? That the tension in our relations with the Muslim world is exclusively tied to the backwardness of the conceptual universe of our Muslim interlocutors—and never to our own behavior towards them.

The principle that Muslims might usefully reflect critically upon their doctrine is not illegitimate as such—far from it. Nor are all the directions staked out by the players of religious reform out of place. This is no matter, then, of rejecting the very existence of a space for interpretive debate concerning the Other's religious norms. Nor is it a question of refusing the idea that such reinterpretations of Muslim references might comprise some part of the change-variables that could pacify the world. All this may be true—provided that all the efforts required to calm tensions are not put into one single basket: "It is the Other who must change." And provided that this reassuring prospect, which has the advantage of exculpating us, should not serve to conceal other prospects that should make us ponder. But most of the epistles reforming Islam produced in the West, from the late Abdelwahab Meddeb to Kamel Daoud, through Abdennour Bidar,[8] and unlike those of Tariq Ramadan (see Chapter 11, pp. 178–80) or of others denied access to the airwaves, are defined by seeking to impose a culturalist interpretation of modes of resistance to change. Whereas such modes of resistance are in fact the markers of disequilibria, political malfunctions, or, more straightforwardly, of fundamentally political injustices.

To pick one example out of a hundred. When listening to some of the Parisian enthusiasts for "reforming Islam," the takeaway has forever seemed to be that, if the Palestinian Hamas so gamely resists Israel's military occupation, this could only be because it failed to master the humanist subtleties of the Quranic text. "Dear friend, might you accept an hour on the show to tell us all about how frightful a moderate Muslim such as yourself finds the radicalism of that ghastly Hamas movement? You see, it's important that such a critique should come from a Muslim." In the 1990s, the same logic was often applied by the Algerian junta's little helpers in the Paris media. These were entrusted with the task of implanting in France the idea that the junta was targeted by Muslim fundamentalism alone—rather than also by a powerful opposition movement that was largely sold on the principle of democracy.

Western discourse on religious reform contributes in the most pernicious way to representing what are in most cases trivially political problems as being cultural ones. Moreover, its key carriers are interlocutors whose influence on the component of society in whose name they purport to speak is extremely limited.

In order to get this fundamental contradiction across, I often use a railway metaphor. Whether these reformers are Muslim or otherwise, their key quality should be that of a good engine. They should pull the wagons along with them. But whether highly scholarly for some, or illiterate for others, the Parisian "reformers" of Islam promoted on the airwaves at peak viewing time are a little like a train engine that whistles away miles in front of the wagons it is supposed to be pulling along. Their driver's main concern is pleasing the spectators who crowd along the tracks—namely, those listeners begging to hear the self-indulgent viewpoints of "fraudulent secularism" be condoned. Whereas their task should be to contradict and to enlighten their audience every time the need arises. It is high time for us to recognize that, far from helpfully pulling the train of reform forwards, all that these commentators produce are mountains of column inches and hot air in our recording studios.

When the Other is Too Close to Home: The Semantic Cost of Proximity

Immigration and the globalization of media produce their share of benefits. They also thrust societies into an abrupt proximity that can also become a source of misunderstanding and tension with the Other. The immediacy of communication does away with forms of distance that had long been preserved by geographical distance. Without filter, it instantly brings into contact with each other societies whose concepts of sacred and taboo differ—in particular concerning their respective relationships to religion, sexuality and gender, and even aesthetics. Yet taking these taboos, norms of the sacred, and other "totems" into account can become meaningful and effective only if they are understood within the terms used by the societies in question.

Let us recall what the French cartoonist Siné considered to be the best cartoon that he had never published.[9] In 1962, he drew a squad of befrocked priests brandishing a giant cross, upon which a man run through with nails and thorns was in his death throes. In the world that they had nearly finished turning Christian, they were breathlessly mocking this "totem" of a "poor" naked native.[10] It is sometimes forgotten that the colleagues of Philippe Val, who was for seventeen years editor then director of *Charlie Hebdo*, elected to draw the Prophet of Islam, naked and in an obscene posture. Part of French society considered this to be the merest schoolboy vulgarity. In a different realm of the sacred, it reverberated in Muslim communities in the ways that, say, a pornographic poster of the Virgin Mary might have done in the Polish, Portuguese, or French countryside of the 1930s.

What a shame, one hears it said, that all "these people" have remained so stuck in the archaism of religion. "Secular" and "modern" France prides itself on having overcome the age of the religious sacred. Yet has it brought an end to the age of taboo for all that? Peer a little more closely, and nothing of the kind is true. To date, France has, in point of fact, merely moved and repainted the frames in which its notion of the sacred is mounted, and the profile of its own totems and taboos.[11] Passionately secular France, which processes sacredness in religion exclusively through the Other's archaism, has in fact remained passionately attached to the "Christian roots" that it never lets slip an opportunity to mention—and to a racial identity that it fully intends to keep "white."

In 2008, in the "temple of irreverence" that is *Charlie Hebdo*, another "schoolboy vulgarity" was concocted. This time, it concerned the supposed desire of one of President Sarkozy's sons to convert to Judaism.[12] This particular version of "irreverence" brought out the peculiarity of the very French inclination to mock the taboos of others more readily than its own. When our Parisian jokers were publishing cartoons of the Prophet of Islam, some regularly proclaimed themselves willing to give up their lives to defend their right to do so. The very same audience suddenly found nothing to laugh about at all in this particular irreverence, which was branded "anti-Semitic." Its author was the great Siné, who died eight years later, "in the flower of old age," as he put it in the epitaph he had prepared for himself. He was sacked on the spot.

And then, in January 2016, in *Charlie Hebdo* again, there was the cartoon showing Aylan Kurdi, the 3-year-old Syrian toddler who was found drowned on a Turkish beach. He was drawn as a potential rapist. Here, our irrepressible Gallic humor appears to consist of assimilating an entire people to a problem and a threat, and rejoicing at the death of one of them. Maybe, just maybe, it might have become part of what one should be (as very few have been) clear-sighted enough to recognize as an appeal towards that which is darkest in our history? For it is as a member of a racialized and criminalized population that little Aylan was vilified here. In the 19th century, this kind of representation was what allowed the trivialization of the massacre of the Native American peoples of North America, the slaughter of Algerians between 1830 and 1962, the pogroms and massacre of the Jews of Europe, and so on. That is to say: what international law has, since 1945, termed "genocide." But if we can't laugh at just anything anymore ... France would be falling apart—right?

Since the 1990s, the relationship of French non-Muslims to the culture of this "not just any Other" has been punctuated by a litany of media-hyped "affairs." Within this great theater play, the fact that the "characters" are Muslim is raised almost exclusively in the register of pathology—if not that of criminality. There was the "affair" of the Union of French Islamic

Organizations (UOIF),[13] an organization that was likely too representative of the sensibility of most believers. There was the "affair" of the supporters of Algeria's Islamic Salvation Front (FIS) who became closely identified with the 1995 Paris terrorist attacks. There was the "affair" of the banning of the Islamic headscarf from public schools, and of the *burqa* from public spaces. Then came the popular protests against the cartoons of the Prophet, which "threatened freedom of expression." And finally, the radical surge that leads us up to the crimes of Mehdi Nemmouche, the gunman who killed four at Brussels's Jewish Museum in 2014, to *Charlie Hebdo*, and the Bataclan ...

The iconic footballer Zinedine Zidane, "Zizou," was one of France's most popular figures. When he scored goals, he became no longer "Muslim"—but just "French." By contrast, any mention of the relationship between France and *its* Islam throws up a long series of antiheroes and dread-inducing figures. Granted, not all of these are terrorists. Like the rector of the Paris Great Mosque or Imam Chalghoumi, a few make themselves fit into the narrow boundaries of the category of "good clients" of the media. With these exceptions, the key figures of Muslim France are all deemed—in the (formerly) best-case scenario of such figures as Tariq Ramadan or the representatives of the UOIF—"controversial," if not "inflammatory." From as early as the mid-1990s, the dominant tone in the media became unbearable to Muslim ears. At the end of a talk, I would be told: "Mr. Burgat, you understand that, when they talk about Islam, Algeria, or Palestine on TV, we have to reach for the remote. Well—our fingers end up hurting from pressing the button so much!"[14]

Sadly, in official speeches and the mainstream media, the negative markers of the "Islamic" vocabulary of the Other's culture almost never interact with a great absentee: the equivalent markers within the culture of the dominant, non-Muslim camp. "Radicalization," "Salafism," and "jihad" are almost never made to rhyme with "Rafale," "F-16," "drones," "missiles," "embargo," "air strikes," or "*Charles de Gaulle*" (the French aircraft carrier). No more so are they made to rhyme with "CRIF" (the very right-wing Representative Council of French Jewish Institutions[15]), or with "Islamophobia." It bears repeating: the one-sidedness with which certain issues are set up as "cultural" prevents us from imagining that non-Muslims, and the powers that be, could bear any share of responsibility. It therefore prevents us from producing an effective explanation of how some young people are unstoppably drawn into the hell of jihadism. Whereas such an understanding would enable responding to it more effectively than the entire arsenal of repression and suspicion that, today, contributes only to worsening it.

The tragic events of January and November 2015 in Paris, of course, gave unprecedented relevance to my initial forays into French Muslim circles. On November 6, 2015, a week before the Bataclan attacks, I was exasperated by the news that the aircraft carrier *Charles de Gaulle* had been dispatched towards Syria. Alarmed at the prospect of "the exploits of our bomber-pilots jeopardizing those of the footsoldiers of the French anti-terrorist system Vigipirate," I wrote in the following terms of the violence that lay in wait for us.

> Tomorrow, or the next day, or in a few weeks, we are bound to encounter the same violence in France as the Russians have in the Sinai.[16] Clutching their election-season calculators, some are likely already celebrating that moment. In truth, the attack itself will not be the worst. The worst will be its terrible aftermath. For let there be no doubt about it: This preordained attack will not only rip apart innocent victims. It will also break the last of the levees that still hold back torrents of sectarian hatred that, today already, gnaw at the heart of our Republic. Friends of Vigipirate: Will you still be there to protect us from *that* terrorism?[17]

There are times when one would much prefer to have been mistaken. That was one.

Notes

1 See Nilüfer Göle, *Interpénétrations. L'Islam et l'Europe*, Galaade Éditions, Paris, 2005; *Musulmans au quotidien. Une enquête européenne autour des controverses sur l'islam*, La Découverte, Paris, 2015.
2 Jean Baubérot, *La Laïcité falsifiée*, La Découverte, Paris, 2012 (2nd updated edition: La Découverte, Paris, 2014).
3 Colloque International des Musulmans de l'Espace Francophone (CIMEF).
4 On said "Problem," see the well-informed books by Vincent Geisser, *La Nouvelle Islamophobie*, La Découverte, Paris, 2003; Thomas Deltombe, *L'Islam imaginaire. La construction médiatique de l'islamophobie en France, 1975–2005*, La Découverte, Paris, 2005; Abdellali Hajjat and Marwan Mohammed, *Islamophobie. Comment les élites françaises fabriquent le problème musulman*, La Découverte, Paris, 2013; Amiraux Valérie, «Visibilité, transparence et commérage: de quelques conditions de possibilité de l'islamophobie ... et de la citoyenneté», *Sociologie*, vol. 5, no. 1, 2014, pp. 81–95; and "Visibility, Transparency and Gossip: How Did the Religion of Some (Muslims) Become the Public Concern of Others?" *Critical Research on Religion*, Special Issue: *The Muslim Question*, vol. 4, no. 1, 2016, pp. 37–56.
5 Éric Zemmour, *Le Suicide français*, Albin Michel, Paris, 2014; Michel Houellebecq, *Submission*, Picador, New York, 2015.
6 François Burgat, "Veils and Obscuring Lenses," in John L. Esposito and François Burgat (eds), *Modernizing Islam: Religion in the Public Sphere in the Middle East and Europe*, Hurst, London, 2003.

7 The effects of this "irruption" have been especially well analyzed in the lengthy study by Nilüfer Göle, *Musulmans au quotidien*.
8 Abdelwahab Meddeb, *La Maladie de l'islam*, Seuil, Paris, 2002; Kamel Daoud, "The Sexual Misery of the Arab World," *The New York Times*, February 12, 2016, www.nytimes.com/2016/02/14/opinion/sunday/the-sexual-misery-of-the-arab-world.html (last accessed June 15, 2019), translated and published the same day in English and Arabic; Abdennour Bidar, *Un Islam pour notre temps*, Seuil, Paris, 2004; and *Lettre ouverte au monde musulman*, Les Liens qui libèrent, Paris, 2015.
9 Maurice Sinet (1928–2016), nicknamed Siné, was among the founders of *Charlie Hebdo*, in which his cartoons expressed anti-Zionist commitments—but also anti-capitalist, anti-clerical, and anarchist ones.
10 This cartoon is reproduced in « Ma vie, mon œuvre, ma mort », a posthumous special issue of *Siné Mensuel*, May 2016.
11 Régis Debray, *Jeunesse du sacré*, Gallimard, Paris, 2012.
12 "Jean Sarkozy […] has just declared that he intends to convert to Judaism before marrying his Jewish fiancée, the heir to the founders of [the electronics-store giant] Darty. The lad will go far!" Siné had written in July 2008.
13 Union des organisations islamiques de France.
14 Quoted in François Burgat, "Veils and Obscuring Lenses."
15 Conseil Représentatif des Institutions Juives de France.
16 On October 31, 2015, flight A381 crashed in Sinai, killing 224 people.
17 François Burgat, "Le *Charles de Gaulle* déployé contre Daech: on affaiblit le terrorisme ou on le renforce?" *L'Obs/le Plus*, November 6, 2015, http://leplus.nouvelobs.com/contribution/1446301-le-charles-de-gaulle-deploye-contre-daesh-on-affaiblit-le-terrorisme-ou-on-le-renforce.html (last accessed June 15, 2019).

Part II

Political Islam: The Stakes of an Alternative Interpretation

9

Being a Political Scientist of the Muslim World

As I entered the CNRS in the wake of defending my thesis, I discovered the world of "full-time" research. The shock came from the fact that this research now had to be conducted "remotely." How was I to keep writing on Algeria when I had just left it? Naturally, I adapted my work methods. But from my first efforts in Algeria, *in situ*, I retained the deep conviction that remaining close to the field was a *sine qua non* of academic research. As obvious as it may seem, this conviction is not universally shared. Overtheorized and "distanciated" interpretations, above any contact with the object of research, have always taken up considerable space—at least in political science. And not everyone has struggled to overcome them.

The CNRS and the World of Research

"On a silver platter, the CNRS provides unrivalled conditions to live in the field ... and there are few takers!" So Jean-Claude Vatin, the architect of the renaissance of the CEDEJ in Cairo, bemoaned to me one day. This was true: there were few takers for what was an extremely comfortable expatriation. For some, the reason was the requirements of conjugal life. For others, it was a genuine existential reluctance ("You're completely mad to go exile yourself in Yemen," a colleague in Aix told me, laughing). Here and there, of course, unfamiliarity with the language still prevailed—but also sociological and cultural ignorance of the distant (the potentially hostile, even) lands of "North Africa." Both the human and the intellectual connections directly inherited from the colonial era still held an important position in the practices and the imaginary of the field of "Arab studies."

Research centers devoted to the study of the Arab world have long nurtured a kind of emotional block with respect to Islamist figures. In 1992, I suggested that the library of the CEDEJ, where I had been based for three years, might purchase a periodical published by the Muslim Brotherhood. The reply came that our institution was dedicated to doing "scholarship, not politics." The argument might not have been completely unfounded had the organs of other political movements endured the same treatment—those that applied themselves to discrediting their Islamist challengers to the ears of our diplomats. This was, of course, far from being the case. When I aspired to bring Tariq Ramadan, who was at the time living in Cairo, to come and speak at the CEDEJ, I received from this same director (for whom my friendship nonetheless remains intact, for he had many other talents) an eloquent grimace of disgust, coupled with a resounding "What? Nooooo!"

True—at least outside of our Catholic institutions—being close to the religious field remains perceived as being radically contradictory with the requirements of scientific method. (This standpoint baffles me rather less than that of the CEDEJ.) "One cannot be a scholar and fast." So a famous Parisian anthropologist asserted, far removed from any historical, sociological, or epistemological reason, to a colleague who had invoked a scheduling constraint tied to his Ramadan fast. Thirty years of attending colloquia and other "international" seminars on political Islam, "Religion and Politics," and so forth, enable me to certify that the recipe applied by universities and the research world unshakably follows an unwritten rule—in France even more so than in the English-speaking world. Whosoever wishes to speak on Islamists must invite their most bitter opponents (whether those in power, or from the left) and ... those opponents only. In other words: one must hear only those who, it is in some sense certain, will (in "scholarly" fashion, of course) unite with their hosts in emotional and partisan simplification of the subject of the meeting—or perhaps one should say: its target.

A few weeks after I arrived at the CNRS I had in a way been warned by what a celebrated university professor confided in me, on the flight that brought us back from a trip to Algeria. We had been hosted there by the Algerian *pères blancs*, who had been as welcoming as they were well-read.[1] In Algiers, moving in the circles of the *pères blancs*, we had met one of the tiny minority of Algerians who had converted to Catholicism. "You see, Burgat," the professor, who at the time presided over one of the most important French academic institutions devoted to studies of the Arab (and Muslim) world, told me: "I have a deep conviction. I believe that these Arab masses are unstoppably on the road to Catholicism. What do you think?" The road promised to be very long indeed before the unstoppable self-assertion of those who were developing in a radically opposite direction was to benefit from a rational approach.

Ghannouchi and Foundations in Tunis

As a matter of fact (and as it did to others), far more than it was the result of a conscious decision, choosing Islamism as a research field seemed quite obvious to me. The choice was governed by reality—and not by some imagined perverse desire to transform that reality, as some would have it who deem that the exaggerated interest of political scientists in Islamists conceals their ignorance of other, more deserving stages in the history of Islamic thought.[2] "Islamism-ologists" have indeed sometimes set themselves up as historical actors, to whom the "political fortunes" of their Islamist research object may be ascribed. This was, of course, to grant them far too much credit.

In the mid-1980s, while I was armed with a still imprecise background understanding of Libya and Algeria, Tunisia gradually took priority over the rest of North Africa in my research agenda. In 1984 already, Tunisia was playing a pioneering role on the scale of North Africa, if not of the Arab world as a whole. Habib Bourguiba had authorized his prime minister, Mohamed Mzali, to attempt an unprecedented experiment. He allowed the Islamists of the Movement of the Islamic Tendency (MIT) to create a party, and so to gain admittance to the legal political stage. Most likely, this was because the MIT was perceived as a possible antidote to the partisan left (and especially the trade union left). It was this context, in which these particular Islamists were designated as new players in a very timid political transition, that provided the catalyst for a personal encounter that was to prove decisive. On August 5, 1985, in the suburbs of Tunis, my interest in this political generation crystallized, and never really left me thereafter.

Amid the torpor of the last week of Ramadan, the summer session of Arabic language classes at the Bourguiba School (the Bourguiba Institute for Modern Languages) was drawing to a close. Since "great" callings always require smaller motivations, mine that year was called Laura B. This American colleague had the gift of sharpening my jealousy. For she had succeeded in obtaining a meeting with one of the mythical figures of "Palestinian" Tunisia. She was to be granted an audience by Khalil al-Wazir, *alias* Abu Jihad, the no. 2 of the Palestine Liberation Organization (PLO), decentered to Tunisia after it had been chased out of Beirut in 1982. The meeting took place in a villa in Sidi Bou Saïd. In that same villa, on April 16, 1988, a Mossad commando landed on Rawad beach to riddle Abu Jihad with bullets after it had killed three of his guards, adding to the already impressive list of extrajudicial executions carried out by Israel.[3]

I, too, dreamed of a high-flying political encounter. On August 3, 1984, to mark the 82nd birthday of the "Supreme Combatant" Habib Bourguiba, a high-ranking political prisoner had just been released. This was Rached Ghannouchi, the founder and leader of the Movement of the Islamic Tendency (MIT) that in 1989, when the authorities banned parties from making any reference to religion, was renamed Ennahda. Despite his having no connection to the MIT, I owed my appointment with Ghannouchi to Salem Ounaïs, my professor in my third year. On the evening of August 5, I put aside my motorcycle to head, at night, for a villa in the southern Tunis suburb of Ben Arous, at the opposite end of town from Sidi Bou Saïd. It was here that the leader of the MIT, who at the time was labeled a "fundamentalist," had set himself up. (I used the same term in my first article on the MIT, having not yet felt the need to distance myself from the terminology conventionally used at the time to label fundamentalist strands in Catholicism.[4]) When the gate of the villa edged half-open, exoticism was in no short supply. At the edge of the courtyard, thirty or so men dressed in their long *jebba*s (a loose male dress) were seated on carpets set up in a circle. Before my eyes, the first formal meeting of the MIT's *majlis al-shoura* (Consultative Council) was just drawing to an end. A few minutes later, I was in one-to-one conversation with Rached Ghannouchi beneath one of the villa's verandas.

The conversation got off to a very bad start: "I don't even know yet if I've decided to answer your questions, and you're asking if you can record me!" A few hours later, in the dead of night, one of his nephews, a student in Canada, drove me back to Tunis in his Mercedes. By then, I had already become deeply convinced. The "fundamentalists" could not be reduced to what the Tunisian or French press had allowed me to understand of them. An unreasoned contempt and fear had, I was now convinced of it, obfuscated a reality that I sensed was more complex, and on which I gradually came to focus my efforts.

A few weeks later, I published my first lines on the subject. Thirty-two years ago now, these read:

> Could Muslim fundamentalists soon officially take part in political life in North Africa? At the close of a summer in which debate concerning the place of Islamists in the political field has been the talk of Tunisia, the possibility can no longer be ruled out. The various roadblocks that until now made the very idea of such a scenario inconceivable have begun to be lifted. Timid as it may be, the current process merits our close attention, regardless of the share of strategic concern that it may contain. Tunisia is conceding that a dialogue might be possible with a political movement—a dialogue that has until now been denied by most other regimes in North Africa, and by most Arab regimes. In doing so, *it is opening up a path that is far from uninteresting: the path towards normalization with a component of North African society that it hardly seems avoidable will reinforce itself in future, if not become hegemonic.*[5]

A lengthy research trajectory had just begun—and with it my troubles.

Four years later, when I presented Rached Ghannouchi with a copy of *The Islamic Movement in North Africa*, the dedication wrote itself: "To Rached Ghannouchi, I dedicate this book, that was conceived of one evening of August 1985 in a villa of the suburb of Ben Arous." From Ghannouchi's individual trajectory, I drew instructive lessons—namely, the encounters and other various factors that came to turn an admiring listener of the materialism of *Radio Tirana* into the leader of an Islamist movement. I filled these out with the career paths of a few other key players who provided my analysis with its major landmarks: the Communist Adel Hussein; the Nasserist Tarek al-Bishri; and the Moroccan Abdessalam Yassine. These four figures were the pillars of the analytical matrix of *The Islamic Movement in North Africa*, which I wrote ten years on from my return from Cairo. In the meantime, without leaning upon such instructive individual paths, analysis of Algeria's FIS came to take up just as important a place in that matrix.

Their Allah (Theirs Alone)—or Our God (Everyone's)?

What led me to diverge from my colleagues' all-but-undifferentiated rejection of Islamism? I have often asked myself the question. The first answer is that very early on, and for the long term, I had the opportunity—the luck—to encounter cultures other than my own. At first unconsciously, I internalized the fact that the most universal values did not necessarily become compromised when their carriers happened to be individuals whose cultural and religious codes differed from those which I had inherited in the shadow of my native church tower. This was one way to absorb one interpretation of the old maxim that "You can't judge a book by its cover."

The second answer is double-sided. It inheres in the fact that my first contacts in the field of political Islam were sociological and human ones, rather than merely reading-based and theoretical. Straightaway, this enabled me to contextualize, and therefore to humanize, the breach that the players of political Islam represented. Further, unlike some of my colleagues, these contacts took place with a very specific component of the Islamist field. This was the Muslim Brotherhood movement (far more than I encountered their Salafi rivals): the most reformist trend of political Islam—and so the least inaccessible one. As Rached Ghannouchi's development has since demonstrated beyond any doubt, this considerably reduced the distance with political Islam as a research object. It made even less plausible the extremely reductive discourse within which it was then confined by the "eradicatory" mindset. On both sides of the Mediterranean, this conditioned any political opening to the pure and simple elimination of any Islamist presence whatsoever.

Beyond this, it seems to me that the belated emergence of my political consciousness, within the borders of France, played an important role. Throughout May 1968, that historic month, I failed to fully convince myself of the urgency of going to liberate the factory workers, prisoners of the shift system. Nor really even to fight the other "excesses"—obvious as these were—"of capitalism." One day in that month of May, the superb 135 mm lens that I had screwed onto the Russian knockoff of a Leica M-3 (purchased a few weeks earlier from a cash-strapped member of the Soviet delegation to the Winter Olympics in Grenoble) was targeted by ... an egg. Thankfully, the egg was still fresh. But it had been thrown by a revolutionary student, and intended for me as a representative of the "corrupt media" with which I had clearly been identified, perched as I was on scaffolding above the "demo." The egg-thrower was not entirely mistaken. In 1968, I observed the student protest and its revolutionary ambitions more than I identified myself with it. In fact, one of my colleagues briefly felt entitled to cast upon me the supreme aspersion in this decade of protest and of the slow rise of the left to power. I was labeled a "Christian democrat."

But there was another, positive side to the coin of my being relatively apolitical. Along with the vocabulary of Leninism, I had not internalized, as if they were sacred verses, the peculiar aversions that have made the overwhelming majority of French communists bottom of the class in understanding the stakes of Muslim Otherness.[6] Granted, Marxism was briefly to feature in my intellectual development. For a few months, the forty-five volumes of the *Complete Works of Lenin*—all but given away by the Editions de Moscou—made an appearance on the shelves of my library in Constantine. They were not often disturbed from their perch. At the time, in his *Critical Introduction to Law* (Maspero, 1976), the jurist Michel Miaille provided an account of the landmarks that had led from historical materialism to the "building of socialism." These correlations for a time seemed to me very convincing. Likely a little too much so. As I have already partly explained, I was to untie this fleeting bond. The primary lesson that I derived from my doctoral fieldwork was that Algeria's plan to proactively transform agrarian structures and the administrative network of the rural world was a patent failure. This was one reason why my empathy for the seductive rigor of Marxist rhetoric came to a swift end. It strikes me that my distance from it had welcome consequences for my later intellectual development.

This "freedom" of mine also saved me from developing the (often entirely irrational) emotional blockage that for so long separated French Communists from any reasoned and effective approach to the Islamist generation, and, together with the Communists, whole swaths of the European and Arab lefts, academics included.⁷ Far from any realistic analysis, this convinced them that the differences between them and the Islamists were irreversible, insurmountable—and irreconcilable. The Arab lefts, "orphans of revolution," found no path to escape from a "frozen revolution" with conservative overtones—as many of those who have analyzed them most clear-headedly characterize their historical development today. They did so neither in their contemporary programmatic texts, nor in their faint-hearted Arab Spring strategy that saw so many of their leaders (and not only in Egypt) miserably run to the protective embrace of authoritarian powers. As Nicolas Dot-Pouillard wrote so pertinently in 2016:

> The revolutionary narratives are on the side of the most radicalized political Islam, that sets itself up as an alternative social model. Paradoxically, the Arab lefts opted for a certain conservatism. This involved preferring the State and the army to armed groups, Pan-Arabism to Pan-Islamism, and the known to the unknown. It was a choice that also favoured one kind of conservatism to another: in this case, Iran's over Saudi Arabia's. For the time being, on the left, "the revolution is frozen."⁸

When I was based in Algeria, my sense of the divides that split the country—or the Mediterranean—was inexorably rebuilt upon new paradigms, my opposition between "good" and "evil" remodeled from new variables and new criteria. The preeminence of "right and left" and "rich and poor" gradually gave way to "endogenous" and "exogenous." Clearly, this interpretative framework was no less ideological than the one it replaced. But I developed a conviction where the players whose motivations I sought to understand were concerned. Examining their identity-based relation with the concept of the endogenous (i.e. with the Western influence channeled by colonization) produced more meaning than did the initial left/right frameworks that I had used to analyze political mobilization.

This choice was to become among the landmarks of my research path. In the eyes of at least some of my colleagues, I have never been quite "scientifically correct." This has often been stimulating—and also sometimes costly. Ever since the Iranian revolution of 1979, French intellectual and political circles, (almost) irrespective of their political standpoint, began to redefine themselves with respect to a new bogeyman in terms of politics, ethics, and, more broadly, identity. Clearly, Iran had accelerated the transposition between ethnic and religious Otherness. It was then that the Other became Muslim. The corporal form taken by the Other was Imam Khomeini. Before he had even taken any decision—say, the decision to eliminate his (violent) leftist challengers by force—he featured as the nemesis of one of *Paris Match*'s most congenial Oriental heroes: the Shah of Iran, husband to the beautiful Farah Diba. The rest is history.

In fact, the "worst" of the stresses in our relationship to the new Islamist generation were yet to come. It was thought that the historical divide of the independence era had confined the Other in the box of his Orient, at a safe remove once again. But, in the early 1990s, the earthquake-like "Return of the Other" spread from distant Iran to infinitely closer Algeria. The onset of the 1990s was in many ways a pivotal moment. It was then that, across several Arab political fields, Islamists displayed an ability that few analysts had foreseen: mobilizing for elections. First came the Tunisian parliamentary elections of April 1989, and the unexpected success of candidates hailing from the forebear of Ennahda, even if this was masked by the crude rigging of the results. Jordan's Muslim Brotherhood followed in November the same year. And (even if political developments in the "Kingdom of the Queen of Sheba" reached us more dimly then than they do today), in Yemen too, where, in the wake of the country's reunification, Islamists made an appearance on the parliamentary scene—even if this was with the support of the regime, which aimed to promote them in order to weaken its Southern rivals.

The Algerian Precursor of the Arab Springs: When "Our" World Discovers That It Is Not Alone

Because Algeria was so close geographically, the spectacular breakthrough of the Islamic Salvation Front (FIS) in the local elections of June 1990 was the turning point of European—and especially French—perceptions of Islamism. These elections exploded a myth that, despite the warning sign of the Iranian revolution, remained firmly anchored in the Western imagination in general, and that of the left in particular. Those who could lay claim to the "orderly" succession of the authoritarian regimes that had followed independence were not the Communists, nor the Nasserists, nor the Baathists, nor any of their ilk. It was the Islamists. When the editor of *Le Monde* entrusted me with deciphering the FIS's election victory that no one had cared to imagine—from Algiers, where I was passing through—his assessment was that "there was only you, Burgat, who constantly said that the Islamists could win elections" ...[9]

I also wrote a Diplomatic Telegram (as it was still called at the time) for the French ambassador Jean Audibert, in which I had ample space to provide my interpretation of the electoral earthquake. This is how I explained the FIS's success:

> Principally, [...] the FIS has successfully co-opted the last and most important of the FLN's political resources: nationalism. This is on various counts. First, in a positive sense—by virtue of the very nature of its discourse. This

discourse is the product of the extension into the cultural and ideological fields of the nationalist dynamic that the FLN had expressed and exploited in the political field (the War of Independence) and the economic one (nationalization). Second, in a negative sense. This is the perverse consequence of the political movements that wield another vocabulary gradually coming to identify themselves with, on the one hand, the French-speaking world; inevitably, with France itself; and, last and most importantly, with a certain social elite. That elite was punished here on two counts: for its economic privileges, and for its cultural proximity with the world of the old colonial power.

In a section entitled "Alternatives," I concluded that: "Neither women, nor the Berbers, nor the army, nor any section of traditional society should be considered [...] to be exempt from the Islamist dynamic."

The scale of the Islamists' victory left very many Algeria-watchers quite astounded—even those who were supposedly awake to social dynamics. This revelation made the FIS all the more alarming as a political player. Received wisdom, bolstered by the blind chorus of local and foreign experts, had long denied that the FIS had any popular base. The conventional portrayal of the Islamists at the time had them as mere groupuscules, who were terrified at the idea of the test of the ballot box, where the *vox populi* would inevitably blow them away. The elections of June 12, 1990, therefore revived the age when the whole political spectrum seized up at the scarecrow of "fundamentalism." Algeria, so close, was no distant Iran. It launched the spectacular career of a media and political traveling circus, both Arab and Western, whose members are powerful and whose approach, on both sides of the Mediterranean, is thoroughly convergent.

All those who felt threatened by this challenge to their power came to grasp the benefits to be derived from labeling those who threatened them "Islamists." This held regardless of the cause of their respective "Islamists'" troubles, whether resistance to domestic military occupations or opposition to authoritarianism. From the long-term incumbents of Arab regimes to those who, on the left, were struggling to preserve their standing as the leaders of the opposition from the Islamist challenge, and from Israel's cabinets to the Western political classes: all joined one vast front. This was united by an interest in emotionalizing, in depoliticizing, and, therefore, in rendering opaque the mechanisms that sustained their domination. In unison, they burst into the same chorus, from the same score. Whatever could conceal the precise and complex nature of the Islamist dynamic was fair game.

In 1990, in Algiers as elsewhere, it was obvious that two worlds cohabited. Sometimes, they never even saw each other at all. These worlds were the product of histories that were in part different. In part at least, they belonged to two distinct social strata. The "Algeria of the Club des Pins"—i.e. the *nomenklatura*, but not only—like the "Tunisia of La Marsa," knew more or less nothing of a broad swath of the rest of society. With Ennahda's breakthrough at the "Arab Spring" elections to the Constituent Assembly in 2012, one Tunisian woman clear-sightedly conceded that "We understood less of Tunisia than the tourists did." In even starker fashion, the same was the case in Algeria. On the eve of the Muslim Brotherhood's breakthrough, it was clear that a certain Algeria, a certain Tunisia, and—with some nuances—a broad component of the French-speaking Egyptian Coptic bourgeoisie (see Chapter 4, pp. 68–9) knew nothing of whole swaths of their own societies.

At the end of June 1990, in the eastern suburbs of Algiers, at Friday prayer time, the great mosque of Kouba could house only a tiny fraction of the faithful. The impressive flood of those unable to enter filled the vast esplanade, allowing me to witness with my own eyes the FIS's startling ability to bring out the crowds. Back in the Glycines Diocesan Center, I was confronted by the surprise of one of its administrators. "Twenty years in Algeria!" he enjoyed telling his guests. "But tell me, Burgat: Where are their voters? Tell me, where are they? And who are they? Believe you me, Burgat, my secretary's father is an FLN member—that says everything, right—and she's as stunned as I am! Who on earth can it be that voted for those people?" One Algeria—the one that was familiar to us—knew (almost) nothing of another Algeria. And neither did we.

"So, Mr. Burgat, what is it that's happening to us?" So I was asked a few days later by Mohamed El-Mili Brahimi, the Algerian minister of education, with kindly irony ... and with highly affected innocence. Along with two of his government colleagues, days after the earthquake of the FIS's victory in the local elections, they did me the honor of soliciting my point of view as the author of *The Islamic Movement in North Africa*. The book had, so it seemed, intrigued at least some of the members of the political class. "Oh, Minister, nothing serious, nothing serious. As you know, these are merely your children! Your children of flesh and blood. And your ... political children. They really are the children of the FLN."

The two worlds that had rubbed shoulders in Algeria oblivious to each other were now set to see one another. But they were mainly to lead battle against each other. The battle was terribly lopsided, given the army's cohesion and the unqualified support of Algeria's European and Arab neighbors. It was to take several more decades—decades that are not yet over—for these two worlds to get back to the stage of cohabiting, without acknowledging one another for all that. The press, in France especially, only very rarely helped to bridge this formidable chasm of incomprehension. Rather, it did quite the opposite. It widened it day after day, in the dailies and the magazines both. There too, the aggressive "ultra-secularism" of Algeria's small minority of "eradicators" of the Other is the root of many misunderstandings—eradicators whom France deigns to acknowledge as its sole legitimate informants. The native informant—better yet, the native informant woman—is she who, armed with the legitimacy conferred upon her by the fact she is called "Rachida," tells us what we want to hear. Namely: that which scarcely helps us to situate ourselves realistically in the world in which we are searching for bearings.

On this front, Europe made no faster progress than France did—far from it. As early as 2006 I presented a report to the European Parliament, in the presence of Michel Rocard. In it, I condemned "the slowness with which the European Union identifies alternative partners within civil societies and the political opposition. It has proved especially and persistently unable to set up any contact at all with the rising generation of moderate Islamist movements." I insisted on the urgency of broadening the EU's narrow and selective understanding of Arab "civil societies," and its reigning doctrine that constrained it to deal only with the components of those societies that wage indiscriminate war against Islamists, whatever shape and form they come in.[10]

The outline of my analysis was unfortunately to be confirmed in the context of the Israeli–Palestinian conflict. When Hamas swept parliamentary elections in 2006, the EU had the wretched reaction we have already discussed (see Chapter 6, pp. 103–4), just as it did later, during the Arab Springs. In July 2013, the overthrow of Egypt's elected president, Mohammed Morsi, and the active and hypocritical support the European Commissioner Catherine Ashton conferred on General Abdel Fattah al-Sissi, very swiftly displayed the flagrant limits to stirrings of flexibility in the EU's policy. Ashton quite clearly considered that Sissi was going to restore "freedoms under threat." Looking back, many Egyptians are rather reconsidering that notion. Had I any remaining doubts on the matter, the words spoken in 2013 by Mrs. Ashton's right-hand man would have burst any remaining bubble. The EU's External Relations office (Relex) had invited me to Brussels for a meeting to evaluate the EU's "Neighborhood Policy." As I outlined my reservations concerning the EU reaction to Sissi's coup, the answer was: "But Mr. Burgat: in Egypt, there was no democratic process—merely a 'majoritarian' process."

And yet: in Paris and Brussels, it takes us an enormously long time to come to terms with the obvious. Why might that be?

Jean Lacouture: "Don't Ask Me to Go Any Further!"

The gap between Europe and the world of the secular Arab nationalism of such figures as Nasser and Algeria's first president, Ben Bella, had very quickly been filled in by part of the European intelligentsia. This intelligentsia fully acknowledged them as legitimate political actors, and accompanied them in their rise. For an overwhelming share of this intelligentsia, the next stretch of road remained closed off: the path that leads to a more rational understanding of Islamism. As the late journalist Jean Lacouture[11] confided to me, during a cordial meeting in Cairo in the early 1990s: "I managed to get all the way to Gamal Abdel Nasser. So please, kindly don't ask me to go any further."

There's none so deaf as will not hear. French society was barely over the shock of the independence era. It was not about to hear out a discourse that was liable to deprive it of the comforts of certainties acquired during its colonial-hegemony phase. For the longest time, the privileged mediators of our relationship with the South of the Mediterranean remained those who were themselves at odds with at least part of their society. In a context in which our fleeting political and cultural hegemony over the South was disappearing into thin air, we constantly caved in to the easy option. We based our understanding of North Africa or the Levant almost entirely on the understanding of those few who thought as we did. These were, first, "ultra-secular" North Africans. Then, in the Middle East, Lebanese and Egyptian Christians—including when these were close to, or members of, the far right. For decades, whenever the moment came to "explain" the Muslim world, it was they who were conspicuously overrepresented in the programming, and even the staffing, of French public service broadcasting.

Only rarely did we concern ourselves with assessing the reality of how firmly grounded (or otherwise) these privileged spokespersons were in democratic principles. To be "one of us," they had only to repeat that, "like us," they were struggling against "Islamists." Since these "Islamists" were, since time immemorial and *ad vitam aeternam*, incompatible with the worldview that we shared. Doubtless not everything that our Maronite, Copt, or ultra-secular friends whispered in our ears was false. Sadly, it was hardly the case that all of it was true, either. In fact, things were a little more complex than that. And this deficit of understanding cost us dearly. Unstoppably, it came to harden up our blind and reckless support for Arab authoritarian regimes, from Zine al-Abidine Ben Ali through Mubarak and now Sissi ... With all the grievously costly consequences that were to ensue.

I had countless opportunities to experience first-hand the symptoms of our difficulty in grasping the dynamics that were transforming our

Arab environment. In Cairo between 1989 and 1993, I used to bring my most distinguished visitors to the peak of a minaret, at the end of the truly magical Moez Eddine Allah Street. The very well-known journalist whose guide I was contemplated Cairo, the city that would not sleep. For several months, based in Algiers, it was he who had been tasked with explaining to the readers of a certain "great French evening broadsheet" why the nasty beardy representatives of the Islamic Salvation Front had triumphed at the Algerian ballot box in 1990—at the expense of the nice secular feminist "members of civil society" whose fears we shared so spontaneously. The journalist was moved. This was the first time in his life that he was entering a mosque. Before him rose a forest of minarets and domes—mosques, but also the majestic palaces of medieval Cairo. All of a sudden, a revelation overcame him. He could not resist sharing it with me. "They *really do* have a civilization!"

Let me invoke (without exaggerating its importance—and with no intention to be malicious, since such is not the point of this exercise) another example to illustrate the extreme empathy sometimes developed by those Western foreign correspondents who are too comfortably ensconced within official portrayals of the tensions inherent to the breakthroughs of oppositions in general—and of Islamist oppositions in particular. ("Islamists are the enemies of democracy, of women, and—where applicable—of Copts" ...) A top editor at the Paris headquarters of the "great evening broadsheet" was passing through Cairo and had invited me to lunch at the table of the imperial Mena House. His paper's Cairo correspondent joined us—a man, for that matter, as charming as he was ... immovable from his posting. The conversation inevitably did the rounds of the favorite subjects of Cairo-expatriate small talk. Very quickly, therefore, we gave ourselves up to the inevitable broken record on the hideous traffic jams of the giant metropolis.

The (too) permanently posted correspondent of the Great Investigative Newspaper launched into an audacious description of the foolproof method he had devised to overcome the problem. "It's very simple! I've found the secret. I live above my office." From the third word onwards, the tone of his voice became hesitant. But it was too late. He could only limp to the end of his terrible confession: "I almost never leave the house." Naturally, such an observation in no way implies that this "armchair analyst" symptom does not also plague the ranks of academics. This includes some of those who have "expatriated" themselves to make their field of research their home for the long term—and who have perhaps made it rather too comfortable a home.

Notes

1 The "White Fathers" ("Les Pères Blancs," officially "The African missionaries") are a congregation founded in 1868 in Algiers, with the specific goal of evangelizing Algeria and Africa.
2 Strictly in keeping with the critiques often formulated by Mohammed Arkoun, George Corm writes: "What I term here Arab anti-national ideology, developed by the new Islamist Arab intellectuals, is spreading rapidly. The media and academic research amplify it to an exceptional degree, often disproportionately so. This contributes even more to rendering barely visible the persistence within Arab societies of an endogenous thought that is energetic, rationalist and critical, including in the religious field." (Georges Corm, *Pensée et politique dans le monde arabe. Contextes historiques et problématiques, xixe-xxie siècle*, La Découverte, Paris, 2015).
3 Gordon Thomas, *Gideon's Spies: Secret History of the Mossad*, St. Martin's Press, New York, 2000, features a (likely incomplete) list. It also details the many methods set up by Mossad to engage in disinformation in the press and in Western political circles. Since the author's idea of violence very coarsely reflects only Israel's perception of it, his mention of some of the methods used by the "only democracy in the Middle East" can in principle be considered to be highly plausible (and certainly short of reality). I encountered these methods in person on several occasions.
4 François Burgat, "Intégristes, la voie tunisienne?" *Grand Maghreb*, no. 33–4, October 1, 1984.
5 François Burgat, "Intégristes, la voie tunisienne?"
6 Pierre Tévanian has faithfully retraced this undeserved diversion of Maxrist thought when confronted with religion (Pierre Tévanian, *La Haine de la religion. Comment l'athéisme est devenu l'opium du peuple de gauche*, La Découverte, Paris, 2013).
7 The best example of the leftist Trotskyist bias is provided by Gilbert Achcar's systematic refusal to acknowledge the pluralistic and evolving dimension of Islamism. Sonia Herbrun (reviewing Achcar's *Morbid Symptoms: Relapse in the Arab Uprising*, Stanford University Press, Palo Alto, 2016) writes: "Achcar retraces the steps of the Syrian disaster. He ascribes to it a twofold cause. On the one hand, US policy; and on the other, all-out 'Islamist fundamentalism.' This interpretative framework, that threads throughout the book, is distinctly lacking in complexity. It fails to take into account the fact that subscribing to parties and movements featuring some reference to Islam was also part of the revolutionary process—and that these parties and movements have been various, and featured internal divisions, something that François Burgat consistently repeats and demonstrates." Along the same lines, Dayan Herzbrun argues: "In a recent article (Nawaat.org, 9 January 2017) the Tunisian intellectual Sadri Khiari observed that 'Ennahda's popular base was no mere question of "religious conservatism" or manipulation. Rather—and whether or not one recognizes oneself in it—it was one expression of the revolution. The real

revolution, beautiful and ugly at once—but not of the counter-revolution.' It is, however, not always easy to admit these facts and to draw their consequences." Dayan Herzbrun, "Grandeur et décadence des révolutions arabes," *En attendant Nadeau*, February 5, 2017, www.en-attendant-nadeau.fr/2017/02/05/revolutions-arabes-achcar/ (last accessed June 15, 2019).

8 Nicolas Dot-Pouillard, "Les gauches arabes orphelines de revolutions," *Moyen-Orient*, no. 29, January–March 2016, https://halshs.archives-ouvertes.fr/halshs-01272224/document (last accessed June 15, 2019).

9 Just this once, it was on the front page of *Le Monde* that I had the privilege of conveying my analysis of the FIS victory in the local elections of June 12, 1990. ("Sous le voile de l'islamisme algérien," *Le Monde*, June 18, 1990). I wrote: "On the cheap—since these local elections do not instantly call into question the institutional balance of one of our key Mediterranean partners—, the electric shock of June 12 may prompt us to lift the veil from a political movement which our perception of has not yet overcome the stage of repulsion for. But we are now going to have to learn to live with it."

10 "What the Arab World Expects from the European Union: The Disappointed Hope of an Alternative to the United States?" Direction générale pour les politiques externes de l'Union, Direction B, Département thématique, October 2006, https://journals.openedition.org/anneemaghreb/409 (last accessed June 15, 2019). The report was commissioned by the European Parliament's Committee on Foreign Affairs, presided over by Stefan Krauss. Part of it read: "Can one earn the trust of a people while being considered the indulgent ally of its two main 'enemies' (Israel and the Arab autocrats)? [...] How can the EU earn the trust of the peoples of Libya, Algeria, Tunisia etc, when it rolls out the red carpets for those countries' leaders—when everything should lead it to condemn them for systematically flouting the most basic right and liberties?"

11 Jean Lacouture (1921–2015) was among the authors and foreign correspondents (for *Combat, France Soir, Le Monde* ...) who, in line with the Communists' commitment, expressed the French left's empathy for emancipatory political dynamics in the Middle East and East Asia, by echoing the aspirations of the "secular nationalist" generation of independence.

10

Saving the Other's "Others": A French Obsession

To this day, the (very) French difficulty in reaching a rational relationship with Islamic Otherness is expressed through a tendency to refuse to communicate directly with the Other in corporeal form. How much cosier it is to not have to look in the eye the hideous Arabic-speaking, Muslim, Arab male, guilty of every sin. So what if, along with his *hijab*-clad wife, they make up the demographic majority in the region? We more or less consciously prefer to deal with those who, in the immediate vicinity of those creatures, have the good taste to be (like us honest folk) in tension or in a competitive relationship with them.

Since time immemorial, we have displayed a consistent tendency. We are willing to enter into this Other's world only through the door of its "minorities," whether these be ethnic, religious, generational, or, more recently, sexual. Anyone, that is, except the Other "in person"—that impertinent, formerly colonized subject! So it is that we have always indulged in a proven fondness for "Berbers," "Copts," and "Maronites." Failing to unearth agnostics in sufficient number, we often also rest great hopes in "Sufi mystics"—forgetting along the way that their Brotherhoods were, in the 19th century, the spearhead of resistance to colonial aggression.

Middle Eastern Christians: "Us" Amidst the "Other"?

Religious minorities have not featured among my key research themes. My inclination has been never to let them overwhelm the perspectives that enable us to understand the dynamics affecting the majority population. Our privileged interest in those among the Other's religious and political fabric with whom we share an ideological, linguistic, or religious solidarity is actually very ordinary. They are those who, amidst the Other, constitute "a little part of ourselves." They provide a path into the Other's world that is less forbiddingly steep than the path that leads to the Other directly. They comfort us in the soundness and the universality of our beliefs and practices. We also like French speakers drowned within the American

English-speaking masses. We like them all the more when they are a minority within a whole that is perceived as being potentially hostile to them. "Long live Free Quebec!" General de Gaulle felt the need to exclaim in 1967. The same scenario applies, in the same way, to Middle Eastern Christians. It is a small step from there to striving to intervene in the status held by these minorities within the political fabric in which they live. All the more so since we are convinced that we are helping them by doing so. Europeans, and the French in particular, have always taken that plunge with gusto. "Defending minorities" in the Muslim world has, then, been a historical pretext for interventions whose goals were not necessarily so ethical or humanist. From 1920 to 1946, France, having been granted its Mandate over Syria, was in a position of colonial hegemony there. It therefore intervened decisively "on behalf of Christians," by creating a state tailor-made for them: Lebanon. In doing so, it set about dividing up the subjects of the former Ottoman province on a religious basis (Alawi, Druze, Christian, etc.). France, world heavyweight champion of secularism, was doing abroad the opposite of what it preached at home.

It may seem as if those days are gone—but are they really? With respect to French attitudes towards Christian minorities in the Middle East, the problem is as much the principle (when such action comes from the state) as (when it comes from the private sphere) it is the method, and its meaning. For instance, the selective interest with respect to visas granted to Christian Iraqis that France's president and his foreign minister expressed, put into practice and made political capital from in 2015, mangles every principle of equality of treatment that the republican framework commands in dealings with citizens of a foreign country.[1]

European NGOs set up in support of the Christians of the Middle East reflect a very commonplace and perfectly legitimate solidarity between co-religionists. Rather less strictly humanist variables are also, however, at play. Such NGOs are often exploited, if not set up from scratch, to serve a political agenda that favors delegitimizing the Syrian opposition. Many Syrian political activists who happen to be Christian (including the very media-friendly Mother Marie-Agnès de la Croix) exert their energies principally to portray the Assad regime as the "protector of minorities." Yet a closer look has long shown that Bashar al-Assad, like his father Hafez, has done rather less protecting of these minorities than he has exploited them to protect himself. Loudly asserting a specific solidarity with Christian Syrians has thereby become a means to divert attention from the very ... "secular" and universal framework of the Syrian crisis, which is very far from boiling down to the purported danger that Islamists represent for Christians. "Long live the Christians of the Middle East!" thus begins to sound like a cry of defiance towards the most legitimate, oppositional hopes of the Muslim majority. It serves to imply that the Syrian opposition has failed to provide sufficient evidence of its "secularism." Granted, it must be understood in this case that what is demanded of Syrians is "French-style secularism." Namely: to be absolutely impervious, not only to the radical strands of Islamism, but to any Islamism at all—if not to any Sunni identity whatsoever.

Among the paradoxes of this French republican fascination for the Christians of the Middle East is that, were these Christians to be transplanted into the European political field, many of them, from the banks of the Nile to Mount Lebanon, would, *mutatis mutandis*, find themselves on the most radical fringes of the National Front—at least insofar as their relationship towards Muslim Otherness is concerned. In Lebanon, "minority syndrome" has produced anti-Muslim tensions that can easily compete with the worst excesses that France produced during the colonial period and in its aftermath. (It has also, through a fantasized "Phoenician" identity, produced anti-Arab reflexes.[2]) A source close to the rector of a major Christian university told me a few years ago that his views "would, if he held them in public, have him shipped off to the International Criminal Court." One day in February, a friend who expressed surprise that the wind from the east had made the snow in a little ski resort in Mount Lebanon melt too fast for his taste earned the following reply from a local notable: "That's the wind that comes from the Arabs; it blows nothing but trouble." In Egypt, certain Christian spokespeople who are among the most reliable fixtures of our grand official meetings with "the Christians of the Middle East" regularly reach for the worst of the shortcuts favored by the French far right when they mention the (Muslim Brotherhood) victors at the ballot boxes of the Arab Spring in Egypt.[3]

These excessive attempts to "defend the Christians of the Middle East" are all the more popular in that they water the very fertile soil of growing hostility, both intellectual and popular, to the Muslim presence in Europe. In practice, the call to "save the Christians of the Middle East" often joins with the various expressions of rising Islamophobia in Europe. The unremitting focus on "Christians of the Middle East" tends to comfort Islamophobia's darkest urges, from criminalizing Palestinian resistance to rallying against attacks "on secularism" or on national "identity." Unsurprisingly, it most often serves to cloud interpretation of political transformations in the Middle East. Which is why I have always tried to distance myself from it.

The Other's Women: Freeing Brown Women from Brown Men Who Resist Us?

In my research, women have held no less important a position than men. But, how can I put this ... no more than that! I have endeavored not to dissociate the study of their trajectory too systematically from that of the rest of society. To the question "How do Arab women vote?" my provocative answer has tended to be: "Just as their fathers, husbands, brothers, and sons do." To the great displeasure of some of my interlocutors—and more so of some of the women among them—who can conceive of the women of this region of the world only as unanimously at war with their men's chauvinism—if not, with none too much nuance, against their own religion.[4]

I have, therefore, often distanced myself from the very French fascination with what I have long ironically termed the "cause of the Other's women." Beyond the "Muslim women" whom we dream of protecting, and for the very same reasons, we French have a repetitive tendency to "love" the Other's "youth" (and more especially, their young women), in impassioned and selective fashion. This French obsession conceals an ancient desire to exorcize the rough edges of our relationship towards the alarming mass of their fathers, brothers, and husbands.[5] We prefer Rachida to her husband Rachid—and, better yet, we prefer their daughter who, like all young Muslim women, must be presumed only to be awaiting our assistance (disinterested, of course) to help her free herself from the violence and chauvinism of her male surroundings.

The "defense of women" trope exploits powerful intuitive expectations: the legitimacy and universality of their rights, and condemnation of patriarchal or male-chauvinist domination. These produce emotional affects that prevent seeing the political backdrop to other processes of domination—and that therefore foreclose dealing with it. Such mobilization in favor of women in political environments that we consider hostile (Afghanistan, Iran, Palestine), when it operates out of context, often serves to mask to public opinion (informed as it is in highly one-sided fashion) another, trivially political mode of domination exercised over their social group as a whole: domination by ... us, or by our unswerving allies. Under the cover of defending one component of society, the rhetoric of some Western and Arab defenders of the "rights of women" serves to conceal assaults on values that are yet more fundamental.

The archetype of this exploitation of what is best in the universal, to serve the worst of political interests, is provided when some in the Western media devote their spreads to the "cause of Palestinian women" who prefer to fight Hamas than to fight the Israeli occupation. (Naturally, it is in that role only that we are invited to support them.) That particular trick is nothing new under the sun: colonial France always promoted its altruistic role as promoter of the colonized subject's women ... Similarly, throughout the history of decolonization, anticolonial activism was frequently denounced as running the risk of endangering ... the rights of those women, as those rights were promoted by the colonizing power. Already in 1988, the Indian academic Gayatri Spivak had demystified this "cause of the Other's women" through the celebrated phrase "White men saving brown women from brown men."[6] Over time, and beyond the independence era, this "cause" very often became exploited, in rightist and leftist rhetoric alike, to conceal the mechanisms of North–South domination again—and again.

For several decades, French diplomacy has, then, had a weapon of mass dissuasion ready to bring out against all those who threaten its material or strategic interests: it threatens to liberate their daughters, wives and mothers, from their intolerable patriarchal or conjugal domination. It is hardly a secret, however, that Western embassies show more interest in liberating Iranian or Afghan women than in liberating, say, Saudi ones. So it was that the promoters of the "War on Terror" (that has, since it was launched in 2001, cost a 2015 estimate of between 1.3 and 2 million victims[7]) justified it by its defending the cause of women. In May 2007, the day he was elected president, Nicolas Sarkozy pronounced the aims of the militarization of his Middle Eastern diplomacy in the following terms: "To all women who are oppressed throughout the world, I wish to say this: it will be France's pride and its duty to stand at their side. [...] France will not abandon those women sentenced to the *burqa*; France will not abandon those women deprived of freedom." On both the right and the left, there is only one kind of violence which it is both politically correct and profitable to condemn and to combat: the only kind that produces victims noble enough to let us temporarily forget our sacrosanct migration quotas. This is not the violence that plays out in Guantanamo, Abu Ghraib, or Gaza. It is the violent chauvinism of Muslim males against their daughters and their wives. And so it is that the tune of the old colonial refrain remains de rigueur: how dare you complain, you whose wives we are so busy liberating?

Finally, the "defense of the condition of women" trope, faithful ally of the rhetoric of colonial domination, has been an intrinsic component of the repressive arsenal of Arab authoritarian regimes. It has long served as a smokescreen for the repression of any Islamist opposition, conducted with perfect impunity. (It was for a good cause!) In Tunisia, it was a key component of Ben Ali's legitimacy. In Algeria, too, during the dark years of the civil war, the "defense of women" trope made great contributions towards justifying an exclusively repressive policy, and the suicidal rejection of any call to allow Islamists to take part in any negotiated resolution to the crisis. Lined up against the "fundamentalists," a handful of intransigent "secularists" were set up as the sole representatives of a society, the struggle of whose women they were very far from being representative of. These were—belatedly—condemned as mere "state feminists." In a blaze of slogans that exploited every timeworn Western fear of Islam, they managed to have the false idea accredited that struggles against these regimes were struggles "against women." As such, the fight to defend the status quo became a fight for the values defended by the West. It took many long years for Europe to start glimpsing a less reductive reality.

As for the sons of those whom the French Republic had imported by the thousands to ensure post-war growth, those were to stay in line, conscientiously kept away from the benches of both government and parliament. They, to be sure, would harm our "national identity." Let them then rot in their ghetto-suburbs. How could those whose wives wear such long garments dare complain of a domination that brings unto them the Enlightenment of modernity? Welcome, however, welcome! to the wives of potentially bearded men—and to those only. Without examining their talents too closely, we are even ready to grant them government positions ... tailor-made for them. It will now be for them to protect us against the common threat, to them and us both, that is embodied in their fathers, their husbands, and their brothers. No surprise here: from Rachida (Dati) to Najat (Vallaud-Belkacem) through Rama (Yade),[8] there is a flagrant male–female gap in the French Republic's achievements in opening up government to include representatives of Muslim and other kinds of "diversity." Mohammed and Rachid? They can wait ...

Spot the mistake. Is it that obvious? Apparently not so, when we witness the zeal with which each new generation replicates it. The "defense of women" in Iran, like that of homosexuals in Gaza or elsewhere, valid as it is in itself, often conceals a refusal to condemn—if not a tendency to condone—the oppression suffered by their societies as a whole, and which those societies' women suffer from too ... One might see in this something of a "hijacking" of the "universal"—to rather ignoble ends.

She Doesn't Critique Her Religion as We Do. All the Same: Could She Be One of Us?

How this obsession with the "cause of the Other's women" plays out opens onto a far broader question than that of gender alone.[9] This is the question, conducive to every analytical shortcut, of how compatible religious practice may be with the dynamics of social modernization. Examining the question attentively allows us to approach the deep roots of the hostility of *homo occidentalus*, who has become dechristianized more than he has become secular, towards his challenger, *homo islamicus*. (*Homo islamicus*, for his part, is "religious" before he even acquires "Muslim" status.) The lessons to be drawn from such an examination are liable to be profitably extrapolated far beyond the question of gender.

In the main, the reason why "secular" feminists refuse to acknowledge the legitimacy of the approach of their "Islamic" fellows is clear enough. They refute the idea that submitting to a religious rule, through which some female Muslims justify some of their social practices (in particular, the wearing of the *hijab*), could possibly have a different valence to that which it had in the historicity of their own experience, and in the individual or collective trajectory of *their* activism. They thereby consider that feminist "Islamic" self-assertion strictly contradicts the ideal of emancipation for which they themselves struggled.[10] In so doing, they refuse to so much as glimpse the possibility that the historical context in which the struggle of these Muslim women has been inscribed for several decades might be somewhat specific.[11]

Yet that specificity is a reality. Since, unlike the feminist mobilization of their Western sisters, the mobilization of "Islamic feminists" has in some sense two distinct targets. First, Muslim women emancipate themselves as women, in a process that is relatively comparable to that of the Christian and Jewish women who often boast of having gone before them. They confront patriarchal and male-chauvinist traditions. Unarguably, to legitimate themselves, those traditions have never been shy in wielding circumstantial interpretations of religious norms. But "Islamic feminists" also happen to be members of a community (the community of Muslims) that is itself collectively engaged in a process of liberation and self-assertion with respect to the political, economic, and cultural tutelage of the West, inherited from the era of colonial domination. This process, however, includes a dimension of identity-assertion within which—and radically unlike in the Western historical process—religion is not an obstacle to be torn down. Religion is thus not a bogeyman here. It is, in context, a foothold and a reservoir of "endogenous" references, mobilized to counter the tendency of dominant Western culture to sustain its hegemony.

The attitude of suspicion that so-called secular feminists direct towards so-called Islamic feminism is thus not so very different from the more generalized attitude of suspicion by *homo occidentalus* towards the use of Islamic "vocabulary" towards ends of assertion of identity and cultural emancipation. These activists harbor the pernicious conviction that the vocabulary which *they* used, and the itineraries that *they* took to express universal (feminist) demands, are the only practicable ones. They fail to recognize the legitimacy of aspirations that emanate from political players who use a different vocabulary and reference points other than their own. Those aspirations are in many ways identical: enhancing the autonomy of women within the sphere of the family on the one hand, and within public space on the other, whether political or economic. Instead, they focus on stakes (clothing, for instance) that belong in the cultural sphere, and that remain alien to the matter at hand: the dynamic of emancipation.

Can she be "one of us," she who abstains from critiquing her religion "like we do"? Such is the question that secular feminists ask themselves. With brutal self-assurance, they answer in the negative, thereby falling into the trap of essentializing their own activist experience. By turning the universal principle of women's struggle for emancipation into an ethnic question, they deprive themselves of the means for a careful, modest assessment that would take the time to decenter itself within the historicity of their Muslim sisters. They would then come to see that their "itch" on the subject has no basis.

Dare one conclude by suggesting that, in the field of cultural and religious codification of dress, the British have made greater steps forward than have their French neighbors—in particular with respect to the *hijab*, but not only that? Can one be a policeman or -woman, even if one wears a funny turban and a long beard—and even if that beard is wrapped in a curious net? When Britain and France were confronted by the decolonization of their respective empires, France, to whom form (the form of the head-covering worn by a public servant) was indistinguishable from content (the content of their task) replied in the negative. The United Kingdom said yes. UK police forces thus hired "Sikhs" in great numbers. Since November 2015, one such Sikh is Canada's defense minister in the government led by Justin Trudeau. I was for a time among the many who accused the Anglo-Saxon system of indulging in the naughty "communitarianism" that "French-style secularism" boasted of having rescued the French Republic from. Today, those still in that camp may well ask themselves the question. How is it that French super-secularism has yet to display its ability to bring to office a black president (as in the United States), a Muslim mayor (as in London)—or a Sikh minister (as in Montreal)?

Notes

1 The political signaling was consistent. Secular France granted visas to Iraqi refugees selectively, on the basis of their being Christian. On March 21, 2015, President François Hollande honored them with his presence, and a speech, during a ceremony to welcome them. A few days earlier, on March 12, he had specifically visited Christian refugees in a church in Erbil, etc.
2 The Phoenicians were traders and sailors based in the cities of Byblos (Jbeil),

Tyre (Sour), Sidon (Saïda), and on the island of Arwad (off the coast of Tartus in Syria). The theme of "Phoenician identity" is often raised in Lebanon by partisans of an alternative to the region's Arabism.

3 See the "demonstration" of the "reality of Islamic fascism" made by Father Henri Boulad at the French National Assembly on May 27, 2015 (invited there by the right-wing Les Républicains parliamentarian Jean-Frédéric Poisson), as he commented on the sensitive issue of the political transition in Egypt. Here is what Sophie Duran, on the far-right *Riposte Laïque* website, made of it: "Islam is totalitarian, supremacist, globalizing. It is a version of fascism. It is not a religion. [...] It is a system, an ideology—worse than Nazism in a sense, because Islam takes religious form, and it is even harder to escape this new religious-tinted fascism than it was to escape Nazism" (www.youtube.com/watch?v=4kSouGyu1qU (last accessed June 15, 2019)).

4 See Lila Abu-Lughod, *Do Muslim Women Need Saving?*, Harvard University Press, Cambridge, MA, 2013.

5 See François Burgat, preface to Laurent Bonnefoy and Myriam Catusse (eds), *Jeunesses arabes. Du Maroc au Yémen: loisirs, cultures et politiques*, La Découverte, Paris, 2013.

6 Quoted in Zahra Ali, "Les Femmes et le genre en Irak," PhD thesis in Sociology supervised by Nilüfer Göle, Écoles des hautes études en sciences sociales, Paris, 2015.

7 By the count of the German NGO IPPNW (1985 Laureate of the Nobel Peace Prize), Physicians for Social Responsibility and Physicians for Global Survival, "Body Count: Casualty Figures of the 'War on terror.' Iraq, Afghanistan, Pakistan," March 2015, https://auratrifu.wordpress.com/2015/05/01/body-count-casualty-figures-after-10-years-of-the-war-on-terror-iraq-afghanistan-pakistan/ (last accessed June 15, 2019).

8 Rachida Dati was justice minister and Rama Yade minister for foreign affairs and human rights, then for sports, under the presidency of Nicolas Sarkozy. Najad Vallaud-Belkacem was education minister under President Hollande.

9 For a sample of this very rich debate, see Rabab El-Mahdi, "Does Political Islam Impede Gender-Based Mobilization? The Case of Egypt," *Totalitarian Movements and Political Religions*, vol. 11, no. 3–4, 2010, pp. 379–96. See also the foundational contributions of Fariba Adelkhah concerning Iran; of Nilufer Göle concerning Turkey; and, of course, Saba Mahmood, *Politics of Piety: The Islamic Revival and the Feminist Subject*, Princeton University Press, Princeton, NJ, 2012; and *Religious Difference in a Secular Age: The Minority Report*, Princeton University Press, Princeton, NJ, 2016.

10 See Zahra Ali (ed.), *Féminismes islamiques*, La Fabrique, Paris, 2012; « Décoloniser le féminisme », *Ballast*, June 11, 2016, www.cairn.info/revue-travail-genre-et-societes-2014-2-page-178.htm and www.revue-ballast.fr/zahra-ali/ (last accessed June 15, 2019).

11 Concerning this debate, cf. also Rabab El-Mahdi, "Does Political Islam Impede Gender-Based Mobilization?"

11

The Political Cost of Dissent

Before he became "Muslim," the Other was once "Arab." Even before the alchemy of the rise of political Islam took us from the era of the *"fellagas"* into the age of the "fundamentalists," the ethnic and linguistic Othering of Arabness had been quite enough to create powerful reflexes of rejection towards it. Things took a distinct turn for the worse, however, once the Other, after he had "spoken Arab" to us, got it into his head to start wanting to "speak Muslim" too.

The Egyptian jurist and writer Tarek al-Bishri was one of the influential landmarks of my education "in Islamism," and one of the most helpful in verifying and intellectualizing my intuitions in the field. "So long as we expressed our nationalist and emancipatory ambitions through the languages of Marxism and nationalism," al-Bishri explained to me in Cairo in 1992, "there was always one or other political strand in the West to understand us and even, sometimes, to support us. As soon as—in order to express very strictly the same political demands—we began to use the vocabulary of Islam, the breach became absolute. We were out on our own." Keeping everything in proportion, I was myself to be left "out on my own" for many long years, in the same way as those who had set about asserting the legitimacy of their "Muslim speech."

Up Against the War Machine of Disinformation

In any event, in Algeria as elsewhere, the ability of Islamist political players to communicate with Western audiences was always especially weak. For good reason. It is difficult, if not counter-productive, to seek out the support of the very audience from which self-assertion requires that one distance oneself. Despite the belated and often clumsy efforts of the Muslim Brotherhood in this regard, this patent weakness in communication terms logically played a part in delaying the emergence of any coherent and rational perception of the Islamist agenda. Incidentally, it also distinctly complicated the task of those few who, as I did, thought it important to bring out a better-informed and more challenging interpretation of Islamism as a process of reactive repositioning. Moreover, the partisans of "speaking Muslim," because they had no centralized organization, and because they were inexperienced and unprofessional, systematically became favorite targets to be set up for infiltration and stings by their powerful foes on both sides of the Mediterranean. Those foes were at the crossroads of the active complicity of the authoritarian regimes ranged against those "speaking Muslim"—and of the growing support for these regimes by their own leftist opposition.

To this day, a strand of the Arab political classes—the one that has easiest access to our media—has remained stuck in a stance of indiscriminate rejection of the Islamist generation. This rejectionism is as emotional as it is schematic. Because the Islamist generation threatens its own symbolic and political hegemony, and, therefore, its material hegemony too, it pushes this strand towards sustaining authoritarian models. In this respect, the Arab Spring constituted a kind of "working-out" of the Algerian precedent of the 1990s on the scale of the entire region.

Granted: from Aziz Krichen[1] to Salima Ghezali[2] through, for a time at least, Louisa Hanoune[3] (before she rallied the regime and sank into an opportunism that prefigured the Egyptian left), a few intellectuals and actors outside of the Islamist camp have avoided the pitfalls of falling into the "eradicatory" narrative. In much greater numbers, however, from Samir Amin[4] to Sonallah Ibrahim[5] and Alaa al-Aswany,[6] many of the "greats" of the Egyptian left have pathetically rushed into the warm embrace of the counter-revolution.[7] In so doing, they aped their counterparts of twenty years earlier in Algeria—in particular those of the PAGS.[8] Through the press and politicians, but also through the devastating contributions of countless artists, writers, and mercenaries of the pen, the breach opened up by Islamist self-assertion was thus exported into Western public opinion—in especially reductive form. No need even to mention the Syrian crisis in this context. Whole swaths of that history remain to be written—in the case of Algeria, but also in Tunisia and Egypt.

Let us take up one exemplary case among so many: the shameless lamentation by the novelist Yasmina Khadra. Khadra also happens to be an "eradicatory" Algerian army officer, who for a long time hid behind the female pen name he wrote under. He was a zealous defender of the spotlessness of the army that employed him, and denied the horrors of its "Condor *bis*" operation.[9] In 2002, in *The Duplicity of Words*,[10] Khadra shamelessly delivered an all-out defense of the Algerian *junta*, invoking his own "truth" and personal "honesty." He brazenly counterpointed these with the supposed "imposture" that he ascribed to the Paris intelligentsia.[11] From his perch in Paris, and for a variety of reasons, Yasmina Khadra was not alone in bolstering the old shortcuts inherited from colonial domination.¹² In the context of the Algerian civil war, some of these intellectuals and artists acted of their own accord, while others were directly exploited by the intelligence services. In the eyes of French public opinion, they benefited from an unshakeable legitimacy, aided by the active complicity of those whom Bourdieu denounced at the time as the "negative intellectuals."¹³ Throughout the crisis, and against all available evidence, Bernard-Henri Lévy and André Glucksmann blindly buttressed an entirely one-sided distribution of the responsibility for violence. Glucksmann went so far as to term any debate as to who was responsible for the outbreak of armed violence "obscene."

When pro-regime Algerian intellectuals were on tour on the French side of the Mediterranean, it was therefore extremely difficult for me to contradict them. As the Algerian anthropologist Tassadit Yassine explained, they held the upper hand in the media with the greatest of ease: "In Algeria [they] were a tiny minority, even while their media exposure was inversely proportional to their social base. They unconditionally backed the most uncompromising fraction of the army and mastered the art of manipulating the language of democracy to make themselves appear respectable in the Paris newsrooms that were their echo chamber ..." The battle was lopsided.

As it concerned me, this isolation expressed itself in multiple ways. Algeria's Foreign Affairs Ministry had not taken kindly to the contents of *The Islamic Movement in North Africa: The Voice of the South*. In 1989, it solicited and funded a counter-volume from the same publishing house, designed to rebut and to discredit my own approach. A few years later, I pointed out some blatant shortcuts in the analytical treatment of the Islamist movement in that volume to one of its three authors (for whom my friendship has remained intact). With impressive candor, he confessed that "In those days, the point wasn't to explain the Islamists! It was to fight them."

The reproach directed at me was always the same. Long before French Prime Minister Manuel Valls,¹⁴ for some, to "explain" already rhymed with "to justify." By deconstructing the causalities and the mechanisms of processes of radicalization, I was thus accused of condoning such radicalization—if not of nurturing it. I therefore became dubbed the "spokesperson" of the Islamists, their 'little drummer boy," their "fellow traveler," and "useful idiot." In the nuanced phrase of Rachid Boudjedra, the Algerian author of *The FIS of Hate* (1992), I was the "friend of the cutthroats." Let us recall that those whose legitimacy as political actors I was defending against the grain of the time belonged to the family of the Ergodans and the Ghannouchis. As such, subsequent events in Algeria did not exactly undermine my analytical apparatus.

As a result, skirmishes of all kinds, and of various importance—some of them grueling, but all of them instructive—multiplied throughout my professional trajectory as a scholar. As early as 1991, a colleague at the CNRS, who was very firmly embedded within the institutional networks of research on Algeria, demanded in the most official terms that I be disbarred from the French Association for the Study of the Arab and Muslim Worlds (AFEMAM). At the time, this was the federation for our small corporation of researchers. She failed to have her request granted—but the tone had been set.

The Media War of Algeria's Women "Eradicators"

Public appearances were the most common theater of various stunts and stings designed to intimidate and destabilize. These targeted the few who ventured too far from the powerfully dominant received wisdom of the time. This consisted of normalizing hatred of the players of Islamist politics. It allowed the "Arab Pinochets" absolute impunity to apply the political option they had settled on: repression—and more repression. Some of these interventions were "programmed"—sometimes very crudely—by the backroom agencies of these regimes. The Tunisian Agency for Communication Abroad (ATCE) very often sent provocateurs as detractors to public events, recruited in the circles tied to their consulates. In at least one case, at the Free University of Brussels if my memory serves me correctly, an entire row of ladies got to their feet and ostentatiously left the room a few moments after I had begun to speak. The message was clear: this man's words are unacceptable to female ears!

These intellectual and civic confrontations took place before the gaze of an audience that was generally predisposed to hear out the provocateurs, that is, those whom we were not yet many at the time to label the "eradicators." According to an unchanging script, public meetings designed to enlighten their participants ineluctably ended up reinforcing their most primal reflexes instead. In 1995, the founder of one of Algeria's two human rights defense leagues was sat at the rostrum of one of the handsome auditoriums of the Great Arch of Paris's La Défense quarter. He was "struggling," for he had imprudently set out on a path that was as sensitive and hazardous as it was ambitious. Namely: to nuance his audience's understanding of the militants of the Islamic Salvation Front (FIS) who had colonized the media. Like his audience, he fought the FIS from the left he had been raised in. But he did so with slightly more discernment, a little less blindly, without borrowing from the crudest shortcuts disseminated by Algeria's military regime. "Not all of them are beyond the pale," he had dared to say. "It's more complicated than that."

Suddenly, a short-haired woman in the audience shot to her feet. How dare he? For the briefest second, the flame of sectarian hatred of the "beardies" had dimmed in the auditorium. A few well-chosen "self-evident facts" were enough to rekindle it. The potential traitor was swiftly silenced by the near-unanimous ovation that greeted the *pasionara*'s intervention. The defeated party got to his feet. He came down from the rostrum, slowly scaled the steps of the auditorium, and ostentatiously came to sit by my side—I, who was (already) close to being a leper. "You see," he told me, "this woman ... In Algiers, she represents 3 percent of society—no more than that, believe me. But you see what she just did!"

Khalida Messaoudi—for she it was—had failed to scale even those heights. At the head of the eradicators of the small RCD party,[15] she had reached 2.9 percent at the 1991 parliamentary elections. I took away one lesson from this experience. The small fraction of North Africans, and more so still of North African women, who whisper in our ears what we want to hear, in the language that we understand, conceal from us a far more complex reality. I had many other opportunities to put the soundness of that lesson to the test—most often at my own expense.

There are countless examples of this obliviousness of a fraction of North African society. In 2006, I was addressing an audience of at least a thousand at the Averroes Encounters, in the hall of Marseille's Exhibition Center. All of a sudden, the audience broke into a loud shiver of disapproval. I had just pronounced an incongruous phrase that had the unacceptable flavor of sacrilege. One of the most media-friendly representatives of the Tunisian Association of Democratic Women was present—the bearer, on this side of the Mediterranean, of our hopes for a secular-democratic future for the region. I had dared to spell out to her my belief that her movement represented no more than 5 percent of Tunisian society. This was a thought-crime of the highest order. At the time, France was firmly convinced that the cream of the French-speaking, urban, bourgeois elite of Tunisia, concentrated in the town of La Marsa and its surroundings, was the only "healthy" component of Tunisian society. Surely it could only triumph at the polls as soon as the tyrant had departed. I did not share this point of view. But I, too, was making a slight misjudgment ... Six years later, Tunisians did indeed discover the joys of filling their ballot boxes themselves. The small eradicatory al-Massar party had made blaring anti-Islamism its key selling point. It wound up very far short of the 5 percent threshold. Instead, it was the Islamists so loathed by "legitimate" polite society who emerged as the top opposition party—and who saw the gates of power open before them.

In at least one instance, I got the feeling that from on high—this is (almost) how I experienced it—some One had decided that enough was enough. It was in Nantes, in the context of the 1994 "Festival des Allumés," that one of these small "miracles" of justice in (female) human form occurred. Khalida Messaoudi, the *pasionara* whose exploits beneath the Great Arch of La Défense I have just described, affected at the time to be a fierce opponent of Algeria's military regime. Later (from 2003 to 2015), having discharged her (dis)information services to the regime's benefit, she became the immovable culture minister of the military's façade civilian government. The Kabyle demonstrators in Tizi Ouzou had not yet expelled her from their ranks while dubbing her "Khalida Lewinsky," to express their dubiousness regarding her being labeled a "regime opponent," and the realities of her relationship to the regime. That evening, she had had no trouble in grabbing the 400 participants in the meeting by the guts. And so to instantly unplug 400 brains, all too ready to revel in being denied any possibility of understanding anything whatsoever to the tragedy that was unfolding in Algeria.

Khalida Messaoudi regaled the crowd with tales of how the Islamists "slit the throats of young women who refuse to wear the *hijab*." "Nadiiiia ... Nadiiiia ... Butchered! Butchered for refusing to wear the *hijab*," she screamed. The long incantatory lament set off an irrepressible shiver of stunned emotion in the audience facing her. The emotional wave had reached its peak. My task promised to be an impossible one. And yet ... And yet. In the fourth or fifth row, a young woman had just risen to her feet. She asked to be allowed to speak. No doubt she meant to fill out the intolerable list of horrors that all members of the FIS were purported to commit on a daily basis. It took some time for the content of her remarks to become clear, since she sobbed as she spoke. Finally, she was handed a microphone that enabled the audience to hear her. Something like a bomb exploded in the auditorium. "Nadia was my friend. It's true that she was assassinated. But it was by her boyfriend, because he couldn't bear her leaving him. It had nothing to do with the veil. And it had nothing to do with the Islamists, either."

Khalida Messaoudi reeled under the formidable blow of the public unveiling of her imposture. She was unable to resume her speech. She left first the rostrum, then the hall. The event was called to a close. She refused to come and dine with "Al-kalb edhek" ("that dog") (that's me) ... I had indeed just provided her with the opportunity to get bitten very hard. Unless I am mistaken, local media did not report the incident. It was too incongruous amid the atmosphere that then ruled unanimously in France, which outlawed any analytical approach to the new "Algerian question." A mighty lost opportunity there, to glimpse a less linear reality than the one that news agencies hammered us with, paraphrasing the press releases of Algeria's very professional "Military Security" who took great care to paint the Islamist bogeyman it purported to protect us from in the most effectively bloodcurdling way.

"General Security" and the Victory of "the Islamics"

A brief encounter with the agents of the forerunner to the Direction Générale de la Sécurité Intérieure (the French FBI/MI5), the late lamented "General Intelligence" service, enabled me to take the measure of how deeply anchored this emotional blockage of every component of our society was in our institutions. Granted: given how low its stakes were, the encounter was more amusing than it was tragic.

After I had spent six years directing the French Center for Yemeni Studies, from 1997 to 2003, I was informed that the French Foreign Affairs Ministry had—in a very commonplace procedure—decided to add my name to the list of recipients of the National Order of Merit. Paltry ex-"'68er" (of the May '68 generation) that I was, I shared my doubts regarding the wisdom of lending myself to such an undertaking with Rémy Leveau, a founding father of our research institutions. He reminded me of the principle laid down by Mauriac: "One does not request a decoration. One does not wear it. But one does not reject it, either." A year later, in the autumn of 2004, back in Aix-en-Provence, I had the surprise of receiving a summons to the police station. "It's nothing, it's nothing," my interlocutor growled on the phone, "it's about your decoration." A few hours later, I was sat in the office of a police chief of the General Intelligence service. I watched him leaf through the contents of a folder, before he asked me: "So, you support the victory of the 'Islamics,' right? That's it? You're all for the 'Islamics'?" Whereupon he made me list my successive postings and publications. There was nothing in those, of course, to change his mind. But there was also nothing to encourage the ironic wariness that he could barely conceal.

I had already had a run-in with intelligence surveillance a few years earlier. This was in circumstances that perhaps better explained the police chief's irritation with me than was this reminder of the "bad company" I kept. Flashback. For some years I had prided myself on frequenting the Tunisian opposition in exile—the same opposition that the leftist activists rather shamefully turned their backs on. This was for familiar research purposes—but also in the framework of the political commitment of a simple citizen. From 1992, keeping this company earned me a ban on entering Tunisia. And still, in 2019, more than eight years after the fall of Ben Ali's regime, I wait for the record to be lifted that, on each of my visits to Tunis, earns me a lengthy hour or two waiting at the border police post.

In the 1990s, the interlocutors of the Islamist opposition had their work cut out for them. Even the human rights NGOs declined to condemn the horrendous treatment suffered by the activists hunted down by Ben Ali and his Algerian counterparts. Not to mention the left, on either side of the Mediteranean. These rivaled each other in discretion—when they were not engaged in one-upmanship by brandishing the unanswerable self-evident truth of the famous slogan "No freedom for the enemies of freedom!" Twice, Amnesty International thus asked me to meet with its activists who refused to advocate for the ultimate bogeyman: the Tunisian members of the Movement of the Islamic Tendency, whom our "great secular ally" could therefore keep torturing in peace.

In this regard, it was said that, in 1994, Jacques Chirac had personally signed an agreement with President Ben Ali to broadcast in Tunisia programs made by France's second public TV channel. And that it was on that occasion that he reportedly granted his partner-interlocutor a personalized favor. This was to keep Salah Karker (1948–2012)—a dissident whose purported contacts within the army were of particular concern to Ben Ali—under house arrest in France.[16] This indeed remained the case for over eleven years, despite a police file that was especially empty, and activist campaigns on his behalf. "The Prisoner of the Two Shores," as I dubbed him in a 2001 op-ed in *Libération*, was conditionally released only in 2005. Only a grave stroke finally reassured his French jailer's Tunisian handler. In the meantime, I had been to visit Karker several times in the second of his two "residences," a hotel (Saint Michel) on the edges of the town of Digne, in the Alpes de Haute-Provence. There, Karker had a bedroom and a small office that allowed him to receive visitors. He was monitored by several policemen who, like him, resided in the hotel.

As I walked towards Karker's office, I glimpsed a black tube about a meter long leaning against the wall of an office that was clearly assigned to his police "guardian angels." At the end of our meeting, I asked these policemen to be authorized to join my host in a brief walk in the countryside. They granted permission—but insisted that we walk instead in the direction of downtown. We sat down at a café terrace. As night began to fall, and we had got through our hot chocolate and our main business, a peculiar setup caught my eye. From the window of a vehicle that was parked 60 or so meters away from us poked out what looked for all the world like the black tube that I had glimpsed in the policemen's office. It was a sound cannon, which was trained on us to record our conversation. Karker spoke only very little French; we were therefore speaking in Arabic. Enunciating with great care, I then pronounced the following sentence: "Allow me, dear Salah, before we continue our conversation, to warmly thank those of our translator colleagues who, tonight or tomorrow, will enable the policemen sitting in the car that is parked under the large tree to understand what we are saying to each other."

The verdict of the General Intelligence of Aix-en-Provence as to whether it was opportune that I should be decorated with the National Order of Merit proved negative. Obviously, I survived it. This was all the easier that my relationship with their useful corporation was not limited to that episode. A few months later, I had the privilege of leading a training session on North Africa and Islam at the headquarters of their main office in Marseilles. Beyond the pleasure of speaking with curious, open, and friendly agents, I had the occasion to understand, as I discovered better-than-the-real-thing "nuns," "plumbers," and other such "electricity-company agents" taking their morning croissant in the police station's cafeteria, the reasons why our rulers had every right to feel that they were well-informed.

From Almost "Divine" Rescuers to Academic Backers

Obviously, there were some cracks in this hostile environment. But only for those who wished to see them, by seeking out the few, rare sources that were not under the direct or indirect influence of the Algerian regime and its powerful allies. Such was the case of a website like Algeria-Watch, a pioneer of the struggle against disinformation, run by Salima Mellah, or of a very small number of journalists who demanded more of themselves than did most of their colleagues. These included José Garçon of *Libération*, Baudouin Loos of Brussels's *Le Soir*, Denis Sieffert of *Politis*,[17] and, of course, from Salima Ghezali to Ghania Moufok through Salah-Eddine Sidhoum,[18] the brave elite of Algerian heroes.

In this field of (nearly) heaven-sent help, Pierre Bourdieu was another reference point—more fleetingly but especially decisively so given, of course, his immense standing. In truth, I was not really a learned reader of Bourdieu in his role as the prestigious sociologist. "My" Bourdieu was primarily the co-author of *Le Déracinement* (translated as *Uprooting*),[19] the volume he had devoted to Algeria when, at the outset of his career, he had studied the French army's policy of repressive confinement of the population of Kabylia. I like to say that *Le Déracinement* is probably the first work that made me realize the power of the social sciences. I believe it is within its pages that I discovered how a little methodology and a few concepts granted access to understanding—to "unveiling"—a social and political reality that was obscured by the screen of the initial perceptions that tend to urge themselves upon us as so much "common sense." Nearly thirty years later, hearing Bourdieu paraphrase what seemed to me to be the terribly one-sided discourse of the "defenders of the Algerian intellectuals" whose International Committee to Support Algerian Intellectuals (French CISIA, founded in 1993) he co-directed with Jean Leca, thus disconcerted me terribly. No. Not Bourdieu! Not him!

So I wrote him, as one sends a message in a bottle. "Professor," I essentially said, "Kindly find enclosed a few recent articles (including an op-ed published in *Le Monde* under the headline "From *Fellagas* to Fundamentalists"[20]). Regarding the crisis in Algeria, I can scarcely bring myself to believe that the author of *Uprooting* should have said his last word." A long wait followed. It came to an end on what resonated for me at the time as a kind of liberating thunderbolt:

> Dear Sir, Forgive me for having been so slow to answer you. I have read the articles you sent me with interest and much benefit. I heard you by chance on television and was able to confirm that my understanding of the situation in Algeria is very close to yours. Perhaps I shall be brought to express it in one of the coming days. Thanking you again, I send you my warmest greetings. Pierre Bourdieu.

Indeed, a few weeks later, in *Télérama*, in a long interview, Pierre Bourdieu kept his word and published a few lines that were as brief as they were decisive. In these lines, he entirely renewed his assessment of the various actors of the civil war, predicting the terrorist spillover that was to come on French soil. Crucially, he crossed a fundamental line that brought him, in spectacular fashion, to the opposite stance from his initial assessment: terming the FIS nothing less than "truly representative" of the Algerian people.[21] But, even in bravely battling the "negative intellectuals"[22] who saturated the media with their falsehoods, no more than the obscure François Burgat could the great Pierre Bourdieu shift the terribly one-sided public perception of these "black years," concerning which whole swaths of lies continue to be circulated to this day.

Being "the Friend of Tariq Ramadan," or: French Drivers of Sectarian Confessionalization

I do not share Tariq Ramadan's religious beliefs. This is for at least two reasons. Most often, he speaks from within a faith that cannot be my own, Christian as my education made me—and a "dechristianized" Christian at that. On the other hand, and to this day, I have more or less unreservedly shared his assertion of the rights of European Muslims, and the mundanely legitimate and wholly ... secular claims that he has formulated in this respect. I therefore regularly presented his theses favorably and, more regularly still, took a clear stand in his favor each time he was attacked.[23] Truth be told, this was quite natural given how often his major detractors have been defined by their bad faith. All this occurred in an atmosphere of great mutual trust and friendship. For those who wished to stigmatize me on the cheap, therefore, for the longest time it was enough to present me as "the friend of Tariq Ramadan." For once, such a "slander," whose effectiveness was proportional to the intensity of the campaign to criminalize the "grandson of the founder of the Muslim Brotherhood," was largely well-founded ...

It was in Egypt that Tariq and I began a long friendship. Tariq is Swiss, and resided in Geneva at the time. In August 1992, he had settled in Cairo, to perfect his and his children's Arabic, and to round out his curriculum in religious studies. We met in that context, before reencountering each other regularly at various gatherings of Muslim associations in France and Europe (in particular in Switzerland, Belgium, and the United Kingdom). Among other encounters, one day he joined me in Luxor. From there, together, we set out along the Nile to return to Cairo. In a hotel we had stopped off at, however, the black uniforms of State Security came to wake us at dawn. An officer ordered us to follow one of their cars towards Cairo. The pretext was that they had to ensure our security in an area of Egypt where political tensions were, it is true, acute at the time. Dawdling was now out of the question. Driving over 100 km an hour in my very ancient Peugeot, our "protectors" compelled us to cut that journey very short. The previous day, near Asyut, we had met with a Muslim Brotherhood parliamentarian, the very remarkable Mohamed Habib. He was a startling figure in every respect—and not only because his electoral base included a significant number of Copts, who were to break with the Morsi camp over the Spring of 2011.

This productive—but very fleeting—meeting in Asyut gave rise to an episode that has remained emblematic of the worst practices of the artisans of the media demonization of the Other.[24] A few years later, in 2002, I was on a bus driving me at night from Zurich Airport to the Swiss resort of Davos where, in the framework of the World Economic Forum, I was to take part in an unlikely "Council of the 100 Leaders" (Western and Muslim leaders who favored bringing their views closer together). My cell phone rang. On the line was Serge Raffy, a journalist from the *Nouvel Observateur* who was then embarked on an umpteenth "great investigation" into Tariq Ramadan. I answered his questions in all candor, with no hidden agenda. It quickly became clear—but I was still naïve, or insufficiently well-informed—that improving his readers' understanding of the intellectual and political world of Tariq Ramadan was the last of Raffy's concerns. He was merely on the hunt for a detail that might put the finishing touch to the hitjob he had concocted against Ramadan.

Clearly, the quickest shortcut seemed to Raffy to be the best. My patient explanations concerning Tariq's personality, and what I believed I had understood of his project, were of no interest to him. Nor was the context of our first encounters, nor even little personalized anecdotes concerning our journey in Egypt. I persisted in repeating to him that "No, no, during our journey in Egypt we did not talk theology." This plainly irritated him. "In Asyut, we went to see a Muslim Brother who represents the wing that is most ..." Bingo! I cannot even finish my sentence. Raffy has just hit the jackpot. Burgat and Ramadan had met a Muslim Brother ... Ooh, the perfect crime! Needless to say, into the trash go context, perspective, and meaning! The terrifying production line of criminalizing rhetorical shortcuts was primed to go into overdrive, to the point of caricature. Henceforth, I would be identified by this one quotation—and this one alone. It was literally screwed onto my online biography.

For a decade, I reencountered the phrase at every turn in the writing of the members of the little club embodied by the journalist Caroline Fourest, the future 2012 laureate of a "Y'a bon Award,"[25] whose half-fawning, half-venomous writings are got up in pseudo-leftist humanism, all the better to feed a very real rightist racism. "Together," she writes of my links with Tariq Ramadan, "*on several occasions* [and all of a sudden my Egyptian journey has multiplied: why refrain from miracles of distortion?] they have journeyed through Egypt, seeking out the Muslim Brotherhood. Nor does Burgat try to conceal this when Serge Raffy questions him."[26] Says it all! The sentence "they journeyed through Egypt seeking out the Muslim Brotherhood" followed on my tail forever. In 2006, *Le Figaro Magazine*, where I have an acquaintance, granted me the fairly prestigious "Guest of the Week" column in which to decipher—as freely as you like, as the page's editor explained to me—the whys and wherefores of Hamas's parliamentary election victory. A few hours later, as I was about to send in my article, an embarrassed phone call came in: "Umm ... The Outreau Affair is taking up a lot of space in the magazine this week. We have to cancel your column." Through my friend in the newsroom, I learned that no sooner had my name appeared on the proofs of the issue as it was being finalized than a trade union representative burst into the newsroom, brandishing the extract devoted to me in Caroline Fourest's pamphlet against Tariq. And that this was enough to instantly have the editor's confidence in me withdrawn.

In 1998, together with his family, Tariq came to Sanaa to take a long holiday in Yemen. We took a high-altitude excursion to the mythical site of Shahara, one of the last strongholds from which the Zaidi Imam Yahya Hamideddin (1869–1948) led his resistance against the Ottomans. From then on, this allowed me to cheerily "threaten" Tariq from time to time with divulging the photographs of one of his young sons brandishing the

Kalashnikov belonging to our friend and guide Hassan. Surely that would cheaply reinforce the worst of the delusions concerning Tariq on the part of all those who find it difficult to endure his intellect, his being French-speaking, his elegance, the quality of his tennis game perhaps. But above all else, his ability to stand up, coolly and unshakably, to the wiliest of our opinion-formers.

Later, at the dawn of the Arab Spring, Tariq distanced himself from the experience of the Muslim Brotherhood more systematically than I have felt the need to, in particular in Egypt. In all likelihood this was to underscore all the more clearly the distance that he meant to preserve, in his trajectory as a European Muslim, from some of the practices of the Egyptian inheritors of the political thought of his illustrious grandfather. He had also often insisted upon the role he ascribed to the Americans. To his mind, US promotion of young Egyptian and Arab activists was suspect.

Here, I could not follow him. The hypothesis that the Arab Spring was at least in part prefabricated from Washington has always seemed to me quite inappropriate.[27] Concerning the Syrian crisis, Tariq sustained a reserve—at the very least, a kind of discretion—that was startlingly far removed from his crystal clear commitment on the question of Palestine. That position could not be my own, either. It alienated those of his closest allies who were closer to the reality on the ground in Syria than he was. As I see it, he took the shortcut of those who failed to refresh their noble-but-creaking anti-imperialist framework. That framework can in no sense account for the deep nature of the Syrian crisis. If only because it amounts to denying any autonomy and any responsibility to the Syrian women and men who fight the battle on their own initiative.

These few differences of opinion were not enough to suspend our relationship, nor to tarnish our friendship. Nor have they discouraged me from consistently denouncing the disastrous intellectual ostracization project which he continues to be targeted by, and that is so terribly counterproductive. Nor has it shaken my respect for him. In April 2016, I traveled to meet Tariq at the Research Center for Islamic Legislation and Ethics (CILE) in Doha, which he directed with determination and brio. There, I was able to witness the quality of the innovative jurisprudential work he had initiated—light years away from the inexhaustible nonsense that the derisory mafia of his kneejerk denigrators in politics and the media ascribe to the purported "doublespeak" of this "agent of Qatar."

Then, in November 2017, came "*l'affaire.*" The outcome of the legal proceedings launched against Ramadan is as yet unknowable. The investigation has revealed a dark side to his personal life—namely, to date, that he was unfaithful. The media, legal, and political treatment of the accusations against him has, however, gone far beyond this. Going beyond any limits, it has exacerbated the rejection that Ramadan's person and his causes always elicited from the French political and media establishments. And it widens yet further the French divide in dealing with Muslim Otherness.

The inevitable consequences will indeed affect both Ramadan and his family—but also hundreds of thousands of Muslims who put their trust in him. The first months of the investigation scarcely encourage the belief that the allegations leveled at him today will be proven. Even if they were to be, it must be insisted upon that they can target him only as an individual. They are irrelevant to the causes that he and others so actively defended. In this context, the extensively documented narrative of the many attacks that targeted both Ramadan and those (including this author) who deigned to defend him (long before his personal behavior came into question) loses none of its explanatory value.

Under Pressure: From Words to Deeds

Denouncing the interpretation of the Algerian crisis that obscured the regime's violence, and its virtuosity in manipulating its audience, involved definite risks. But my proving effective in the same way on the subject of the Israeli–Arab conflict was more risky yet. This became especially true from the second half of the 1990s, in the wake of the anti-terrorist summit of Sharm al-Sheikh in March 1996. Then, two of the key enthusiasts of the eradication of the Islamic Other, Algeria and Israel, began to forge links to cooperate in security and communications terms that were almost flawless. It was thereby safest—and best advised—to hold to a single analytical framework. In the best of cases, this held that there was little to choose between the occupied and the occupier. The Director of the French Institute for International Relations (IFRI), Pascal Boniface, learned this at his cost—as did many others.[28]

Preferably, this narrative made a fundamental part of the history of the conflict rest exclusively upon the—Muslim—religion of the rebellious occupied people. It was more or less this interpretation that our "sweet" national symbol cartoonist Plantu embedded in the imaginary of the readers of *Le Monde*. Among the recurrent tropes of Plantu's cartoons are little black flies that float around the world's evildoers, enticed by the nauseating emissions that they exhale. (The figures whom these flies orbit around run the gamut from Hamas leaders to Tariq Ramadan.) For the longest time, these flies had the unfortunate habit of more easily finding their way to buzzing over the heads of the dominated, or the occupied, than they did over those of the dominant and the occupier. They were also rather less often to be found buzzing over the heads of the perpetrators (whether military or civil) of the gruesome policy of eradication of Algeria's Islamist opposition than orbiting those of the tens of thousands of victims of the eradicators' policy.

Likely it was because I had too consistently condemned this falsely "analytical" representation of the conflict that, in 2004, I was targeted by an attack whose unexpected efficiency suddenly excluded Pakistan from the range of my comparatist's trajectory within the Muslim world. One fine day, a diplomat friend warned me that I had just been targeted by an *ukase* from a certain obscure Union of French Jewish Professionals.[29] He sought to reassure me that "We get one a week at the Ministry." "The last time," he explained, "It was because we were planning to host a Palestinian journalist 'whose hands,' according to the press release, 'were covered in Jewish blood.'" And yet: political violence had just burst into my private sphere. In one of its most anodyne shapes. And yet, for once, also one of its most destructive versions.

The charge sheet was not exactly sophisticated (see boxed text below). In fact what marked me most lastingly was the relationship between the absolutely trivial nature of these accusations and their terrible "efficacy"— as well as the near-total absence of reaction from my immediate superiors. On the scale of the various expressions of political violence suffered by so many elsewhere in the world, whose fate I have devoted my professional career to, this was, of course, nothing serious. Such episodes are very banal within the political systems whose failings my work aspires to explain. And yet—this time, it wasn't those others. It was me. One of my two employers remained quite calm concerning the matter. But the ironic silence within my work environment in Aix-en-Provence gave me the smallest of glimpses into what can be felt by the thousands of women and men who, whether in the Occupied Territories or in every national context where

---

Press Release from the Union of French Jewish Professionals

The Union of French Jewish Executives and Professionals has learned with consternation that François Burgat is to be nominated for the position of Director of Research within the "Political Science" section of the CNRS. The UPJF is surprised at such a promotion for a defender of the Islamist cause, at the key institution of French academic research.

Burgat actively took part in the UOIF congress in April 2005. Beyond this, he has for example stated, concerning September 11: "Monstrous as the attacks were, [...] Arab public opinion, independently of its political leanings, broadly perceived them as a kind of 'anti-imperialist' reaction. To my mind, this behaviour is explained far less by the purported spread and influence of a reactionary interpretation of Islam than it is by the arrogance of domination by one camp: by the feeling of being collectively victims of policies that are systematically and exclusively aligned with the interests of the United States, and with Israel's most intransigent positions."

Were this nomination to become confirmed, the question would then have to be raised of François Burgat's legitimacy to train future generations of French academics. It would then become the responsibility of François Goulard, the new Minister of State for Academic Research, to put this absurd situation to an end.

Claude Barouch, President

Arab authoritarianism persists, pay an infinitely greater price than my own.

At the CNRS, the rapporteur of my application for Director of Research status received the charge sheet in her personal mailbox—as she explained to me nearly a decade later. This was evidence that the sting had been initiated by somebody very well versed indeed in the mysteries of French academic administration: an insider, in fact, whose name it was not hard to guess. The President of Section 40 in question was notified. He nobly shrugged his shoulders. And refused to follow up in any way. Long live France! Alas! At the time, I was a candidate to be posted to Pakistan, this time by the Foreign Affairs Ministry. I had been offered the position of Director of (the Pakistan-based equivalent of) the French Center for Yemeni Studies, to take up that challenge once again. For reasons I have already explained, I was tempted by studying the contrast between, on the one hand, the religious framework of a country that was more or less specifically founded to gather Muslims and, on the other, by the unstoppable diversification among its citizens of the means by which they expressed their religious belonging in the political field.[30]

The verdict came very quickly. It was pitiful—and said much about how fragile is the French Republic's ethical spinal column. On the spot, a courageous consensus was forged between the Ministry's central administration and the minister's cabinet: "Prudence! We'll think it through later!" My nomination had been settled in principle—but it had not yet been formally notified to me. It was therefore withdrawn. Three years later, the Foreign Affairs Ministry revisited this dark episode, and overcame it. As a candidate to direct the Institut Français du Proche-Orient (IFPO), I had to explain myself several times concerning all the ins and outs of this affair, in person, on every floor in the Ministry's headquarters, and right up to the top of the minister's cabinet. But on that occasion, reason and equanimity prevailed.

Notes

1 Krichen is a Tunisian sociologist close to the far left, the founder in 1967 of the journal *Perspectives*, and a pioneer of the call for unity of action between the Islamist opposition movements and the left. Krichen was later minister-counselor to Tunisia's temporary President Moncef Marzouki before resigning in 2014. He has published an account of that experience: *La Promesse du printemps*, Script Éditions, Bordeaux, 2016.
2 Ghezali was editor-in chief of the daily *La Nation* and, like Ghania Mouffok, a brave and principled opponent of the Algerian junta's "eradicatory" policy.
3 Hanoune founded the Trotskyist Algerian Workers' Party and was one of the signatories of the historic 1995 Sant'Egidio Pact, before she accepted being elected to parliament in 2004, to be a candidate for the presidency, and to allow herself to become co-opted by the system.
4 Amin is a French-Egyptian Marxist economist settled in Dakar.
5 Ibrahim is a very widely celebrated Egyptian author, close to the Communists, the author of *That Smell* (1959) and *Zaat* (1992), an impassioned critique of Mubarak's Egypt.
6 Aswany is the author of many bestselling novels, including the celebrated *Yacoubian Building* (2002), and another impassioned critic of the Mubarak regime. He became especially active in the international campaign to discredit the Muslim Brotherhood, and gave passive support to the 2013 military coup that killed off the democratic transition.
7 This is a paradox that Nicolas Dot-Pouillard has analyzed with great nuance (see, in particular, Nicolas Dot-Pouillard, "Les gauches arabes orphelines de revolution").
8 The Party of the Socialist Avant-Garde, heir to the Algerian Communist Party.
9 "Condor" was the name given in the 1970s to the joint operation between the "special services" of the dictatorships of the Southern Cone of South America (Argentina, Bolivia, Brazil, Chile, Paraguay, and Uruguay) to track down their "subversive" opponents. For the purpose, they used the murderous methods of "counter-insurrectionary warfare" taught them by their French and US partners. (See especially Marie-Monique Robin, *Escadrons de la mort, l'école française*, La Découverte, Paris, 2004; and John Dinges, *The Condor Years: How Pinochet and His Allies Brought Terrorism to Three Continents*, The New Press, New York, 2005.)
10 Yasmina Khadra, *L'Imposture des mots*, Julliard, Paris, 2002.
11 The book accused François Gèze, director of the La Découverte publishing house and a contributor to the Algeria-Watch website, ad hominem, of having lent credence to the testimony of Sublieutenant Habib Souaïdia, one of the first Algerian army officers who took the risk of breaking the *omertà* concerning the massacres and other horrors perpetrated by some units of the army, or by "Islamist groups" manipulated by the army. (Habib Souaïdia, *La Sale Guerre. Le témoignage d'un ancien officier des forces spéciales algériennes*, La Découverte, Paris, 2002.)

12 Following in the footsteps of the work of Frantz Fanon (*Peau noire, masques blancs*, Seuil, Paris, 1952), the Iranian-American academic Hamid Dabashi has shown how many immigrant intellectuals more or less consciously replicate the frameworks that bolster Western domination in the countries they came from. (Hamid Dabashi, *Brown Skin, White Masks*, Pluto Press, London, 2011.)
13 Pierre Bourdieu, "Les intellectuels negatifs," a previously unpublished essay included *in Contre-Feux*, Raisons d'agir, Paris, 1998, www.homme-moderne.org/societe/socio/bourdieu/contrefe/lintellect.html (last accessed June 15, 2019). As for Gilles Kepel, he had already shown an inclination towards an over-ideologized reading of political dynamics in Algeria, and a willingness to interpret those only through the prism of his conclusions regarding Egypt. Let us take one example among others: the June 1992 assassination of President Mohammed Boudiaf by his peers. The reasons why this president—whom the "secular" generals had raised to power and found too enterprising—was eliminated were clear enough. Kepel preferred to invite his readers to marvel at how "Boudiaf's assassination by the Islamists" confirmed the arguments concerning Egypt that Kepel himself had developed in *Le Prophète et Pharaon. Aux sources des mouvements islamistes*, Gallimard, Paris, 2012 (First edition: La Découverte, Paris, 1984), translated as *Muslim Extremism in Egypt: The Prophet and Pharoah*, 2nd ed., University of California Press, Berkeley, 2003.
14 French Prime Minister Manuel Valls claimed, in January 2016, that "to explain is already to justify a little."
15 Founded in 1989, the Rally for Culture and Democracy is a Berber-centered party (slightly) rooted in Kabylia.
16 Karker had hoped to forestall Ben Ali in 1987 by deposing Bourguiba with the help of a few army officers. (See François Burgat, *The Islamic Movement in North Africa*.)
17 Or civil society activists such as Rabha Attaf and Fausto Giudice, the authors of "La grande peur bleue," *Les Cahiers de l'Orient*, 1995, http://tlaxcala-int.org/article.asp?reference=9111 (last accessed June 15, 2019).
18 Sidhoum, an Algerian surgeon and human rights activist, bravely documented the black decade of the Civil War. In 1997, he was sentenced to twenty years in jail, and for a long time went underground. He is currently the editor of the online newspaper *Le Quotidien d'Algérie*.
19 Pierre Bourdieu and Abdelmalek Sayad, *Le Déracinement. La crise de l'agriculture traditionnelle en Algérie*, Minuit, Paris, 1964.
20 François Burgat, "L'Algérie, des fellagas aux intégristes," *Le Genre humain*, 1991; also published as "Le nationalisme arabe, des fellagas aux intégristes," *Libération*, January 14, 1995, www.liberation.fr/tribune/1995/01/14/le-nationalisme-arabe-des-fellaghas-aux-integristes_119840 (last accessed June 15, 2019).
21 "Indeed, the Algerian question seems to me to take priority. Not only in ethical terms—but also in political ones. From a cynical point of view—very much including that of our own interests—Algeria is France's number-one problem today. [...] The Algerian civil war can, from one day to the next, transport itself

to France, along with its murders and its terrorist attacks whose perpetrators will not always be those labelled as such by journalists. This is why one must support the Rome Accords by any means available: accords between the democratic parties and the representatives of the FIS, *whom I consider to be truly representative* [my italics]." (*Télérama*, no. 2353, February 15, 1995).

22 Pierre Bourdieu, "Les intellectuels négatifs."
23 See François Burgat, "Invitation au dialogue," *Le Monde Diplomatique*, January 1996, www.monde-diplomatique.fr/1996/01/BURGAT/5127 (last accessed June 15, 2019). In a review of Tariq Ramadan's volume *Islam, le face-à-face des civilisations. Quel projet pour la modernité?* (Tawhid, Lyon, 1995), I wrote: "Perhaps because he knows us so well, the questions the author directs at us come across less as a challenge or as a provocation than as a reasoned and reasonable invitation to communicate."
24 Concerning this practice of "demonization," see Thomas Deltombe, *L'Islam imaginaire*.
25 Since 2009, an organisation ("Les Indivisibles") has awarded a yearly prize to the public figures who have distinguished themselves by declarations that it deems to be racist. Caroline Fourest has been selected twice.
26 Caroline Fourest, *Frère Tariq*, Grasset, Paris, 2004.
27 Concerning this debate, see Asef Bayat, *Revolution without Revolutionaries: Making Sense of the Arab Spring*, Stanford University Press, Palo Alto, CA, 2017, and Emmanuel Karagiannis, *The New Political Islam: Human Rights, Democracy, and Justice*, University of Pennsylvania Press, Philadelphia, PA, 2017.
28 Boniface was the victim of a violent campaign of intimidation for having defended a critical stance towards Israeli policies. This sought to have his institution's public funding sources cut off. (See his book, *Est-il permis de critiquer Israël?*, Robert Laffont, Paris, 2003.)
29 Union des Professionnels Juifs de France.
30 See Christophe Jaffrelot (ed.), *Le Pakistan*, Fayard, Paris, 2002; *Le Syndrome pakistanais*, Fayard, Paris, 2013.

12

Between Judges and Spooks

Several times, then, I really did feel the hostile breathing down my neck of the goons behind-the-scenes of one or other of the regimes in question. This was especially the case when I agreed to testify as an expert witness before foreign courts, in the United States, Canada, and New Zealand, where I was called upon to defend Islamist refugees seeking asylum. There were other troubles of the same kind. These autocrats were sensitive to international public opinion. The stakes of these international legal cases were high enough that they sought to influence the verdicts. At its core, the public relations of the "Arab Pinochets" towards their Western partners rested on the deterrent power of the "fundamentalism" of their bogeyman dissidents. The idea was thus absolutely unacceptable to them that some of these bogeymen might be declared innocent—or that their "crimes" might be reduced to the level of the counter-violence of an opposition forced into legitimate self-defense. The indispensable gullibility of the North was at stake.

The "Arab Pinochets" (and Their Allies) vs. Their Political Opposition in Exile

The Tunisian Agency for Communication Abroad (ATCE), Algeria's DRS, and its Moroccan counterpart therefore devoted considerable means to this strategy. Libyan methods were more summary, directly inspired by the Ben Barka Affair. (The Moroccan nationalist leader had been disappeared in 1965 in Paris by Morocco's intelligence services, with the complicity of their French counterparts.) These concentrated on the exploits of its "Operations Division," which were most often delegated to the Palestinian groups maintained by Gaddafi, who had those he termed "stray dogs" assassinated or disappeared.

I "frequented" one of the victims of these methods. I had wished to make the acquaintance of Mansour Kikhia, the former minister of foreign affairs (1972–3) and UN ambassador, who had joined the ranks of the opposition exiled in France. In 1992, I met him in the bar of Cairo's Safir hotel where he was staying. The former minister was kidnapped soon after by Libya's intelligence services. He was thrown into a convoy of Mercedes that returned him to Tripoli, where a long agony of torture awaited him. It is said that Gaddafi personally attended the torture sessions. Former detainees assert that he forced Kikhia to crawl on the ground while barking. In 2012, Kikhia's frozen corpse was found in a secret morgue where Gaddafi had had the bodies of several of his opponents preserved, to deprive them of the peace of the grave and to keep defying them even unto death.

From 1990, the tide of political exiles who arrived in Europe or the United States from Tunisia, but also from Algeria, increased considerably. I was therefore regularly solicited to assist in the examination of applications for political asylum made by exiled Islamists from the Islamic Salvation Front (Anwar Haddam in Washington, DC, Ahmed Zaoui in Auckland) and (Tunisia's) Movement of the Islamic Tendency, which became Ennahda in 1989 (Mohamed Zrig in Montreal). The regimes in question largely sustained themselves through the intense repression that their Western partners tolerated, when they did not directly join in. These regimes therefore did not hesitate to take action, both on the media front of course, but also in the political and judicial arenas, to preempt any kind of support for their opposition in exile—or even any normalization of their reputation.

The regimes' aim was to discredit these opponents in order to prevent their being welcomed into exile—or at least to make it impossible for them to mobilize Western public opinion, or so much as to inform it. Various legal investigations were thus set in motion, whose purpose was to inform judges as to the precise political context of the countries the petitioners had left. What was at stake was to allow these jurisdictions to determine whether the petitioners' belonging to an "Islamist" party—a nomenclature that the regimes did everything in their power to have identified with "terrorist"—was compatible with refugee status in the United States, in Canada, and in various European countries. These cases all required lengthy auditions or, in the Auckland case, very lengthy written preparation. They were instructive as to the methods used by the Algerian and Tunisian governments to blacken their opponents' names by any number of means—and, in the process, and in equal proportion, to conceal their own misdeeds.

The role of the defense, and of the foreign experts it called upon, was thus decisive. In at least one case, the Zaoui affair, the relevant Algerian Ministry highly significantly preferred to throw in the towel, confronted by the number and the quality of the testimonies presented by the defense to contradict its one-sided argument, including on the part of its own security agencies.[1] It failed in the case of Anwar Haddam, too: the accused was ultimately granted asylum in the United States. And in the Zrig case, as we shall see, it had to rely on the intervention of powerful "local" and foreign allies to achieve its ends.

The Shadow of Mossad's War on Hamas Exported Abroad ...

When I was called upon as an expert witness for the defense by the Montreal administrative court, I was questioned for three days, in an atmosphere that was oddly hostile. The case was a relatively ordinary one. It consisted of documenting the ins and outs of the political strategy of the Movement of the Islamic Tendency (MIT, founded by Rached Ghannouchi) to determine whether one of its members had a case for political asylum in Canada. This was Mohamed Zrig, who was later to become an Ennahda parliamentarian, in the wake of the 2011 Spring. Such a determination was impossible if any act liable to be considered a "crime against humanity" could be ascribed to the party (of the Islamic Tendency) to which he had belonged. Very soon, however, the case came to unveil an extremely political backstory that went beyond the context of Tunisia alone.

Going against my expectations, this time it wasn't the minions of the Tunisian Agency for Communication Abroad, whom I had often had the occasion to see in action, who were on the case. In all likelihood, it was the defenders of Israel's interests. Two highly revealing incidents put their stamp on the trial as it unfolded. They led to the testimony of the two expert witnesses called on by the defense, the British academic George Joffe and myself, being ruled inadmissible. Much more surprisingly, the testimony of the two expert witnesses put forward by the prosecution was also ruled inadmissible. Mohamed Zrig's appeal against the ruling that denied him political asylum in Canada was also rejected.

The charge was formulated by Canada's Ministry of Citizenship and Immigration. It so happened that the minister, Lucienne Robillard, had spent three years (1969–72) in an Israeli kibbutz. Throughout the trial, it was difficult not to wonder as to the relationships she might have developed with the authorities of her host country at the time. When my hearing took place, George Joffe's had already occurred. He had not traveled to Canada, but spoken from the Canadian embassy in London via a secure phone line. As early on as the segment to ascertain his identity, the magistrates' questions became curiously focused on the expert witness's wife, a doctor who was born in the Palestinian territories and regularly returned there to practice medicine. The questions soon turned insidious. Would a female doctor practicing in the Palestinian territories not, by definition, be led to "treat Palestinians"—and therefore, among those, "certain terrorists"? "I'm Jewish!" Joffe exploded in the court's face. "I'm Jewish! [...] How *dare* you? You are not worthy of presiding over a court! [...] I do not recognize you as a jurisdiction, you are not worthy of it!" Exit the first witness for the defense.

I was soon to "join" Joffe's company among those disqualified by the court. My own itinerary to get there was far longer. It involved over fifteen hours of testimony. But a single sentence extracted from my testimony was adjudged to express empathy with the MIT. From the MIT's already-lengthy political trajectory, the court would, throughout most of its investigation, retain only a single episode. It concerned the death of a janitor at an office of the ruling party, the RCD, that was set on fire in the Spring of 1991 by two MIT activists. This had occurred at a time when political repression, including deaths from torture, was scaling the heights of violence. This was enough to have the leaders of the movement filed under the rubric of those responsible for "crimes against humanity." Had this stringent—but distinctly one-sided—interpretation of who was responsible for political violence been raised to the standing of a criterion by which to judge the governments of a region where rapes, deaths from torture, and extrajudicial executions piled up, very few of the members of those governments would then have been able to set foot on Canadian soil. But at the time one maxim reigned supreme. It was unanswerable. Received wisdom brandished it unerringly whenever the rights of Islamist activists were invoked to justify the efforts devoted to their defense: "No freedom for the enemies of freedom!" One could not reasonably protect political activists whose agenda, in the collective imagination, boiled down to denying their opponents these same rights.

The case of the prosecution's expert witnesses was far more unusual—and yet more revealing of the very particular political environment of this trial. As it turned out, criminalizing the potential partners of the Palestinian Hamas seemed to be the main driver of the Canadian government's legal strategy. The first of the two experts, who has since passed away, was one Khaled Duran (1939–2010), a German citizen converted to Islam. It was very easy to track down the traces of his activity as a Muslim representative within "interreligious dialogue" conferences that were organized in rather particular frameworks. These were distinguished by having a "Muslim" voice condone the shortcuts of the discourse of the Israeli occupier with respect to its occupation of Jerusalem. The second witness, A. H., was a Tunisian academic who taught at the University of Virginia at Tampa. Like Duran, he was a great specialist in "interreligious dialogue." Both would be at the heart of the second of the two major incidents of the Zrig trial.

A few weeks before the case reached the appeal stage, to which I was associated, it emerged that both were involved, in a southern US town, in a sting that had patently been set up by Israel's Mossad. An appealing young woman named Melina Carlson had been recruited, her mission being to approach a Palestinian leader during his stay in hospital. She was unmasked, and made a very extensive confession. In order to be hospitalized herself, she had obtained a fake medical certificate signed by a real doctor. In a first surprise, the Tunisian academic A. H. who transferred to Melina Carlson, in cash, the sums that allowed her to be hospitalized was the very same whom the prosecution had called as a witness in the Zrig case. The two experts then sought to evade. Claiming that they feared for their own security, they both refused to show in person before the court. Moreover, they demanded considerable fees. Khaled Duran provided a medical certificate to justify being unable to travel. Coincidentally, this fake certificate was signed by the very same doctor who had signed Melina Carlson's certificate ... Exit the two witnesses called by the prosecution.

But a heavy smell was left hanging in the air: the trial's being politicized to the benefit of all those whose driving motive is criminalizing the political family to which the Palestinian Hamas belongs. Zrig's appeal was turned down. In the name of the "right to be forgotten"—and there was plenty to be forgotten here—those who didn't exactly emerge from this affair with their credit intact have since meticulously made any trace of this inglorious (and—unsurprisingly—undercovered) episode disappear from the internet.

... and the Double Footprint of Algerian Intelligence

In October 2007, the Rachid Ramda affair came to trial before the special Paris circuit court in charge of terrorist cases. (The jury of the court is entirely made up of magistrates.) This provided me with a fleeting satisfaction. I was able to publicly tell the court's prosecutor that it would be a shame for her jurisdiction to be the only place in Paris where the identity of the perpetrators of the Paris terrorist attacks of the summer of 1995 remained a mystery—including the terribly deadly attack of the Saint Michel RER (commuter train) station. Like the case of the murder of the monks of Tibhirine, that file was easily seen through. The man who gave the order—a certain Ali Touchent—had been clearly identified. It was just as clearly settled that he was affiliated with the backroom agencies of Algeria's DRS (the Algerian regime's Political Security Agency). A number of French politicians, including Jean-Louis Debré and Lionel Jospin, refused to be duped. Through various "leaks," they had even sent precise signals to their Algerian counterparts. They had also made enquiries as to the instruments that could be deployed if the French government determined to strike at the personal assets of Algeria's leaders. (Nicole Chevillard, the editor of the confidential economic newsletter *Nord-Sud-Export*, came to the bar to say as much.)

But none of all this could be spoken out loud. In some sense, it was a truth that was worth several billion euros. That is, approximately the considerable share of the profits of the Algerian hydrocarbon industry that France's economy harnessed more or less directly. And this was enough to make many decision-makers balk ...

In the media-saturated context of the trial in Paris, the victims' pain was largely harnessed—and perhaps even exploited—by an "Association for the Victims of Terrorism." As elsewhere, its agenda appeared to be very closely conflated with that of criminalizing Palestinian resistance. The true stakes of the special circuit court's proceedings should have lain in establishing whether Rachid Ramda, who was said to have been the "financier of the attacks," had been directed by members of Algeria's Islamist opposition—or, rather, by the representatives of the regime's backroom intelligence networks seeking to smear that opposition. But Ramda was sentenced without the court debating this point. That dimension of the case was by far more fundamental if my French compatriots were to grasp the precise ins and outs of "Islamic violence." To this day, it remains hidden away in the shadows of France's financial interests—like many other cases on both sides of the Mediterranean.

Yasmina Salah and the Fake Interview

Finally, I had at least one more of these encounters "of the third kind." Once more, it was with Algerian intelligence—and no less startling. One day in January 2006, a friend brought to my attention the "excellent interview" that I had given to the Arabic-language magazine *al-Mujtamaa*. I was surprised. Rather quickly, I tracked down the magazine's website. It was published from Kuwait City, was close to the Muslim Brotherhood, and had quite a respectable circulation. I had good reason to be surprised: I had never granted any interview to *al-Mujtamaa*. Yet the interview with "the French intellectual François Burgat" was adorned with a photograph, a few biographical details, and several arguments that could undoubtedly have been passed off as my own. A peculiar saga was just beginning.

The text of the statements ascribed to me was curious. After a few general points that I could indeed have taken it upon myself to pronounce—and that were even personal enough that they could scarcely be ascribed to anyone else—the tone of my purported answers flew off the rails. I read myself announcing a forthcoming volume whose activist title, *The New*

Islamic Society, was utterly at odds with the register of my own work. More intriguing still, I then allegedly shared my conviction that, after September 11, the citizens of the United States "converted to Islam by the thousands." The bizarre interview was presented as having been translated from the original French by one Yasmina Salah. She in turn had supposedly copied it from issue 105 of a magazine called *La Vérité* ("*The Truth*").

In that magazine, which was purported to have published over 105 issues to date, my alleged interviewer was a certain "David Sardinan." There was a slight problem: the magazine did not exist, in any shape or form. "David Sardinan" the journalist was also a figment of the imagination. Yasmina Salah, on the other hand, was very much a creature of flesh and blood. She described herself as a "woman of letters, journalist, and translator," who had written some novels in Arabic and was a former contributor to the FLN's newspaper *El-Moudjahid*. She had appeared in public on several occasions, in her capacity as a "feminist activist." In her presentation of my imaginary interview, she affected to have taken the initiative of making it available to the Arab reader given "the importance of the ideas that are expressed in it."

Yasmina Salah was no stripling in her career as an author of forgeries—what would today be called "fake news." In the next issue of *al-Mujtamaa*, published the week following my fake interview (the second week of January), she gave an encore to her intriguing performance. This time around, imaginary figures of the French intellectual scene (including a certain Maurice Miniard, who was supposed to be a "well-known" politician and writer) wielded the most unlikely references (including the fake "bestseller" *La Vérité Française* ("*The French Truth*"). These offered up sensational revelations as to the "real reasons" that had allegedly "really" led France to abstain from joining the war in Iraq—and that were less humanist than they were tied to oil and business interests ...

A few pitiful exchanges then sought to convince me that I had not been subject to an elaborate sting operation. Yasmina Salah sent me a lengthy letter of apology and of "great esteem," in which she offered that we collaborate again. She also provided a startling explanation. She claimed to have been the victim of an error committed by the magazine *La Vérité*, which had supposedly wrongly credited an interview that had in fact taken place, with a certain "François Bourgeois," a "journalist and writer" who was said to "have directed French Cultural Centers in several countries of North Africa." The chief editor of *al-Mujtamaa* magazine then forwarded me a copy of a letter written in a peculiar style, and that had allegedly been addressed to him by one "Bernard Leucate." "Leucate" introduced himself as being the director of the magazine *La Vérité*, thereby buttressing the theory of mere mistaken identity.

In another issue, however, that was published nearly a month later (in February 2006), the editors of *al-Mujtamaa* magazine demonstrated that they had never been duped. The disinformation sting had been operated with their full knowledge. The magazine was duly informed of the whole business, both by myself and through the intermediary of a colleague who lived in Kuwait City. At first, it offered to publish a retraction. In fact, it did quite the opposite. It published a new piece from Yasmina Salah in the shape of an interview—a "real" one this time—with Rabah Kebir, a former leader of the Islamic Salvation Front who had fallen into the clutches of Algerian intelligence. This latest piece was quite clearly designed to "restore Yasmina Salah's credibility." The magazine's Egyptian chief editor, Abderrahmane Shaabane, had committed himself in person to part with his Algerian contributor once and for all. His behavior in publishing her once again indicated his personal involvement in the whole strange business—an affair that was, in passing, fairly typical of the disinformation stings so beloved of Algeria's DRS.

Why was I deserving of the honor of such treatment? At the time, I was involved in the defense of Ahmed Zaoui, a former FIS leader who was applying for asylum in New Zealand. In the course of his interminable trial, I had argued that Algerian authorities were subjecting him to nonsensical accusations of "crimes against humanity," which they sought to have accredited in order to have him extradited. In all likelihood—and lame as the sting was—its purpose was to undermine my testimony by having the magistrates of the Auckland court take me for an ideologically committed activist in favor of the applicant, and whose testimony could therefore be presumed to have been provided as a service to him.

Note

1 See Ahmed Zaoui, *Refugee Appeal no. 74540*, August 1, 2003, New Zealand Refugee Status Appeals Authority, Human Rights Foundation, Auckland, 2005.

13

Wrestling with the Research of Others: Olivier Roy, Gilles Kepel, and Islamism

Over the course of a scholarly career, the nature and the quality of interaction with those who share the same field of research is a thorny and important question. To my mind, my two main rivals (or partners) in the field have always been exemplary. Why so? Because, in our loneliness as scholars, we survive only inasmuch as we manage to preserve the reality—or the fiction—of a certain originality. My "distinguished colleagues" have, to varying degrees, always had the elegance to produce substantially different analyses to my own in our shared research field. Those who wish to enter into this debate at its lowest level see only a "war of the Islamist scholars" and "ego battles." It would of course be unrealistic to deny that narcissistic considerations may have slipped into how scholars express their disagreements. Yet to see only those would be entirely beside the point.

The question of which of the representations of the Muslim Other is to dominate the public sphere is altogether more important than the individualized ego-quarrels which the hastier (and often the laziest) commentators of academic debates wrap it up in. Nothing less is at stake here than our relationship with part of the globe—and, therefore, our relationship to ourselves. Should this be spelt out once again? This debate does not, of course, belong to three scholars. To clarify my own interpretation, in this chapter I have adopted the practical method of counterpointing it to those of two of my most high-profile colleagues in the field. Needless to add, this is in no way to minimize the essential contributions of all the others who have magnificently contributed to these debates.

From One Islamism to Another

Gilles Kepel and Olivier Roy have enjoyed much greater media exposure than I have. The task of periodically outlining our differences has fallen upon my shoulders—since this has been the only means to assert the legitimacy of the contrarian interpretations that I have sought to defend.

Kepel and Roy have enjoyed greater media exposure for two reasons: one good one—and one less so. The first is that media attention is largely driven by book promotion. Both of them have, in this respect, had a higher publication rate than mine, something that I respectfully salute. Whether from lack of will or distracted by administrative responsibilities, I have published my own books at a less sustained rate. In retrospect, I allow myself to think that this has spared me from having to disavow my successive approaches to the subject. This is hardly the case for Roy or Kepel, who have been repeatedly and brutally caught short by the developments of our research object. The second, or "less good" reason for this major gap in media exposure is that both authors have produced explanations of the Islamist phenomenon that are closer than mine are to French norms of "political correctness." Clearly, to take some recent examples, emphasizing the responsibility of the dominant political players is less likely to lead to being hailed as a "serious" scholar. "Serious" scholars focus on the purported tendency of the dominated "to play the victim." Or they assert that the radicalization of young—and older—French Muslims has no connection to the Israeli–Arab conflict. Or they emphasize the "religious" dynamics of urban revolts whose causes are more straightforwardly socio-political.[1]

Naturally, a scholarly approach to so complex a phenomenon cannot be inscribed in "black and white." Gilles Kepel's thesis ascribes a decisive role to the influence of religious doctrine on society—in this case, to the so-called Salafi interpretation of religious doctrine. Naturally, this thesis cannot be rejected wholesale. I decline to accept that the paradigm of French *jihadi*s as "small-time crooks"[2] (to reprise Olivier Roy's evocative description) is analytically effective. But nor does this imply rejecting wholesale what this thesis of "desocialization" enables one to grasp of the various components of the process of radicalization.[3] Yet it strikes me as being essential both to lay out an exhaustive inventory of the respective causes of the emergence of the "Islamist phenomenon" that we have each identified—and to rank them, setting aside falsely consensual appeals to accept that our approaches might instead be "perfectly complementary." How could such a thesis be consensual, when it fits within the "simplicity" of the thesis of American neoconservatives, to whom those responsible for anti-Western violence can only be those who commit it? (The scale of the social constituency of these perpetrators is, in passing, much overstated.[4]) The logic here is that their motivations cannot be *political*. They must therefore be deemed purely ideological, that is, *religious*. The policies of states targeted by such violence are deemed "wholly unrelated" to its production—since its purely ideological origin makes it strictly one-sided. How, say, could a thesis that "explains" that the appallingly lopsided management of the Israeli–Arab conflict by our media and political classes has nothing to do with the increasing exasperation of some of our compatriots be "complementary" with my own, which has always asserted the opposite?

Going against the grain of a complacent syncretism, then, I mean to state here why the explanation that I put forward must be reasserted as being the primary cause of our collective dilemma. That is: the deep dysfunctions of the political institutions of societies struck by a violence that is instead described as exclusively "religious" or "psychosocial"—but without specifying its political and historical backgrounds. Only such an explanation is able to take into account an absolutely decisive variable in analyzing the latest avatars of the Islamist trend: the responsibilities of non-Muslims in the making of *jihadi* violence. Those responsibilities are fundamental—yet they are too often if not systematically obfuscated.

Where did this difference of analysis arise from? I am firmly convinced that what we write as scholars is lastingly determined by our first experience of field research. I have often warned my students to take special care with the first pages they write as budding authors: those pages are likely to weigh heavily in their career. Consciously or otherwise, we all—all too human—find it enormously difficult to renounce our past conclusions.

With respect to Kepel in particular, our core difference is indeed one of method. I did not start out in the study of Islamism by reading its core programmatic texts, but by meeting its players in the field. I began by speaking with participants in the movement—whereas Kepel himself explains ironically that for a long time he devoted himself to the "opuscules of the groupuscules" in Egypt that assassinated President Anwar Sadat in 1981. Sadat's death, and the contrasting reactions to it in Kepel's circle, convinced him to shift his research in that direction. The players he wished to study were, however, all imprisoned. This de facto made any direct contact between the analyst and the sociological object of his analysis impossible. It seems to me that this is why he based his perception of the Islamist phenomenon as a whole on its most literalist and most radical component—and, to my mind, limited the range of his perception to that component for far too long.

The political players I came to know, through long encounters in the flesh, came from North African societies (especially Algeria) rather than Middle Eastern ones. It is in North Africa, and in Algeria in particular, that the paradigm of the culture of "resentment" is most explicitly asserted—a resentment born of the traumatizing and still-bleeding wound of total colonial conflict. As we have seen, I put this variable front and center of my approach to the Islamist response to it. Finally, among these players, duly "humanized" by my proximity to them, it was with the Muslim

Brotherhood and its supporters that I developed my first contacts, more systematically than I encountered their challengers from the Salafi or *jihadi* margins. The Brotherhood movement, which to this day remains the mainstream of the Islamist political spectrum, also had a median position in the doctrinal field. Conversely, this is likely why I wrestled from the outset with the differences between my primary research object—the Brotherhood movement—and its literalist Salafi or *jihadi* challengers.[5]

It strikes me that what distinguishes Olivier Roy's encounter with Islamism is the centrality to it of, first, the Afghan, then the "Persian" worlds. In neither of these regions did history witness colonial conflict in its most direct form. Nor, thereby, did it produce the same culture of resentment that colonialism produced almost everywhere else, in the Middle East and North Africa. Roy's autobiographical work, which is as revealing as it is absorbing, brings this out very explicitly.[6] Entering into the subject from the distant angle of Afghanistan, his analysis has almost no sociological or linguistic roots in the Arab world, which in truth he knows very little, and not well. And yet—by the magic of a generalization that falls into the trap of essentializing—since most inhabitants of the Middle East and North Africa are, like Afghans, "Muslims," the geographical range of the core of his "Islamist field" swiftly scaled up to the level of the globe. It is the extreme brittleness of his relationship to the Arab "pulse" of Muslim societies that led to what I consider to be real analytical dead-ends, to which I will return.

Yet, at first, I felt great empathy for Roy's output. Far more explicitly so than Kepel's, it featured an awareness of the significance of the "nationalist"—or more precisely, the "anti-imperialist"—variable to those who opted for the Islamist lexicon. His initial approach towards the Afghan version of Islamism was embedded in a framework that I immediately considered to be highly enlightening: Islamism as a "process of cultural reappropriation of modernity."[7] Curiously, since he set out this perspective, Roy has used it only occasionally. On very many points, however, our perceptions long remained very close. My approach later diverged from his, first with respect to this thesis of "the failure of political Islam"; then on how to interpret the "Arab Spring"; and finally, and more sharply, on our interpretations of the *jihadi* phenomenon.

Roy: Did Someone Say "Failure of Political Islam"?

Our first disagreements derived from Olivier Roy's statement in 1992 of his key thesis: "the failure of political Islam," or its having become obsolete. He then adopted an almost exclusively "pathologizing" standpoint towards it, close to Kepel's. The Islamist trend struck me as being more ambivalent. These disagreements then deepened each time Roy had to restate these same terms and to reassert their soundness, against all evidence to the contrary. Our differences were initially limited for the most part to questions of appropriate terminology. The entire world worried about the rise of those whom we thought to keep calling what they called themselves: "Islamists." Whether these were moderate or radical—and whether they rose through elections or as armed guerrilla groups. Roy, meanwhile, unshakably repeated his thesis that they belonged to the past—terminologically at least.

To Roy, the rising battalions of "beardies" were an avatar of the latest in the crowded field of "post-" concepts: "post-Islamism." They had, he felt, abandoned the hope of applying a literalist reading of their religious dogma in the political field. I in fact shared this viewpoint—without drawing quite the same conclusions from it. The rub was that, in order to be able to assert that Islamism was obsolete, and that we had therefore entered into the era of "post-Islamism," Roy had to take on an extremely reductive and highly impractical definition of the heart of the matter. To be very clear, conceptually, his literal definition reduced Islamists to their proclaimed desire to set up their religious dogma as political ideology, through the creation of an "Islamic state." And this thesis had the rhetorical advantage of taking the discourse of at least part of the players in question literally.

Curiously, Roy was not reproached with what many colleagues at the time accused me of having unwisely adopted: a "literalist" relationship to how political players positioned themselves. That criticism would have been rather more justified had it been directed at his analysis than at mine. Granted, Roy's statement was not wholly inaccurate. Yet it struck me, and others, as being more theoretical, or archetypal, than it was sociological or based on observation of dynamics in the field. As Baudouin Dupret has emphasized concerning Roy's approach (an argument that is also applicable to Kepel's, who, as we shall see, developed a similar thesis a few years later):

> One gets the feeling that both authors ascribe a revolutionary project to political movements, [then] assert that these movements did not reach the goals they set themselves. They therefore conclude that these movements failed. In so doing, however, it strikes me that they lose sight of two things. First, that the revolutionary project was perhaps not the project of these movements (at most, it was the project of a few of their representatives) so much as it was the project that these authors ascribed to them. [...] Yet it was not the Islamists who proclaimed themselves to be utopians, thereby preparing the way for their own failure as such, and their conversion into conservative ideologues. It is, rather, these scholars who, collectively and globally, ascribed such a project to the Islamists—in order to be able to

derive the conclusion that it had ultimately failed. In this sense, the only failure here is the failure of political science.[8]

Roy's thesis once again excluded wholesale from the initial inventory of the Islamist field an absolutely foundational articulation of Islamism: that of Hassan al-Banna's Muslim Brotherhood movement. The logic of this Brotherhood version of Islamism was to interpret the Islamic norm in context. This did not lead towards an indiscriminate rejection of the elements of "Western" political thought—but, rather, towards its reappropriation. Notwithstanding its highly emblematic slogan ("Islam is the solution"), it could in no way be reduced to the simplifying paradigm (the literal application of dogma in politics) that Roy sought to proclaim was "obsolete." Had Muslim Brotherhood discourse in the 1940s not defended constitutional monarchy as being the political system closest to the "Islamic state"?[9] Had al-Banna himself not stood for election (in 1944)? In the Syria of the 1950s, had the Muslim Brotherhood not entered parliament with the support of a part of the Christian community, who saw in them a shield against Baathist "socialism"? Did they not field ministers scarcely distinguishable from their "liberal" colleagues from the same Damascus or Aleppo bourgeoisie? In short: if such was the definition of "post-Islamism"—had this not begun from the very dawn of Islamism?

Even if we set aside the emergence, in 2015, of new militants of an "Islamic state" whose disappearance Roy had thought he could announce, this definition was far too restrictive and far too distant from facts in the field. Yet again, it excluded the "metaphorical" dimension of Islamists' "religious" self-assertion. It glossed over the essential fact that their core motivations were at least as much identity based as they were religious. Behind the literalist façade of their discourse, what their approach aimed at, far more than at setting up an Islamic state, was restoring the legitimacy—and more so, the centrality—of this endogenous (and not merely sacred) lexicon in political discourse.

In other words, Olivier Roy's approach struck me as flawed in that it shrank the realities of Islamism to a literal appropriation of the slogans of its political players. To my mind, this rhetorical façade—while it did indeed draw upon their discourse—was more the perception of an observer (very) distant from realities on the ground than it was a realistic description of the deep roots of a far more ambivalent movement. I therefore considered that the reality of the "re-Islamization" dynamic, even in the very first ways in which it expressed itself, was not limited to the players' wish to set up the literal reading of their dogma as a political constitution.

My differences with Olivier Roy's vision were expressed very peacefully, and in a rather constructive manner—in particular, in a 2001 special issue of the journal *Esprit* in which, to his credit, he gave me the space to lay them out. Those differences on substance were ultimately only chronological or terminological. Beyond these, in practice, we both asserted that most of the footsoldiers of this movement—I called them "Islamists," he preferred to call them "post-Islamists"—could not be reduced to literally adopting the religious norm as a political doctrine.

Kepel: Social and Religious Trees to Hide the Political Forest— Once More unto the Breach

To come straight to the point, I distanced myself from Kepel's approach, more radically still than from Roy's, for the same reasons that brought me to distance myself from the American tradition identified with the historian Bernard Lewis. Lewis was among the first proponents of the specter of the "war of civilizations"[10] and of the political expressions of an intellectually highly reductive, and humanly unacceptable, neoconservatism. Kepel's approach is also very bookish, in the sense that, in his work, the founding texts shed light on the practice and political imaginary of the players, and not vice versa. Our differences were thus immediate and frequent. These concerned substance, of course—a substance with respect to which his approach has changed on several occasions, without too much concern on his part for consistency. Increasingly, however, we differed just as much, or more so, concerning form. The ways in which Kepel related to the human foundation of the Islamist field were often ironic and condescending, if not downright contemptuous—which, for my part, I was accused of harboring a guilty empathy for. Finally, Kepel's writing drew on a register that has always seemed to me to be closer to that of self-fulfilling prophecy—or the arsonist playing fireman—than it is to the patient deconstruction characteristic of the social sciences. From my lofty perch, Kepel seems to tell us, with barely concealed glee, I take part in a process of stigmatization whose "benefits" I then revel in, even while purporting to look away, quietly humming "I told you so." These differences became exacerbated as the "Arab Spring" wore on, then, in 2015, as the *jihadi* phase entered the scene, something I will come back to.

Kepel's thesis on the assassins of Anwar Sadat was his entry point into political Islam.[11] It was also, however, his only "long-term" immersion in a field outside France's borders. Kepel never diversified his one and only doctoral immersion in the field outside of France. Nor did Roy. Moreover, very quickly, Kepel's "field" trips came to take the shape of highly official, half-diplomatic, half-media-driven tours, in which the back seat of the French ambassador's official vehicle took the place of the mythical "flatbed of the Toyota" from which his predecessor, Bruno Etienne, saw the world.[12]

In June 2002, Pascal Ménoret, an exceptional observer of Saudi society, was posted at the Cultural Office of the French embassy in Riyadh.[13] Kepel was glimpsing that society on the occasion of a visit. Distressed at his own behind-the-scenes glimpse of the field "investigations" of his guest for three days, Ménoret was impertinent enough to write up the high-society fraud that these investigations consisted of. He did so in a short, private pamphlet, in a style whose irony was all the crueler in that it was impeccably well documented. Thanks to the internet, this quickly made the rounds. "GK in Wonderland" made its unwilling hero so furious that, during a reception in Washington in November 2008 on the sidelines of the annual meeting of the Middle East Studies Association, he went for Ménoret with his fists, and was in some danger of being shackled by police, who took down the testimonies of stunned students. Only the leniency of the victim of his assault (and his colleagues) spared Kepel from spending a long weekend (or more) in a jail of the nation's capital.

While my relations with Kepel have never been exactly friendly, this has not prevented me from recognizing that he has real talents. These range from his remarkable fundraising ability and his publishing power to the quality of his writing. Beyond this, unreservedly and quite unironically, I concede to Kepel a genuine ability to attract many of the excellent scholars who will follow us—from Stéphane Lacroix through Loulouwa Al Rachid to Thomas Pierret and many others. He has, moreover, found them excellent publishing opportunities, which the entire scholarly world can be grateful for.

In part, my first differences with Kepel likely also derived from the fact that, unlike Roy, he was never content with accumulating the capital of mere knowledge. Whereas the overwhelming majority of his colleagues are content to have their work achieve some recognition, Kepel, whom Roy dubbed a "top-notch professional Rastignac,"[14] has tirelessly hustled throughout his career to be granted the exercise of formal powers over French research institutions on the Arab and Muslim worlds. Sometimes none too subtly—and to this day, without any great result to show for it.

I had expressly distanced myself from Roy's thesis that Islamists had "failed." I did the same when, in his 2000 book *Jihad: The Rise and Decline of Islamism*,[15] which met with unprecedented media coverage, Kepel made the peremptory announcement that Islamists were in "decline." (Kepel, in passing, quite simply neglected to take due note of the content of the book in which his colleague Roy had, some years previously, set out the narrative that led towards the "failure of political Islam.") "The last twenty-five years have witnessed both the waxing and waning of the militant Islamist movement—a phenomenon whose emergence was as spectacular as it was unforeseen.[16] [...] Islamist movements have entered into a spiral of decline that has accelerated since the beginning of the 1990s."[17] Barely had he set out this thesis than its credibility was shredded by the tragedy of September 11.

The decline of Islamism, which was so dramatically contradicted by events, purportedly resulted from the breakup of the contingent alliance forged in the 1970s and 1980s between three social groups: underprivileged youth, the pious bourgeoisie, and Islamist intellectuals. This explanation left me skeptical on several counts. The first was that before—very late in the day—he chose to take the part played by a "pious bourgeoisie" into account, Kepel had long refused to concede what should have been a foundational, self-evident fact—namely, that one can be both "bourgeois and an Islamist." With little concern for the obvious exception of Saudi militants comfortably ensconced in their oil rent, Kepel had long sustained the "economicist" *doxa* according to which Islamists recruited only among those left behind by development policies. "In Algeria," so a special correspondent sent by *Le Monde*, Jacques de Barrin, had already thought he could enlighten his readers on December 27, 1991, "the Islamic Salvation Front recruited most of its followers on the fringes of society—among those who had nothing to lose in giving the Front a chance, and who are ready to take every risk."

From very early on, I made the choice to analyze the movement through the infinitely wider angle of its identity-politics dimensions. I therefore never adopted this overly restrictive approach. This never led me to deny that an oppositional movement, including, where relevant, its more radical offshoots, could have a specific and potentially evolving social base, which it clearly matters to understand within each national context.[18] Tracking how the social base of opposition movements develops is in no way beside the point. (So long as these developments are not extrapolated into a socio-economic explanation of the reasons for which such protest movements take up the lexicon of "re-Islamization"—or let go of it.) It remains no less crucial to dissociate the social variables of a protest movement from the identity-based variables that determined the political vocabulary through which its members expressed their protest. Sidelining the fact that the identity-variables that determine the choice of the Islamic lexicon are potentially trans-social is all the less likely to lead to a pertinent analysis.

Knowing Too Much ... or Too Little? Flaws in the Drift towards Formalism

In another expression of our differences, Kepel's approach strikes me as obfuscating the drivers of the fundamentally oppositional dimension of the Islamist trend, concealing these behind the façade of laying out its formal characteristics. This patent inclination towards formalism strikes me as organically linked to the process whereby the political framework of Islamism becomes blurred. With respect to jihadism in our generation, refusal to address its fundamental political causes is once again displayed by overstating its social variables. The idea is—to restate the point— that only economic deprivation could make one become a *jihadi*. This approach, sidelining any political factors, uncontrollably leads towards a focus on hypothetical intellectual genealogies, leaning on doctrinal texts or founding programs, linked to one another by human or technological carriers. The general atmosphere of such a scholarly project can only tend towards coming closer to the genre of a police investigation than it does to the scholarly construction of the complexity of the research object. Among analysts of the *jihadi* phenomenon, Kepel is among a very few to ascribe such broad explanatory powers to the key figures of radicalism—whereas, say, very few ISIS militants refer to Abu Musab al-Suri. This fetishism tends to reduce the explanations for a mass protest dynamic to the part played in it by a few individuals. Yet who could believe that, without these individuals, none of this would have come to pass?

Kepel's approach features a further methodological flaw: it overestimates the ideological variables that lead to conflict—in this case, the religious variables, namely, Salafism. In May 2016, the *Revue des Deux Mondes* published a long interview in which Kepel asserted that "these are not 'red brigades' turned 'green.'" 'To Gilles Kepel, radicalization does not come before Islamization'—or so the journal condensed his argument here. Overestimating the part played by ideological carriers, Kepel laid out his thesis according to which the rise of Salafism denotes a cultural breach: a trend that can turn those imbued with it against the society that produced them.[19]

Finally, Kepel grants disproportionate weight to the technological carriers of thought that Islamists use in the most mundane fashion, no more nor less so than do their rivals or opponents of all stripes. Granted, the emergence of audiocassettes as a tool to spread the militant word had been raised to the status of a key explanation to the rise of Islamism in the 1980s. As analysts were confronted with the emergence of Al-Qaeda, the role played by the internet became subject to the same obsession.[20] During the "Arab Spring," this slanted reading found a new lease of life: it was all the internet's fault! Social media, a mere auxiliary to these revolts, was elevated to the status of a driving force of protest movements—when, as events would demonstrate, such protest fundamentally derived from rejection by society *as a whole*, Islamists included, of the four decades of dictatorship that had come before.

Fixated upon the *form* in which hostility to the Other is expressed (its carriers, modes, and the itineraries it follows), Kepel's reading hews close to received wisdom. As a whole, it thereby sidelines investigation into, or that takes into, account the fundamental causes of radicalism—that is to say, of the roots of the rising hostility towards the Western world across whole swaths of the Muslim world. In so doing (unless that is precisely what it seeks to achieve), this reading once again buries precisely the variable which I insist time and again is central to analyzing the phenomenon. This is the multifarious effects of North/South domination, which the close of the colonial era has in no way expunged from international relations. This slant is nothing new, far from it. It fits within the tradition of the Western gaze and, more broadly, of the blinkers through which masters of the world of all kinds gaze upon the Other. In overstating ideological variables for the Other's behavior, we circumscribe how this hostility expresses itself, restricting it to causes exclusively derived from cultural or religious belonging ("Palestinians resist, not because they are occupied, but because they are Muslim," and so on). This selective fascination is very far from being the preserve of a single scholar. But Kepel is a remarkable embodiment of it. The drift towards formalism reveals itself all the more easily when, as is characteristic of Kepel's work, no significant distinction is made between the political appropriation of religion in the dominated Muslim South and its parallel in the reigning Judeo-Christian North.

1991: The Revenge of God—or of the South? The *trompe l'oeil* of the "Three Fundamentalisms"

Yet another disagreement with Kepel is perhaps more structural. This relates to the ways in which he minimizes how persistent North/South relations of domination remain. A case in point is his recourse to the trope of a universal "revenge of God" to characterize how the political and religious fields of the Abrahamic religions relate to one another.[21] From very early on, I favored inverting the terms of this trope by positing a "revenge of the South"—or rather, simply the South's return to center stage. This enables us to draw a crucial distinction between the contexts of the "North," weakened but still dominant, and the "South" that, even while it is in rebellion, still belongs to the side of the dominated. Moreover, the political system in each is substantively different. By contrast, the idea of a "revenge of God" obfuscates, among other things, the deep differences between, on the one hand, the socio-political context that produced the assassin of Anwar Sadat—and on the other, that which produced the assassin of Yitzhak Rabin. Yet these differences are fundamental. First, they account for the relationship (in the present case, a relationship of domination) that persists between the respective societies of each assassin. Second, they account for the deep discrepancy between the status of an Israeli citizen within a truly democratic society (democratic at least, that is, for Israeli Jews) and of an Egyptian who was reduced to a struggle for survival amid the all-out repression that Sadat had just unleashed against the intelligentsia of his country, whatever shade their politics was.

This extremely reductive approach would last until, in 2015, the time came to account for the latest offshoot of the *jihadi* phenomenon. Before applying his logic to the trade unionists of France's largest, Communist-oriented trade union, the Confédération Générale du Travail,[22] Kepel came to invite his readers to entertain the thought that a congruence might be discerned between the supporters of the National Front and those of the Islamic State.[23] Granted, ISIS and the National Front are two radical and sectarian offshoots of human societies that most of us find deeply unattractive. They also, however, differ rather fundamentally. For one thing because, subject to exceptions, National Front activists—let us be grateful to them for that at least—do not (yet?) put into practice the fantasies of violence that their rhetoric promotes. These offshoots differ all the more so in that they have emerged from two political geographies whose historicity, and whose place in the world, stand in stark contrast to one another. In particular (and perhaps especially) this is because the one that produced the National Front still dominates the other. The political imaginary of Parisian *jihadi*s relates to the dominated South. That of National Front voters is more or less consciously mobilized in the service of perpetuating the hegemony of the North. Seeking to draw an analogy between the two is thus a hard sell. In any event, the invitation to consider their "congruence" throws out what may, to the National Front's voters, be a mere detail of history,[24] swiftly forgotten, but it remains a painful open sore to millions of the globe's other citizens. Namely: the violence of sixteen years of occupation and war in Iraq, and the one to two million Afghans, Pakistanis, and Iraqis killed through the "War on Terror" which the West has fought in their countries. Those are the variables that make the analogy between the National Front and ISIS not only clumsy and mistaken—but also, in many ways, truly unseemly.

A final stratagem enables conjuring away the various effects of the persistence of North/South relations of domination. The neoconservative approach has a fail-proof mechanism to deal with the demands for recognition that now and again, inevitably, slip through the wall of media indifference. In order to discredit the protests of the dominated, and to perfect the denial of their ability to represent themselves, it turns out to be enough to invent an illusionary "competition" between the attacker and the attacked. The effect is to obscure the skewed balance in power between them—and the differences in how far each "victim" can be held responsible for its own situation. What should be done should you happen someday to accidentally—or worse, deliberately—run over your neighbor's hedge and ruin his flowerbeds? Or even, as the Israeli Defense Forces frequently do in Gaza, destroy the very pillars his home is built upon? Simple: calmly wait for him to dare to complain in public. Then, in a tone of unrestrained exasperation, copiously condemn his unbearable tendency to "play the victim."

Since 2011, then, for the sum of these reasons, which are somewhat different according to whether they apply to Kepel or Roy, I have distanced myself very clearly from how each of these authors assesses the part played by Islamists in how the Arab Spring broke out. Both ascribed a more strictly religious basis to the Islamist trend than an identity-based one. Both underestimated the depth of its social basis during the first weeks of the Arab Spring. Most likely for these reasons, they felt themselves able not only to announce, but also to "explain," that the Islamist capacity for political mobilization had supposedly collapsed. This is a theory to which I never subscribed.[25] In point of fact, this fragile speculation, which was very widely taken up in the media and beyond, went down in flames shortly afterwards.[26] To Gilles Kepel, Islamists had once and for all become "old-fashioned" (as his students "had been telling him for some time"). To Olivier Roy, they were being overtaken by a spike in religiosity for which he left out any specific explanation ("When everything is religious, nothing is religious"[27]) and that had cut the (political) grass from under their feet. Who in the region could now "vote for those who were not at the rendezvous of revolution?"[28] Those rash lines were written a few weeks before Egyptian Islamists (whose various parties amassed nearly 70 percent of the vote) swept the elections, followed in short order by their Tunisian counterparts.

The test of the ballot box revealed more than just the limits of political forecasting. That is always a risky business, even if none of us, myself included, can resist indulging in it. Moreover, it emphasized the structural fragility of the concepts and the analytical toolbox that had enabled both Roy and Kepel to shape such forecasts. A few weeks later, I read Kepel's answer to a journalist who had asked him to explain why Egyptian Islamists had triumphed at the ballot box (thereby shredding his predictions): "We've known for a long time that the Islamist parties are better organized than the others." Sadly, I was probably among only a few to be left speechless.

Notes

1 In the case of the 2005 riots, Kepel minimized the death by electrocution of two adolescents who were being chased by police in Clichy-sous-Bois. Rather, he emphasizes an alternative trigger. Three days later, a tear gas canister was shot close to a mosque. According to Kepel, these riots presaged the terrorist attacks of 2015. Gilles Kepel (with Antoine Jardin), *Terreur sur l'Hexagone. Genèse du djihad français*, Gallimard, Paris, 2015, pp. 36–7, translated as *Terror in France: The Rise of Jihad in the West*, Princeton University Press, Princeton, NJ, 2017.
2 Olivier Roy, "Ces terroristes sont des pieds nickelés, les mettre sur le même pied que la nation française est une insulte à cette dernière," *Atlantico*, December 2, 2015, www.atlantico.fr/decryptage/2472911/olivier-roy-ces-terroristes-sont-des-pieds-nickeles-les-mettre-sur-le-meme-pied-que-la-nation-francaise-est-une-insulte-a-cette-derniere-olivier-roy (last accessed June 15, 2019). "Pieds Nickelés" refers to the characters of a comic strip created in June 1908 by Louis Forton and reprised to this day (more discreetly) by various authors. Its lightweight heroes want, above all else, to keep their feet "nickels" (perfectly clean), i.e. to not dirty them through work. They thus live on the margins of society—and at its expense.
3 One could likely usefully substitute for "radicalization" such terms as "commitment" or "rejection."
4 In *Islamopsychose, pourquoi la France diabolise les Musulmans* (Fayard, Paris, 2017), Thomas Guénolé interprets the "reductio ad islamum" that, to his mind, characterizes Gilles Kepel's approach when Kepel neglects the quantitative dimension that should enable him to distinguish a thoroughly marginal (radical) phenomenon from a quite distinct mass phenomenon (p. 75).
5 The assertiveness of the literalist, Salafi wing of the Islamist movement inexorably came to respond to the blanket ostracism of the Brotherhood. Salafis had always denounced the latter's "lax" strategy of reappropriation of the Western political apparatus. (See François Burgat, "Salafistes contre Frères musulmans. Un changement dans la continuité," *Le Monde diplomatique*, June 2010, www.monde-diplomatique.fr/2010/06/BURGAT/19235 (last accessed June 15, 2019).)
6 Olivier Roy, *In Search of the Lost Orient: An Interview*, foreword by Jean-Louis Schlegel and Olivier Mongin, Columbia University Press, New York, 2017.
7 Olivier Roy, *Islam and Resistance in Afghanistan*, 2nd ed., Cambridge University Press, Cambridge, 1990.
8 Baudouin Dupret, "Avec une touche de nuance: à propos de Gilles Kepel, *Jihad. Expansion et déclin de l'islamisme*," *Annuaire de l'Afrique du Nord*, no. 38, 1999 (quoted in François Burgat, "De l'islamisme au post-islamisme: vie et mort d'un concept: les non-dits du 'déclin islamiste,'" *Esprit*, August 2001).
9 Brynjar Lia, *The Society of the Muslim Brothers in Egypt: The Rise of an Islamic Mass Movement, 1928–1942*, Ithaca Press, Reading, 1998.
10 Raphaël Liogier helpfully reminds us that the origins of the concept made

famous by the American political scientist Samuel Huntington (1927–2008) predate Bernard Lewis's use of it (Raphaël Liogier, *La Guerre des civilisations n'aura pas lieu. Coexistence et violence au xxie siècle*, CNRS Éditions, Paris, 2016). It was first used in 1926 by one Basil Matthews, as the title of a book in which, paraphrasing Renan, he set out his observer-traveler's utter conviction that Islam and modern science were implacably incompatible.

11 Gilles Kepel, *Muslim Extremism in Egypt*.
12 Bruno Etienne, *L'Islamisme radical*, Hachette, Paris, 1987.
13 See Pascal Ménoret, *The Saudi Enigma*; *L'Arabie. Des routes de l'encens à l'ère du pétrole*, Gallimard, Paris, 2010; *Joyriding in Riyadh*.
14 See Cécile Daumas, "Olivier Roy et Gilles Kepel, querelle française sur le djihadisme," *Libération*, April 14, 2016, www.liberation.fr/debats/2016/04/14/olivier-roy-et-gilles-kepel-querelle-francaise-sur-le-jihadisme_1446226 (last accessed June 15, 2019). The author of this article also mentions the "other major explanation, dubbed a 'third-worldist'" one (which Roy and Kepel agree to denigrate). Its starting point is "the geopolitics of the Middle East, the post-colonial inheritance, and its consequences in terms of racism and discrimination in European societies." She adds that this is "mainly defended by the third major figure of French [scholarship on] Islam, François Burgat, a renowned specialist based in Aix-en-Provence." On Kepel's critiques of Roy, see Gilles Kepel and Bernard Rougier, "'Radicalisations' et 'Islamophobie': le roi est nu," *Libération*, March 14, 2016, www.liberation.fr/debats/2016/03/14/radicalisations-et-islamophobie-le-roi-est-nu_1439535 (last accessed 15 June, 2019).
15 The English title was *Jihad: The Trail of Political Islam*, revised ed., I.B. Tauris, London, 2009.
16 Gilles Kepel, *Jihad: The Trail of Political Islam*.
17 Gilles Kepel, *Jihad, Expansion et déclin de l'islamisme*, Gallimard, Paris, 2000, p. 11.
18 See, for instance, a useful study of the social base of Tunisian Salafis: Olfa Lamloum and Mohamed Ali Ben Zina (eds), *Les Jeunes de Douar Hicher et d'Ettadhamen. Une enquête sociologique*, Arabesques, Tunis, 2015.
19 For a well-argued approach to the specific contribution of Salafi movements to the dynamics of the Arab Spring, cf. the excellent volume by Francesco Cavatorta and Fabio Merone (eds), *Salafism after the Arab Awakening: Contending with People's Power*, Hurst, London, 2017.
20 One too often forgets how, from the telephone to social media, the use by radical groups of the weapon of technology cuts both ways. Syrian authorities responded to the very first weeks of the Syrian "Arab Spring" of 2011 by lifting their restrictions on Facebook. This was perfectly synchronized with the fact that the regime had recently acquired (from a French company) the technology that was to enable it to sow devastation among activists. Similarly, the first harbingers of US success in its counter-insurgency campaign in Iraq came after an extensive mobile phone network was set up. (See Toby Dodge, *Iraq: From War to a New Authoritarianism*, Routledge, London/New York, 2013.)

21 Gilles Kepel, *La Revanche de Dieu. Chrétiens, juifs et musulmans à la reconquête du monde*, Seuil, Paris, 1991, translated as *The Revenge of God: The Resurgence of Islam, Christianity, and Judaism in the Modern World*, Penn State University Press, Philadelphia, PA, 1993.

22 See "Gilles Kepel: 'On assiste à une guerre au sens de l'islam,'" *L'Express*, June 21, 2016, www.lexpress.fr/actualite/societe/gilles-kepel-on-assiste-a-une-guerre-sur-le-sens-de-l-islam_1804424.html (last accessed June 15, 2019), and the virulent critique of Kepel's stance by Alain Gresh, "Gilles Kepel, l'islamo-gauchisme, la CGT et les hooligans," *Nouvelles d'Orient*, June 28, 2016, https://seenthis.net/messages/messages/503730?fbclid=IwAR2se76Il_FI7T9Z4_eUcCTPJRM0alqS8G5InYd5TRSW0_oi_XwWHfyCNTs (last accessed June 15, 2019).

23 See Gilles Kepel, *Terror in France: The Rise of Jihad in the West*, and his many media interviews, for instance with the interviewer Jean-Jacques Bourdin on BMTV/RMC, December 16, 2015.

24 Translator's note: a reference to the National Front's founder Jean-Marie Le Pen calling the gas chambers a "detail" of the history of World War II.

25 See Baudouin Loos, "Quel islamisme face à la révolution?" *Le Soir*, February 25, 2011, www.cetri.be/Quel-islamisme-face-a-la (last accessed June 15, 2019) ("The specialist in political Islam François Burgat considers that the Islamists are far from being absent from the current Arab revolutions").

26 At the outset of the "Tunisian Spring," before realizing the scale of her mistake, a certain colleague reproached political scientists (Burgat, Kepel, and Roy thrown together) with driving the disproportionate interest in Islamist politics. This was at a time when she thought she could triumphantly announce (nor was she alone in doing so) that the Tunisian and Egyptian case studies had (at last) revealed their weak social basis. (Sarah Ben Néfissa, "Révolutions arabes: les angles morts de l'analyse politique des sociétés de la région," *Confluences Méditerranée*, no. 77, 2011.)

27 Olivier Roy, "Révolution post-islamiste," *Le Monde*, February 12, 2011, www.lemonde.fr/idees/article/2011/02/12/revolution-post-islamiste__1478858__3232.html (last accessed June 15, 2019): "As paradoxical as it may seem, re-Islamization made the religious variable banal and depoliticized it: When everything is religious, nothing is religious"; and Olivier Roy, "This is not an Islamist Revolution," *New Statesman*, February 15, 2011: "What has been perceived in the west as a great, green wave of re-Islamization is in fact nothing but a trivialization of Islam: everything has become Islamic, from fast food to women's fashion."

28 Olivier Roy, "Comme solution politique, l'islamisme est fini," *Rue 89*, January 2011: "Why would they vote for people who failed to show up for the revolution? This is not Iran in 1979, when the revolution was made by Islamists, or Algeria in 1991, when the Islamic Salvation Front led the way. Islamists were at the forefront of those movements. Today, they are entirely absent from the political challenge."

14

The *Charlie Hebdo* Attacks: Failure of Islam, or: Failure of Politics?

Of course, the scale of the two events cannot be compared. Yet the attacks against *Charlie Hebdo* and the customers of a kosher supermarket by Amedy Coulibaly and the Kouachi brothers really were a kind of French "September 11." On January 7, 2015, this violent, painful electric shock thrust the question of our relationship with the Muslim world as a whole back into the spotlight. From Yemen to Syria through the Israeli–Arab conflict and France, the counter of a rational, scientific understanding of the Islamist phenomenon was reset. Not only that: the whole spectrum of our interaction with Muslims was brutally "called upon" by this episode. The massacre of *Charlie Hebdo*'s journalists set into motion—or, rather, accelerated—a process of "cognitive withdrawal," back to the old binary certainties of "us" and "them." In a worst-case scenario that cannot be entirely ruled out, this was perhaps what historians of Europe will someday identify as the "beginning of the end" of the road towards including Islam and Muslims on the Old Continent. In the heat of the moment, I set out the framework of my reflection in a blog post (see boxed text below).

"Of All Those Who Did Not Deserve to Die …"[1]

At one end of the chain, before our eyes, lies the execution of twelve people. After joining without any reservation in the emotion aroused by this event, it becomes terribly difficult to add anything more. If not, for my part, and speaking for many others too, that … fucking hell … Cabu … Cabu didn't deserve that. Nor did the others, I know. But I wouldn't have the indecency to speak of that. I didn't know them. I didn't know them, because I had long since radically broken with their newspaper's curious conception of freedom of expression.

What more could be said, after that absolute condemnation, that would not be likened to defending the indefensible? At one end, then, we have twelve men and women who did not deserve to die.

At the other end are those who took upon themselves the right to kill them—a right which they perhaps even elevated to a duty. Over there, at the other end, lies all that what we know to be most evil. And that, be it only to understand it and, when we have to, to seek to prevent it (which does not mean to forgive it), we desperately need to comprehend. Our misfortune is that, over there, there are no spotlights. Or rather, there are only dim spotlights, that only selectively light up some of the victims, or some of the perpetrators. [...] It is in those shadows that the information deficit risks being felt.

Any attempt to fill that void here is ... mission impossible. One would have to recall the existence of a fathomless breach. Far from being a novelty, this has never really healed since the colonial era. A chasm that excludes from France's politics, not just a few handfuls of extremists—but also millions of Muslim citizens (including Ali Baddou;[2] Michel Houellebecq makes him, like me, want to "throw up") and some specific features of those politics, both internal and external. In short, this exclusion ranges from Hollande's prolonged passivity in reacting to the massacres in Gaza, whose root causes he encouraged, through allowing tens of thousands of Syrians to be killed, to his sudden bellicosity faced with the far fewer executions in Mosul—but those were of "Christians," not "just" Iraqis!

What I mean to address here is all these "brave battles," led with much waving of flags and many a Rafale fighter jet when they are in the service of the few. By contrast, in the name of the very same principles of the selfsame Republic, other such battles are endlessly deferred when they would be in the service of others. Inextricably linked to these patent underachievements of the French Republic is the way in which certain social trends accompany them—or indeed, through their euphemisms, condone them. Here, it is not Houllebecq or Zemmour who need to be checked off when we survey the cast of characters that led inexorably to the catastrophe of *Charlie Hebdo*. Alone, they have no such power. It is, rather, the endless cohort of those who blissfully handed Houllebecq or Zemmour the microphone. It is all those about whom one has to wonder whether they might not in fact rejoice to hear said out loud what they themselves whispered to us for so many years—and through such hypocritical rhetorical contortions, too.

The latest episode of this lengthy and lethal face-off [...] may be logically considered as having a more or less direct link to the events in Paris. This is clearly the French decision, in August 2014, to go to war with one of the new political players of the post-colonial reconfiguration of the Middle East: the armed group that, under the name of Islamic State, lays claim to the mantle of at least part of the Syrian and Iraqi states. Since August 2014, our planes bomb night and day, with the precision for which air strikes are famed, targets that an especially wide national consensus has designated as being legitimate. To date, this policy had caused several hundred deaths through the bombing of the Mosul "caliphate." Today, we now have to add to that number twelve new victims, in Paris this time—though in a separate category, since these victims wielded no other weapon than the pen.

At first, the Paris attacks united us in a wave of emotion and condemnation for this new irruption of armed violence within the intimate space of our national political domain. First a targeted attack. Then, a few months later a blind and especially large-scale one. But since the "*Charlie Hebdo*" demonstrations of January 11, 2015, interpretations of the "Paris September 11" have driven us a little further apart still than we already were.

"Salafis"—or "Small-Time Crooks"? Divergent Interpretations of the Paris 9/11

To come straight to the point: Kepel's approach, like Roy's, exacerbated an already apparent contradiction. This consisted of minimizing the impact of ancient and ongoing North/South relations of domination on the behavior of the players concerned—if not ignoring it altogether. Kepel, as usual, concentrated on meticulously describing the vectors, modes, and instruments of expression of this deep hostility elicited by the West. He also, however, persistently abstained from lucidly seeking out the causes of that hostility. To arrive at a nearly identical result, Roy, almost from thin air, created a *jihadi* who sprung from nowhere. He asked us to believe that this figure was entirely disconnected from its original milieu (Muslims in France). The result was to make it impossible to think through any short-term or historical correlation with the injustices of all kinds endured in this milieu. Kepel, for his part, mentioned such suffering only in passing—all the better to gloss over it.

Both authors, then, sideline the heart of the matter: the deep historical roots and the endlessly renewed, mundanely political causes that drive the misunderstanding between "Islam and the West." Keeping a great distance from these interpretations, I stuck to a phrase that I first used in 1997 to the European Parliament: "We will have the Muslims we enable ourselves to have."³ I persisted in thinking—and in trying to convince others—that such violence was the end product of a malfunction that Kepel and Roy more or less entirely sidelined.⁴ Each after their own fashion: culturalist for Kepel, "psychosocial" for Roy. Namely: the malfunctioning of the political sphere, and the dysfunction of the mechanisms of representation and resource distribution among the various components of the political field. Only this thesis struck me as able to account for the variable that no one wanted to hear mentioned: our obvious share of responsibility in our *jihadi* misfortune. I meant to set our own world and its dysfunctions at the core of the chain of causation—and not only, like an overwhelming majority of analysts, to restrict it to the Other's world or, more mistakenly still, the Other's religion or culture.

Like his previous ones, Kepel's book published in December 2015, entitled *Terror in France*, is very well written.⁵ Even if I have little taste for the condescending and contemptuous tone he wields towards the "ill-educated" when he professes to explain to us how they operate. He delivers unto us a mass of details worthy of attention, some but not all of them of a police-like nature. Mainly, however, he upholds the thesis that sectarian radicalization precedes political radicalization—and not vice versa. The origins of the Paris attacks must, he argues, be sought first of all in the fact that a "deviant" interpretation of one or other *sura* of the Quran (Salafism)—if not these *sura*s themselves—has unstoppably spread among some French Muslims. (God knows how—as, indeed, does Kepel, who has tracked the spread of these *sura*s.) With the greatest meticulousness, he thus charts the intellectual and territorial genealogies that connect Muslim conservatism to political violence. Coming from such and such a country, radicalization passed through such and such an individual or militant, then through another. It transited, in his account, through such and such a neighborhood of such and such a town—and even from the fourth to the third floor of a certain French prison!⁶

The "communications" of the Other (here, ISIS) are once again brought forth as the secret of that Other's appeal. Kepel's interpretation had previously ascribed an excessive centrality to Ibn Taymiyya's⁷ Egyptian readers (Sayed Qutb, Choukri Mustapha, and Abdessalam Faraj) (already) overshadowing the terrible (Nasserist) repression that they had all endured.⁸ The time has now come for Abu Musab al-Suri to take up the task of confusing the issue. (He too, as we have seen, only departed from the mainstream Muslim Brotherhood trend after the carnage of Hama in 1982.) This highly atypical figure is now raised to the rank of quasi-"ringleader" or even "detonator" of revolt in part of the globe. Step by step, the carriers, mediators, and ancillaries of a revolt thus (falsely) become its causes.⁹ By the same token, other, real causes disappear from our field of vision, obfuscated by the minutiae of tracking everything (carriers, intermediaries, financing, etc.)—except the heart of the matter. Here, the details of the *why* of this revolt stand in dramatic contrast with the vagueness, if not the relative vacuum, that surrounds the *what*.

Far removed from the culturalist atmosphere that defines Kepel's mental universe, Roy distinguished himself by avoiding the Salafi variable altogether. He would in fact be reproached for this in unusually violent and personalized terms, going beyond the usual tone of even the most impassioned academic debate: "The emperor has no clothes," "majestic ignorance," and so on.[10] Roy sets up an analogy between jihadism and such protest movements as the Baader-Meinhof Gang or Maoism. His analytical apparatus has at times been enthusiastically taken up by some of those who rightly denounce the wholesale incrimination of France's Muslims as being collectively responsible for the tragedies in Paris. Not everything in that apparatus has seemed to me incompatible with my own perceptions.

First of all, I subscribed unreservedly to the strategy for fighting ISIS that Roy sketched out in a superlative formula: "ISIS's worst enemy is ... ISIS!"[11] The inevitable downfall of ISIS will come about from the inherent contradictions of the extreme authoritarianism of its leaders. On the other hand, whenever political players as illegitimate as Westerners are in this part of the world strive to assert themselves as ISIS's "Enemy Number One," their intervention runs every risk of reinforcing its prestige and the mobilizing capacities of those whom it purports to weaken. This is to say nothing of the fact that such intervention can end only by bringing to power, in the wastelands created by our life-saving bombs, Kurdish or Shia militias that are terribly ill-equipped to lead the societies they operate within out of their crisis. I also embraced Roy's welcome condemnation of the dichotomy of the absolutely contradictory demands that the "Republic" (or those who speak in its name) impose upon French Muslims.

The *Charlie Hebdo* episode witnessed the latest iteration of a flagrant contradiction. The injunction regularly addressed by the vox populi to French Muslims to dissolve themselves into the national fabric, or else be accused of "communitarianism," goes hand in hand with another injunction. The latter is heavy with insinuation. It reverses the first, and "communitarianizes" their condemnation of violence inflicted anywhere in the world by any of their co-religionists—especially when such violence targets "Westerners." Roy thus quite rightly insists upon the latent contradiction in enclosing French Muslims within the identity of a "Muslim community" that, to his mind, "does not exist."

The aims of those who support this reading may be laudable. The reference to a community does play some part in making it impossible to think through the diversity of those whom it is made up of. The phrase, however, strikes me as having its limits. It fails to convey an essential feature of the reality lived by *all* French Muslims, in their infinite diversity. This is the very tangible reality of the "glass ceiling," or barbed-wire fence that somehow means that, whether one is called "Mohammed" or "Rashid," one encounters more trouble in exercising social or political mobility than when one is called "Gilles," "Olivier," or "François."

We come back to the amiable tendency of all those who think it necessary to deny the relevance of the terms "East" and "West," in the name of better coexistence among peoples. East and West do, however—in the short term at least—differ in a highly tangible way, that has nothing to do with culture, and which our proactive humanism should never allow us to forget or underestimate. The one dominates the other! Yet perhaps it is this unspoken (still less accepted) dichotomy that unstoppably makes those who are not authorized to feel "fully French" run the risk of searching for the ideology that will allow them to feel French in "fully separate" fashion.

A Nihilism of Small-Time Crooks?

My key disagreement with Roy, however, lies elsewhere. It is in the fact that he sees the rise in European jihadism as merely a kind of psychosocial spasm on the part of individuals who are relatively, historically, and socially detached from their environment. He considers this spasm to be relatively extraneous to the religious variable—a point on which I am happy to follow him. He also, however, considers it to be no less extraneous to the political variable—and this position, I absolutely refuse to condone. Roy accounts for the origins of this violence through a paradigm of "riffraff" or, to reprise his own terminology, a paradigm of "small-time crooks." To leave no room for misunderstanding, he completes this by specifying that "to put [*jihadis*] on the same level as the French nation is an insult to the latter."[12] The "small-time crooks" paradigm sets up a category of socially "fallen" individuals, intellectual and political inverterbrates, whose key characteristic is to be radically cut off from the worldview of Muslims in France or elsewhere. Their only pathology, then, is an individual one that could simply be termed "nihilism,"[13] with no need to be more specific.

The "small-time crooks" paradigm can be liberating when it is deftly used as a humorous trope.[14] It seems to me to be rather less credible as a scholarly trope. Young "outcasts" of French society, the overwhelming majority of them of Muslim heritage, purportedly seize upon the *jihadi* pretext just as they could grasp hold of any other: to escape the drabness of their social failure. Such is the thesis of the "Islamization of radicalism" that was first formulated by the anthropologist Alain Bertho.[15] Clearly, this thesis partly lays out a reality. The ranks of *jihadi*s may include such specimens, especially but not only among recent converts. Yet to my mind two things must be refuted here: first, the caricature of this desocialization, which goes together with the concurrent hypothesis of depoliticization. Second, extrapolating this into the pivot of an explanation, when—at best—it can illuminate only one of its components.

Among others (including, incidentally, Gilles Kepel), the sociologists Farhad Khosrokhavar and Ouisa Kies have emphasized the obvious. If these youth were not politicized before they went through jail, all aspirant-*jihadi*s were very strongly politicized by the time they left it.[16] Roy completely occludes this fact. He raises one of the many facets of this phenomenon to the status of a sole explanatory pivot-variable. This leads him to deny that not only European jihadists, but also the Iraqi cadre of ISIS officers, most of whom are veterans of Saddam Hussein's army, might be self-conscious political players. In both of these types, Roy sees only "nutters"—if only because they have the impudence of wanting to "found an Islamic state."[17] This is a project that Roy had long since proclaimed to be outdated—since, after all, the era of "post-Islamism" had begun. Here, the shortcuts of a depoliticized analysis throw together not only the "demand" for jihad among some Europeans, but also its Iraqi "supply"—whereas the latter can hardly be reduced to some "nihilist" itch.

As such, this abrupt extrapolation of the social periphery of a revolt to the status of its overall explanatory principle leads to insurmountable contradictions. The "small-time crooks" paradigm rests on the premise of the absolute "nihilist" isolation of *jihadi*s: the isolation is deemed to be not merely generational, but also "nihilist" isolation with respect to their milieu, that is, with respect to all Muslims, in France or elsewhere. We are to understand that Amedy Coulibaly, the killer of the Hyper Cacher supermarket in January 2015, had "no connection to the problems of Muslims in France." Nor was he interested in "the concrete struggles of the Muslim world (Palestine)." That theory rests upon especially fragile processes of observation and reasoning.[18] The hermetic social isolation of European *jihadi*s is to be demonstrated by their small numbers and, far more so, because, according to Roy, their family environment radically rejects them. After all: when one of their children leaves for Syria, instead of joining them there, do their parents not immediately go "complain to Dounia Bouzar"?[19]

In *Jihad and Death*, published in November 2016, Roy emphasizes his argument that *jihadi*s are not the direct victims of violence against Muslims.[20] They are thereby presumed to be not in touch with Western policies. Not within the European societies in which their rebellion takes root—nor in the East, whether in Syria, Iraq, Palestine, or Afghanistan.

No attempt to explain the behavior of those rejected by their milieu could thus be suffered to invoke history, on any account. Nor could it take stock of the deprivations of all kinds suffered in that milieu. To use Roy's terms, it is out of the question that the *jihadi* phenomenon should be correlated with "post-colonial suffering, youth identification with the Palestinian cause, their rejection of Western interventions in the Middle East or their exclusion from a racist and Islamophobic France."[21] Nor could it be correlated with colonization. Since, in startlingly abrupt fashion, Roy claims that they didn't live through it! That whole thesis is, to his mind, an "old third-worldist broken record" to be treated with disdain.

Positing this chasm between the revolt of a tiny minority of France's Muslims and the rest of their co-religionists does have a commendable advantage. It nullifies the thesis of the collective guilt of Muslims as a whole, which so many political players—and not only on the far right—tend to take up systematically. Yet this approach also comes at an especially high analytical cost. In a startlingly direct way, the argument also obfuscates the relations of domination endured by the Muslim component of the population, masking what I consider to be the deep roots of the problem. Does the fact that "our" jihadists are only a "tiny number" allow us to prejudge with such certainty that there is no such thing as a malaise that is potentially felt by all those who do not rebel, merely because they condemn the methods used? Let us first take the time to recall that the sample of departure-for-jihad-life narratives, such as those collected by, for instance, Dounia Bouzar's Center for Prevention, take into account only those families that spontaneously asked for help. Concerning other families, we know nothing that supports such a hypothesis. Nothing—except, of course, that for those families that did ask for help, any standpoint other than condemning the radicalized son is politically unsayable. If, that is, they do not wish to find themselves nose-to-the-ground in handcuffs at dawn. For my part, I had to search no further than Aix-en-Provence (not exactly far from my own home) to find the case of a father following his son to Syria where he had just been killed, and himself being seriously injured there ...[22]

Does the fact that some parents of *jihadis* go and complain (to Dounia Bouzar) mean that, by condemning Coulibaly, they subscribe without any nuance to "being *Charlie Hebdo*"? That they are proud of the brainless TV appearances of Imam Chalghoumi who supposedly represents them? That they embrace the French phobia for the *hijab*? That they admired François Hollande's indulgence towards Abdel Fattah Sissi and those who butcher Gaza? That they approved of Nicolas Sarkozy's military arm-waving in Afghanistan, or of François Mitterrand's blind support for the "eradicators" of the Algerian junta—that is to say, for Sissi's predecessors? That they are indifferent towards the glass ceiling and the barbed-wire fence of contempt that, where jobs and housing are concerned, lock them up in the social ghetto of this "community" which they are then so often kindly requested to emerge from?

Psychologizing Protest to Hide Its Political Roots—Revisited

The tendency to reduce a protest movement to the mundane presence on its periphery of members in a state of social or individual failure is hardly new. In fact, faced with the Islamist generation (and its predecessors: let us not forget the Algerian *"fellaga"* thugs), it is a very recurrent drift on the part of the Western gaze. The opaque accusation of "nihilism" was already used, with just as little basis, against the Russian "populists" who, in (very politically) confronting the Tsar's absolutism as early as 1860, were the predecessors of the Bolshevik revolutionaries.[23]

Among the many forerunners of this drift, the "analyses" that were expediently produced throughout the 1990s in France by some "state psychoanalysts" cannot go unmentioned. At the time, these explained to us the roots of the Algerian civil war in terms that are unlikely to survive the verdict of history. To a captive audience, they delivered an inventory of the pathologies that supposedly affected the general psyche and (already!) the sexuality of the members of this Islamist opposition which the inhuman "eradication" policy of the Algerian military had succeeded in radicalizing. In their book *The Meeting of Civilizations* (Seuil, 2007), Youssef Courbage and Emmanuel Todd too, setting aside the effects of Israeli military occupation, thought they could correlate "Palestinian violence" to the fact that, in Palestinian society, the patriarchal social structure delayed marriageble age beyond adolescence, thereby nurturing sexual tension.

The flaws of approaches restricted to the prism of psychoanalysis (if not of psychiatry) steadily help to discredit the political status of mundanely oppositional dynamics—and with it, their legitimacy. The latest of the tools developed to euphemize popular revolts is the category of the "uber-Muslim."[24] Highly significantly, this loses a good share of its scientific credibility when one takes the time to notice that, in explaining violence the world over, it is paired with no inferred theory of the "uber-Jew" or the "uber-Christian." Yet the latter would potentially be no less relevant than the former in isolating the variables behind the racist violence of Avigdor Lieberman, the identity-fixations of a Nadine Morano,[25] or those of then-Prime Minister Manuel Valls and some of his advisers. To shed light on this highly revealing selectiveness, and on the terribly dangerous nature of this approach (more precisely—since it undeniably contains a grain of truth—the dangers of limiting oneself to it, or of overestimating it), it may be especially enlightening to consider a more "noble" mobilization: one that is perceived as legitimate.

What explanatory weight do we ascribe to the psyche, and more specifically to the state of psychological disturbance, of those who went to Spain to fight for the Republic? Or to those who, in their wake, "went up" to the French *maquis* to fight against France's Nazi occupiers? Was Nelson Mandela's sexuality decisive to his political activity? Do we reach for a conceptual toolbox involving a purported "super-Jew" to explain the "acting out" of European volunteers in Israel's army, who head abroad to kill in illegally occupied territory? When we reduce the motivations of those who revolt to their troubles of all kinds, even while these may have hastened the moment of their "acting out," tightly correlating these to their religious belonging, how can it not be obvious that the result can only be a terrible deficit of understanding?

This "psychosocial" reading has been especially applied to Muslim converts who joined ISIS. Insistence upon the relatively high number of converts (around 25 percent) among the ranks of French *jihadi*s has long been brandished as "proof." These youth, it was argued, could not be said to have any relationship to the whole question of colonial as well as community suffering. Such suffering could not therefore be "scientifically" ascribed any significant standing in the inventory of the variables that lead to radicalization—a radicalization that could thereby be termed "nihilist."

As time went on, the socio-economic data regarding these converts became unarguably more precise. This data has all but nullified the hypothesis that, taking as its evidence the presence of radicalized converts, glosses over (or simply denies) the part played by processes of colonial and community exclusion. Not only do the testimonies collected by David Thomson confirm that most converts come from the same socially deprived environments as their neo-co-religionists from Muslim backgrounds. More importantly, they show that these converts also endure being ostracized on a basis that may not be religious, but that certainly is ethnic and that is, in every case, identity based. "One factor stands out particularly in this group," Thomson asserts:

> most come from working-class families and at least half are minorities. Jihadist converts are more often named Kevin than Jean-Eudes. And when they are named Jean-Edouard, Jean-Michel or Willy, they are generally West Indian. The proportion of those raised in Christian homes from sub-Saharan immigration, or from Portuguese households, or, to a lesser extent, from Asian families (Korean or Vietnamese), is very high. France's overseas territories are also well represented among jihad converts. Recruits from the Travelers community have also been noted.[26]

The relative importance of converts should not, of course, be underestimated. But nor can it be imposed as a primary interpretative framework. Not without harming understanding of the ISIS phenomenon as a whole. Not in its European version—the "demand" for jihad. And not in its Middle Eastern theater, in Iraq or Syria, where the "supply" of this jihad is manufactured. With respect to recurrent attempts to decenter analysis in favor (once again) of one of its marginal phenomena, it strikes me that an objection on principle can be entered. As political players, involved in a protest mobilization whose roots are in the Middle East, these converts define themselves as passengers climbing onto a moving train. One cannot, however, expect of such "five-minutes-to-midnight" passengers that they should account for the rationality of a movement in whose shaping they took no part whatsoever—that is, in how the train was built, and where it is bound. The "converts" variable requires a specific explanatory apparatus. This is a field that I have only partly explored.

Doubtless, the variable of rejecting one's origin group, a question inherent to any conversion mechanism, is all the stronger when the distance separating the convert's origin group from his new belonging group is greatest. Clearly, the zeal inherent to newcomers, and their tendency to internalize the imaginary of the chosen group, or even to outstrip its expectations in order to be recognized within it and to merge more naturally into it, must be taken into account. Neither, of course, should the effects of the strategy of the "reception group" be underestimated: its interest in showcasing its "war spoils" won from the enemy, as the ultimate proof of its appeal—and so of its superiority. Yet while the presence of converts grants us access to one component of a complex phenomenon, it cannot be raised to the status of generic explanatory framework. (Converts tell us more about the societies in which the "demand for jihad" develops than they do about the societies that provide the "supply.") Nor can it make any claims to a decisive intervention in how the *jihadi* object itself is to be constructed.

In Their Own Right—or On Their Own?

As for what remains—that is, the motivations of the bulk of ISIS troops—where is the data that would allow us to proclaim with such certainty the principle on which Roy's argument rests: that *jihadi*s are absolutely isolated from their original milieu? The "Arab Spring," Roy's thesis continues, restricted political dynamics to strictly national theaters and reasoning. It thereby slowed inter-Arab dynamics of regionalization or internationalization, if not eliminated them altogether. The supposed proof is that ISIS has "more Belgian *jihadi*s than Egyptians"—itself a doubtful claim. What, then, of the thousands of Tunisians and Saudis who provided the first groups of foreign "volunteers," independently of nationality, who enrolled in the army of the "caliphate"? If Palestinians seem to abstain from joining ISIS, should this not above all be correlated to the fact that they have neither the need nor the ability to go and fight a "distant" American enemy? When Israelis regularly parade even unto the courtyards of their homes, obviously embodying an (extremely) "close enemy," more than enough to use up their capacity to mobilize politically? If Egyptians are less present on the stage of global jihad, is that not also because a good number of them are fighting Sissi in Sinai? And even those "national" *jihadi*s have, ignoring the old state-borders, pledged allegiance to Abu Bakr al-Baghdadi's utopia of a "free Sunnistan," which recruits volunteers from nearly eighty nations, most of them from the Arab world.

Roy's demonstration thus rests upon arguments about which one has to wonder what planet their data comes from, so far removed are they from the "Muslim street." His argument to justify the supposed political alienation of *jihadi*s is that "They never experienced colonization." Doubtless—but who would dare to apply this reasoning to the struggles of the descendants of Jews or Armenians who didn't live through the martyrdom of their ancestors? Or to criticize them for having nonetheless kept alive their forefathers' commitments, or for feeling themselves to be its inheritors?

To pinpoint the political component of the breach opened up by the Paris attacks, it is essential to "zoom out" in ways that domestic French interpretations so systematically fail to. Instead, we need a reading that enables us to interpret the phenomenon within its territorial and temporal contexts. Those are *sine quibus non* to understand it—and, wherever required, to respond to it with some hope of curbing it, rather than worsening it. The temporality required is far longer than the chronicle of incidents related to the caricatures of the Prophet of Islam. The territorial dimension is far broader than Paris in January or November 2015, and those who fell there under the bullets of Kalashnikovs. The timescale must encompass the colonial fracture and its countless victims. The territorial dimension cannot exclude the Middle East and the thousands of victims of F-16s, Rafale fighter jets, and other French and Western drones. Reaching for sociology or psychoanalysis doubtless allows for more precise analysis of the motivations of "our" *jihadi*s, or more precisely of the "auxiliaries" and "accelerators" of their acting out. But to go thus far and no further also runs the risk of obfuscating the heart of the matter: the political matrix of the battle which they have joined.

The "Islamization of radicalism" narrative has met with wide approval and resonance far beyond scholarly circles. It has done so for a simple reason: this analytical framework sets up the violence that hit the streets of Paris as disembodied, and utterly divorced, from the most dubious policies of our governments. As such, it shares an especially fatal flaw with its culturalist rival ("It's all the fault of Islam")—the version towards which Kepel's analysis leans. "(Our) bombs away!" can be read between its lines with a little care—since "their bombs have nothing to do with ours."

The thesis I have defended here is the polar opposite. It searches for the roots of jihadism where those roots actually are: deeply political ones, at the heart of the *malaise* of the poorly chosen targets of our foreign policies, or of those excluded from whole swaths of our nations that hold them at such a distance. It reminds us of what should be the obvious: that whenever our own world, in France, in Iraq, or elsewhere, fails to allow anyone to live fully, "in their own right," the risk will remain high that they will join the ranks of those who want to live "absolutely alone"—regardless of which Prophet they might favor.

Notes

1 François Burgat, "Parmi tous ceux qui ne méritaient pas de mourir …," *Grotius International*, February 2, 2015, http://hoggar.org/2015/01/08/parmi-tous-ceux-qui-ne-meritaient-pas-de-mourir/ (last accessed June 15, 2019).
2 French-Moroccan journalist Ali Baddou.
3 Hearing of the Cultural Commission of the European Parliament, entitled "Islam and Europe," January 1997.
4 François Burgat, "Réponse à Olivier Roy: les non-dits de l'islamisation de la radicalité," *Rue89*, December 1, 2015; "Djihadisme: Kepel et Roy oublient l'essentiel. Une troisième voie est nécessaire," *L'Obs/Le Plus*, July 7, 2016; Public hearing at the French National Assembly, January 12, 2016, www.nouvelobs.com/rue89/rue89-parti-pris/20151201.RUE1504/reponse-a-olivier-roy-les-non-dits-de-l-islamisation-de-la-radicalite.html (last accessed June 15, 2019).
5 Gilles Kepel (with Antoine Jardin), *Terreur sur l'Hexagone*.
6 "The example of Fleury-Mérogis [a prison in Paris's southern suburbs] is incredible: Djamel Beghal, an Al-Qaeda militant, is in isolation on the fourth floor, but has no difficulty in communicating through the window with Kouachi and Coulibaly, who are imprisoned on the floor below. All this happens under the nose of French authorities, who understand nothing of what is happening." ("Entretien réalisé avec Gilles Kepel à l'occasion de la parution de *Terreur sur l'Hexagone*," Gallimard, January 2016, www.folio-lesite.fr/Media/Folio/Entretiens-ecrit/Entretien-Gilles-Kepel.-Terreur-dans-l-Hexagone (last accessed June 15, 2019).)
7 Yahya Michot, *Muslims under non-Muslim Rule: Ibn Taymiyya*, Interface Publications, Oxford, 2006. Cf. the theologian Ibn Taymiyya's writings online, as well as the publications concerning him.
8 François Burgat, *Islamism in the Shadow of al-Qaeda*.

9 "In January 2005, the 1,600 pages of the *Call to Global Islamic Resistance* appeared online: a composite of militant encyclopedia and third-generation *jihad* handbook, written by Suri, a Syrian engineer in his 40s who had obtained Spanish citizenship. It set its seal on the next decade." (Gilles Kepel, *Terror in France*.)
10 Gilles Kepel and Bernard Rougier, "'Radicalisations' et 'Islamophobie.'"
11 Vincent Rémy, "Olivier Roy, politologue un peu Tintin," *Télérama*, November 9, 2014, www.telerama.fr/monde/olivier-roy-politologue-un-peu-tintin,118746.php (last accessed June 15, 2019).
12 Olivier Roy, "Ces terroristes sont des pieds nickelés, les mettre sur le même pied que la nation française est une insulte à cette dernière," *Atlantico*, December 2, 2015, www.atlantico.fr/decryptage/2472911/olivier-roy-ces-terroristes-sont-des-pieds-nickeles-les-mettre-sur-le-meme-pied-que-la-nation-francaise-est-une-insulte-a-cette-derniere-olivier-roy (last accessed June 15, 2019). The expression "Pieds Nickelés" refers to the characters of a comic strip created in June 1908 by Louis Forton and reprised to this day by various authors. More than anything else, its lightweight heroes want to keep their feet "nickels" (perfectly clean), i.e. to not dirty them through work. They therefore live on the margins of society—and at its expense.
13 "It is with respect to 'nihilism,' the product of Western thought, that these youth choose to join ISIS. Their real obsession for the aesthetic of violence is at odds with Islamic tradition." (Olivier Roy quoted in Abdou Semmar, "Radicalisation: Olivier Roy réfute la thèse de l'échec de l'intégration," *Algérie Focus*, March 30, 2016.)
14 After the fashion, for instance, of Yassine Belattar (cf. his online sketches, www.youtube.com/watch?v=HMWg0dY3iyI (last accessed June 15, 2019)).
15 Alain Bertho, "Une islamisation de la révolte radicale?" *Regards*, May 11, 2015, www.lespunaises.info/alain-bertho-une-islamisation-de-la-revolte-radicale/ (last accessed June 15, 2019); see also Alain Bertho, *Les Enfants du chaos. Essai sur le temps des martyrs*, La Découverte, Paris, 2016.
16 Farhad Khosrokhavar, *Radicalisation*, Maison des sciences de l'homme, Paris, 2014; *Inside Jihadism: Understanding Jihadi Movements Worldwide*, Paradigm Publishers, London, 2009; *Quand Al-Qaida parle. Témoignages derrière les barreaux*, Grasset, Paris, 2006. See also Ouisa Kies, "Processus de radicalisation et de déradicalisation en milieu fermé," Conférence au Centre international de criminologie comparée, Montréal, April 2016, www.youtube.com/watch?v=R_oap9rulvc (last accessed June 15, 2019).
17 "How should one react when faced with these new types of guerilla? Above all: without intervening too much. If crushing ISIS means destroying Sunni towns and villages, it creates new enemies. Better to let the *jihadi*s of ISIS make themselves detestable, as they already are—since only terror lets them hold on. Let us make do with helping their many enemies." (Vincent Rémy, "Olivier Roy, politologue un peu Tintin.")
18 Fabien Truong, *Loyautés radicales, L'islam et les « mauvais garçons » de la Nation*, La Découverte, Paris, 2015. Scott Atran, "ISIS is a Revolution," *Aeon*,

December 15, 2015, https://aeon.co/essays/why-isis-has-the-potential-to-be-a-world-altering-revolution (last accessed June 4, 2019).

19 Dounia Bouzar is an activist who, in 2014, founded a Center for the Prevention of Sectarian Trends Linked to Islam. There is very far from being a consensus concerning the scientific nature of its methods and the strictly pathologizing approach that it adopts (an approach that is also wholly depoliticized).

20 "From that standpoint, François Burgat's objection that radicals are motivated by the 'suffering' experienced by Muslims who were formerly colonized, or as victims of racism or any other sort of discrimination, US bombardments, drones, Orientalism, and so on, would imply that the revolt is primarily one led by victims. But the relationship between radicals and victims is more imaginary than real. Those who perpetrate attacks in Europe are not inhabitants of the Gaza Strip, or Libyans, or Afghans. They are not necessarily the poorest, the most humiliated, or the least integrated." Olivier Roy, *Jihad and Death*, Hurst, New York, 2016, p. 8.

21 Olivier Roy, "Le djihadisme est une révolte générationnelle et nihiliste," *Arrêts sur Info*, December 5, 2015, https://arretsurinfo.ch/olivier-roy-le-djihadisme-est-une-revolte-generationnelle-et-nihiliste/ (last accessed June 15, 2019).

22 See the director Stéphane Malterre's documentary, *Au nom du père, du fils et du djihad*, CAT & Cie and TAC Presse, 2015, https://rutube.ru/video/5eabc077a626ddf36265587d7ec35868/ (last accessed 15 June, 2019). The film retraces the involvement of the Syrian-French Ayachi family of Aix-en-Provence—first the son, then the father—in the conflict in Syria.

23 In 1860, Russian intellectuals wanted to "move towards the people," i.e. the peasantry. They were accused of being "nihilists," whereas their project was already a truly political one: to abolish Tsarism, and mobilize intellectuals, students and youth towards the peasant class (see Francesco Venturi, *Les Intellectuels, le peuple et la révolution. Histoire du populisme russe au xixe siècle*, vol. 1, Gallimard, Paris, 1972).

24 Fethi Benslama, *Un furieux désir de sacrifice. Le surmusulman*, Seuil, Paris, 2016.

25 A right-wing MP typical of the populist scene in France.

26 David Thomson, *Les Revenants*, Seuil Les Jours, Paris, 2016, p. 283, translated as *The Returned: They Left to Wage Jihad, Now They're Back*, Polity Press, Cambridge, 2018, p. 238.

Conclusion: Where Do We Go Now?[1]

In September 2011, the French Communist Party ordered a poster celebrating the Arab Springs, to promote its traditional *L'Humanité* ("Humanity") Festival.[2] For once, this painted the old party as in perfect tune with French public opinion as a whole, regardless of political creed. The poster portrayed a very young North African teenager. In her hair, unsurprisingly freed from any veil, the muse of the new Arab world wore a long garland of flags, including France's, symbolizing the long-awaited healing of the colonial divide. To increase her dramatic presence, the garland also included the Israeli flag. No narrative of coexistence was to be left behind.

Fleetingly, the Arab Spring allowed us to glimpse a world painted in the colors of our wildest dreams. A world from which any oppositional expression of Arab and Muslim difference had been expunged. A world in which our own political and cultural hegemony had been internalized; in which everyone had, at last, come around to our way of seeing and acting. Exit bearded males, their veiled wives and their constantly protesting moods. Exit their "pro-Palestinian" and "anti-Western" slogans. Had the ideal Muslim finally been born?

The dream died—and the awakening was brutal. The Other returned: the Muslim, the Muslim woman, and their protests, in the shape of "political Islam." They were back to tirelessly denouncing the shortcuts that we take to make the interests of a few prevail, time and again, over those of others. Once the euphoria had cleared, an admission had to be made. First in the ballot boxes of Arab Spring elections, then beyond them, the vocabulary of political Islam had not vanished. Far from it. Rather, it had displayed a kind of "omnipresent diversity."[3] The protest phase of the Arab Spring, followed by counter-revolution and internationalization, witnessed the range of Islamist positions spread out across the entire political spectrum, from Rachid Ghannouchi (in Tunis) to Abu Bakr al-Baghdadi (in Mosul). In the Western imagination, however, this diversity and complexity were largely blurred out.

A single, extremely minoritarian extreme of this spectrum has now stolen the limelight from the Islamist phenomenon as a whole: the one preached from Mosul by Abu Bakr al-Baghdadi. At the opposite end of the spectrum—and as distant from the caliph of Mosul as it is from the members of the Egyptian Salafist Nour party who more or less explicitly joined in Sissi's coup—lies the movement led by Rached Ghannouchi, who had been a political leper in the 1990s. Since 2011, Ennahda has asserted itself within the legal framework with rare equanimity, to the extent that it made a decisive contribution to the adoption of the most democratic and secular constitution in the Arab world. But one can never be too careful. France and its Western allies thus gave their backing to the army's ousting of Ennahda's "counterpart" Mohammed Morsi. It thereby encouraged the spectacular democratic leap backwards that we are now familiar with. Ennahda's exemplary political path, both in and out of power, first as majority then as minority, went back to being of no more interest than was the political equanimity of Indonesia's millions of Muslims.

On the eve of the 10th Congress of Ennahda, the successor party to the Movement of the Islamic Tendency founded in June 1981, Rached Ghannouchi implemented a thoroughly interesting decision. This was to explicitly broaden his action beyond the political field—in particular, by separating the party's political wing from its proselytizing one. No more imams in the party! Interesting as this decision may be, there was nothing truly revolutionary to it. It merely crowned a reformist trajectory that had been begun several years before. Ennahda had won the first democratic elections in contemporary Tunisia. This development was accelerated by Ennahda's decisive contribution to the process of political transition and institutional reconstruction. In these respects, Ghannouchi's party made important concessions. In particular, it enabled the passing of a strictly secular constitution that crowned the institutional basis of Tunisian democracy.

Ghannouchi's decision will certainly not "put an end to the era of political Islam," as some hastily wish to claim. For reasons of several kinds, it will have very little effect on the political factions that do not recognize themselves in that label. Indeed, it will even deepen the divide between them. This will likely be the case in Tunisia, where Ennahda is far from having a monopoly on Islamist constituencies, and where its shift towards the center is leaving increasing political space to more radical political mobilization.

Nonetheless, this development signals an interesting trend. A substantial part of the Islamist political spectrum is approaching a historical threshold. The initial, strictly reactive aim was to restore the social role of a religious identity that was long perceived as being under threat. This is gradually losing its centrality. For the time being, in the case of Ennahda, this transformation affects only one "extreme" of the very broad spectrum of Islamism. For my part, "From Rached Ghannouchi to Abu Bakr al-Baghdadi," I persist in describing Islamist staying power in terms of its "omnipresent diversity." Ghannouchi's adjustment extends the range of this diversity still further. On its margins, it adds a borderline category to all those that allow accounting for the current "plural" state of Islamism: a "post-Islamist" one. The premature use of the term, by Olivier Roy in particular, had, to my mind, distorted it; it now becomes effective. This reference to a "Muslim democracy" that could be plausibly compared to historical "Christian democracy" now becomes more meaningful than previously. The future effects of the formula ushered in by the leaders of Ennahda will, however, be governed by the attitude of some of their "partners"—first among them the president, Beji Caïd Essebsi. It is how seriously or otherwise he chooses to share power that will either lend credibility to the moderate option chosen by his "ex-Islamist" partners—or that will, on the contrary, discredit it. But Western countries will also be important partners in this transition, if not essential ones. In Europe, unsurprisingly, every spurt of Islamophobia and every episode of culturalist frenzy reinforces the radicals, and discredits those who strive to weaken them. It remains, however, too soon to draw full conclusions from these latest developments.

Against the Terrible Inertia of Prevailing Wisdom ...

The inevitable mantra of "one man, one vote, one time" was—as so many experts kept telling us—supposed to "demonstrate" that any Islamist movement that came to power through the ballot box would be unable to handover power peacefully. The mantra proved itself to be a vacuous scarecrow. True, we seldom like to stare in the face the scale of our past errors. Nor, faced with the violent fracture in jihadism that Al-Qaeda and its successors opened up, did anyone think to formulate an answer to Bin Laden's provocative question of 2004: "Why did we not attack, say, Sweden?"[4]

In the three decades since I began problematizing my approach to Islamist difference, I have been overcome by a discouraging feeling. Not only has the prevailing wisdom not "progressed." Rather, it has gone spectacularly backwards, with respect to all the great questions born of our encounter with the Muslim world in general—and with the Muslim world's "Islamist" generation in particular. Year after year, a few Western thinkers are enjoined to answer the same nagging questions. Are "Islam and democracy" compatible? Are "Islam and the rights of women"? "Islam and civil liberties"? And so on. They stand in for the millions of "voiceless"

Muslims who (unless these are carefully formatted) are left at the door of TV studios. I sometimes bitterly confess that this terrible inertia of prevailing wisdom, in its most grossly reactionary forms, has constrained me to "ramble." So much so that I have the exasperating feeling of having been giving the same, single lecture throughout my entire career. What has most affected me is this chilling impassiveness: this absence of any reaction, even a critical one, from the artisans and partisans of the dominant discourse. It is only with infinite slowness that broadly proven hypotheses have been allowed to emerge from the academic sphere to interact with prevailing wisdom.

What is it that I—among others!—have been tirelessly repeating for three decades? That the precondition of the long-awaited democratic transitions is not excluding Islamists from the political sphere. Nor is it bypassing them through some hypothetical third force. Much less is it hoping that they disappear. The solution is integrating them into the political sphere.[5] What is it that I have struggled to persuade audiences of? That "Islam is nothing more nor less than what most Muslims alive today wish to make of it."[6] No essentialism, therefore, can scientifically account for the role that the Islamist reference point plays in the political lexicon of those individuals who feel the need to adopt it. Contrary to every assertion (by at least some) of its political players as well as its observers, in no shape or form is the "Islamic reference point" a dogmatic, intangible dead-end, divorced from history. It is not impervious to progress. It does not bar the way to the social and political history of the societies that surround us, or of the communities whose fates we share at the national level. Like all dogmas, both sacred and profane, Islam becomes an earthly reality only through its social articulation—that is to say, as the result of a strictly human mediation. This mediation is perfectly liable to work through every kind of development and adaptation within itself—and within the bounds of necessary respect for a symbolic relationship to its founding text.

Provided, that is, that the world of the powerful—and to this day, we remain the powerful—does not sing too contradictory a tune in this respect. The stakes are high when one is finally willing to realize (as I have tried to persuade us) that, in many ways, we will have "the Muslim [neighbors] that we grant ourselves." In the main, Europe and the United States still share in determining the behavior of whole swaths of their political environment. Unwavering support for regimes like that of Marshal Sissi; for anti-religious elites marginalized by their own societies; or even for the most abrupt ethical and political shortcuts of our Israeli ally: these lead only to exacerbating the radical, reactive threat which these policies are precisely supposed to preserve us from.

Where do we go now?

CONCLUSION: WHERE DO WE GO NOW?

... Sharing—or Terror

What is it, then, that I have, it seems, failed to convey over these three decades? That the weapon of mass destruction against terrorism has already been invented. One thing lies at the root of the repeated failure of our "war" against the terrorist scourge: a blind refusal to put that weapon into practice. Granted, the weapon is especially expensive. The privileged of the world order of the 21st century, great and small, "Western" and "Muslim," seem unwilling to pay its price. The weapon has a name which those who hold power in all its forms have little time for. That name is "sharing." The weapon takes aim at precisely that which the privileged have no intention of sharing. First, of course, sharing economic and financial resources, whether on a world scale or on national ones. Second, sharing political power, which a whole generation has been deprived of, monopolized as power has been by veteran leaders who hobble from "election" to "referendum" and back. Third, the sharing of Palestine, too, promised for so long, and today has become a pipe dream. Yet beyond all this, what would most require sharing is ... feeling. Feeling for every victim of every kind of violence. And in the process, denouncing the contemptuous monopoly that double standard humanists exercise in this respect.

"Sharing" here also—perhaps even more so—means sharing the right to make one's own truth be known and valued: one's history great and small, and one's vision of the world: at prime time, whether on our screens or in the pages of a press that is less and less diverse.

To share does not always mean to give. It can also mean to learn how to receive. Such is the case for the opinion of others. If, however, we "manufacture" our information instead of collecting it; if the voices of the world arrive at our ears and eyes only through channels over which we have taken control; if we can no longer hear anything except the sound of our own voice—we deprive ourselves of the benefits of a vital commodity: the Other's outlook. It is that very outlook that allows us to understand ourselves through our own relativeness and, ultimately, through our own weaknesses and errors. Doubtless this self-confinement is what prevents us from taking up the challenge of accepting our own share in the responsibility of the terrorist phenomenon—when to do so is the only way to banish its ghost.

We must share with one another, then—or die of terror.

Notes

1 The title of a film by the Lebanese director Nadine Labaki (*Wa-halla la-ween?*, 2011).

2 The Communist Party's newspaper is called *L'Humanité*.
3 See François Burgat, "De Ghannouchi à Baghdadi. Le printemps an IV, entre contrerévolution et confessionnalisation," *Carnets de l'IREMAM*, April 20, 2015, https://iremam.hypotheses.org/5734 (last accessed June 15, 2019).
4 Osama Bin Laden, "The Towers of Lebanon," message to the American people of October 30, 2004, in Bruce Lawrence (ed.), *Messages to the World*, Verso, London, 2005, p. 238.
5 See François Burgat, "Le partage ou la terreur," *Libération*, July 13, 2005, www.liberation.fr/tribune/2005/07/13/le-partage-ou-la-terreur_526512 (last accessed June 15, 2019).
6 See François Burgat, *Les Acteurs islamistes en 1997, entre participation politique, résistance armée et diaspora. Synthèse*, Ministère de la Défense, Direction des affaires stratégiques, Paris, 1997.

Index

Abbas, Mahmoud (Abu Mazen) 105, 107
Abdelkader, Emir 35
Abdu, Mohammed 4
Abu Salim Prison (Tripoli), 52
Afghani, Jamal al-Din al- 4, 14
Ageron, Charles-Robert 35, 47
Ahmar, Abdallah Hussein al- 84, 87
Aleppo 25–6, 32, 124–5, 130, 201
Amin, Samir 170
Amiraux, Valérie 139–40
Arafat, Yasser 10, 55, 99–100, 105, 107
Ashton, Catherine 155
Assad, Bashar al- 23, 50, 57, 59–60, 71, 77, 80, 81, 83, 92, 108–10, 114–17, 119, 122, 124–5, 129–31
Assad, Hafez al- 114, 131, 181
Assad, Rifaat al- 116
Aswany, Alaa al- 170, 186
Atatürk, Mustafa Kemal 53
Awlad haratina 63, 72

Bachir, Omar al- 55
Baczko, Adam 130
Baghdadi, Abu Bakr al- 4–6, 15, 122, 223, 227–9, 232
Banna, Hassan al- 52, 73, 78, 201
Bassil, Rita ix
Bataclan attack 139–40
Beaumont, Robin x, 107, 131
Bechara, Souha 106
Belhadj, Abdelhakim 49
Ben Ali, Zine al-Abidine 49, 64, 67, 69, 71, 81, 113, 117, 156, 164, 175–6, 186
Ben Barka, Mehdi 57, 188
Ben Bella, Ahmed 64, 156
Bendjedid, Chadli 40
Bennabi, Malek vi, 35–6, 27
Bin Laden, Osama 7, 10–11, 87, 229, 232

Bishri, Tarek al- vi, x, 69, 78, 149, 169
Bonnefoy, Laurent ix, 92, 168
Boumediene 40, 42–3
Bourdieu, Pierre 35, 171, 177–8, 186–7
Bourguiba, Habib 43, 53–4, 67, 147, 186
Bouti, Muhammad Said Ramadan al- 129
Bouvier, Nicolas 17
Bouzar, Dounia 218–19, 228
Burgat, François vi–vii, 13–14, 32, 48, 50, 61, 73, 91–2, 106–7, 109–10, 112, 128–31, 139–41, 146, 152, 154, 156, 158, 168, 178, 180, 183–4, 186–7, 193, 209–11, 224–6, 232
Bush, George W. 7, 89

Cabut, Jean (alias Cabu) 212
Chalghoumi, Hassen 127, 139, 219
Charlie Hebdo attack 212–26
Chirac, Jacques 69, 73, 80, 176
Clinton, Bill 88

Dahlan, Mohammed 107
Debray, Régis 93, 106–7, 141
d'Estaing, Valéry Giscard 38, 40
de la Croix, Marie-Agnès 211
de Lamartine, Alphonse 22, 31
Denoix, Sylvie ix
Dhawahiri, Ayman 70
Dik, Majd al- 129–30
Dirèche, Karima ix
Dorronsoro, Gilles 130
Dot-Pouillard, Nicolas ix, 107, 151, 159, 185

Ennahda 5–6, 14, 120, 148, 152, 154, 158, 189–90, 228–9
Erdogan, Recep Tayyip 5, 124

INDEX

Faisal, Turki al- 83
Fatah 101–3, 105, 107
Finkielkraut, Alain 94, 106
Fourest, Caroline 29, 180, 187
Free Syrian Army (FSA) 118–21
Front Islamique du Salut (FIS) 8, 39, 139, 152, 157, 172, 189, 195, 204, 211

Gaddafi, Muammar 21, 49–60, 67, 188–9
Gaza Strip 95, 98, 105, 107, 164–5, 208, 213, 219, 226
Geisser, Vincent x, 140
Gèze, François x, 130, 185
Ghannouchi, Rached vi, x, 5, 69, 147–9, 171, 190, 227–9, 232
Ghezali, Salima 170, 177, 185
Ghouta 121, 124, 126
Göle, Nilüfer 140–1, 168
Gresh, Alain 116, 211
Guignard, Xavier 10, 107, 131

Habib, Mohammed 179
Hadi, Abdelhadi Mansour al- 85
Halévi, Ivan 106
Hamas 9, 94, 98, 100–5, 107, 136, 155, 163, 180, 182, 190–2
Hamieddin, Yahya 76, 78, 91
Hanafi, Sari x
Haniyeh, Ismail 107
Hanoune, Louisa 170
Hariri, Rafiq 112, 115
Hassoun, Ahmad Badreddin 26
Hawrani, Ali al- 108
Hezbollah (Lebanese) 23–4, 71, 79, 85, 92, 94, 108, 111, 118–19, 128–9
Hill, Thomas W. ix, 107
Hollande, François 167–8, 213, 219
Houellebecq, Michel 134, 140, 213
Hourani, Albert 4, 14
Houthi, Hussein Badr Eddine al- 84–5
Houthis 85–7, 91
Huntington, Samuel 210
Hussein, Adel x, 69, 149
Hussein, Saddam 12, 82, 85, 218

Ibrahim, Sonallah 170
Iherchane, Omar x
Islamic State in Iraq and Syria (ISIS), the, Islamic State Organisation, the, Daesh 4–5, 9, 11–12, 14, 45, 53, 59–61, 70, 73, 86, 90, 92, 102, 112, 114–15, 117–19, 122–7, 129, 130–1, 141, 161, 165, 170–1, 178, 181–2, 205, 207, 214–16, 221–3, 225–6
Israeli Defense Forces (IDF) 98, 107, 208

Jarari, Mohamed 51, 56
Jazeera, al- 46, 82, 98, 115
Joffe, George 190–1
Jospin, Lionel 192

Karman, Tawakkul 86, 92
Kepel, Gilles v, x, 7, 14, 186, 196–200, 202–11, 214–16, 218, 224–5
Khadra, Yasmina 170, 185
Khamenei, Ali 125
Khomeini, Ruhollah 49, 182, 151
Kikhia, Mansour 69, 188–9
Krichen, Aziz 170

Labaki, Nadine 231
Lacroix, Stéphane x, 203
Lahad, Antoine 95
Lévy, Bernard-Henri 59, 100, 115, 171
Lewis, Bernard 100, 202, 210
Luizard, Pierre-Jean 14, 128

Marzouki, Moncef 185
Mbembe, Achille 1
Ménoret, Pascal vi–ix, 10, 13, 14, 91, 203, 210
Mermier, Franck 74, 90, 92
Messaoudi, Khalida 172–4
Mitterrand, François 48, 73, 219, 224
Mohamedou, Mohamed Mahmoud Ould x
Mohammed VI 72
Morsi, Mohammed 119, 155, 179, 228
Movement of the Islamic Tendency (MIT) 147–8, 176, 189–91, 228
Mubarak, Hosni 49, 54, 56, 70, 81, 84, 113, 117, 156, 185
Muslim Brotherhood 2, 4, 11, 52–3, 55–6, 69, 73, 78, 84, 86, 92, 100, 103–4, 117, 128, 131, 145, 149, 152, 154, 162, 169, 179–81, 185, 193, 201, 215

Nached, Rafah 109
Nasrallah, Hassan 23
Nasser, Gamal vii, 4, 44–5, 49, 52, 54, 58, 69–70, 72–3, 78–9, 104, 149, 152, 156, 215
Netanyahu, Benjamin 93
Nusra, Jabhat al- 120

INDEX

Obama, Barack 120–1
Omar, Jarallah 82–3
Ouchaklian, Minas x

Palestine Liberation Organization (PLO) 100
Palestinian Authority 99, 101, 103
Palestinian Islamic Jihad (PIJ) 101
Paoli, Bruno 129–30
Partiya Yekîtiya Demokrat (Democratic Union Party, PYD) /Partiya Karkeren Kurdistan (Kurdistan Workers' Party, PKK) 114, 124, 129
Pasqua, Charles 72–3, 132
Pélissier, Julien x
Pétain, Philippe 105
Picard, Elizabeth 14, 129
Pierret, Thomas x, 129–30, 203
Plantureux, Jean (alias Plantu) 182
Pompidou, Georges 50, 72
Putin, Vladimir 118

Qahtan, Mohamed x, 78, 91
Quesnay, Arthur 141, 160

Rabin, Yitzhak 206
Rafale 139, 213, 223
Raffy, Serge 179–80
Ramadan, Tariq 133, 136, 139, 146–7, 178–82, 187
Reagan, Ronald 51
Rey, Mathieu 10, 14
Rida, Rashid 4
Roy, Olivier v, x, 32, 95, 102, 196–9, 201, 208, 210–11, 224–6, 229

Sadat, Anwar al- 45, 54, 198, 202, 206–7
Sadr, Musa 56, 131
Said, Edward 35, 104–5, 107
Salah, Raed 93
Salah, Yasmina 193–5

Saleh, Ali Abdallah 80, 82–8, 91, 110, 117, 128, 130
Sarkozy, Nicolas 25, 57, 59, 109, 112, 138, 141, 164, 168, 219
Sarout, Abdelbasset 115
Senussi, King Idris 21, 50, 53
Setmarian Nasar, Mustapha Ben Aldelkader (alias Umar Abd al-Hakim, alias Abu Musab al-Suri) 73, 117, 130, 205, 215
Sharon, Ariel 10, 98
Sinet, Maurice (alias Siné) 138, 141
Sissi, Abdel Fattah 70, 87, 156, 219–20, 223, 228, 230
Soghanalian, Sarkis 82
South Lebanon Army (SLA) 95

Tagamu al-Islah (party) 78, 82, 84–7
Tel Al-Zaatar (Lebanon) 111
Tlass, Ahmed 117, 128, 130
Trabelsi, Seif Eddine x
Trudeau, Justin 167
Trump, Donald 105
Turabi, Hassan 70–1, 73

Union of French Islamic Organizations (Union des organisations islamiques de France, UOIF) 138–9, 183
Utvik, Bjorn x

Val, Philippe 137
Valls, Manuel x, 29, 171,186, 220

Wazir, Khalil-al (alias Abu Jihad) 147

Yassine, Abdessalam x, 149

Zahar, Mahmoud al- 98
Zemmour, Eric 29, 32, 134, 140, 213
Zola, Émile 1
Zrig, Mohammed 189–92
Zubeiry, Mahmoud 76–8

EU authorised representative for GPSR:
Easy Access System Europe, Mustamäe tee 50,
10621 Tallinn, Estonia
gpsr.requests@easproject.com

www.ingramcontent.com/pod-product-compliance
Lightning Source LLC
Chambersburg PA
CBHW070237240426
43673CB00044B/1828